T0380786

Where Are We Going?

URSULA CHIRICO-ELKINS

WESTBOW
PRESS®
A DIVISION OF THOMAS NELSON
& ZONDERVAN

WestBow Press books may be ordered through booksellers or by contacting:

WestBow Press
A Division of Thomas Nelson & Zondervan
1663 Liberty Drive
Bloomington, IN 47403
www.westbowpress.com
1 (866) 928-1240

ISBN: 978-1-9736-0513-3 (sc)
ISBN: 978-1-9736-0514-0 (e)

Library of Congress Control Number: 2017916470

Print information available on the last page.

WestBow Press rev. date: 11/6/2017

Contents

Part 5

Part 6

Part 7

LET NOT YOUR HEART BE TROUBLED

John 14:1 and 27

My friend, in your world of indifference and haste

I bestow serenity and peace.

If you endure injustice and prejudice

I offer you my unconditional love.

Do your trusted friends disappoint or deceive you?

I embrace you as my cherished friend.

If sorrow and suffering overpower you

Remember the radiant lights of hope and joy.

Does fear of illness or death haunt and trouble you ?

My friend – I died and resurrected for you.

Part 1

Part I

Chapter 1

The Coming of the Messiah

Isaiah 9:2, 40:1-13, 61:10-11,

"The people that walked in darkness have seen a great light: they that dwell in the land of the shadow of death, upon them hath the light shined".

The hope for the coming Messiah, the Anointed-one, has always upheld the people of Israel in their times of trouble and suffering. The people of Israel expected the Messiah to be a man of military authority because Israel experienced so many invaders of their country. Judas Maccabeus was high-spirited and patriotic who, with his band of devoted men, drove the Greeks out of Israel. The celebration of Hanukkah retells the story of the purification of the Temple. The oil, supposed to last for one day of purifying the Temple, lasted eight days instead. The idea of a Messiah who redeems Israel from its suppressors has its basis in the books of Ezekiel who was of priestly lineage and had been deported to Babylon in 587 BC after Judea fell under the rule of the Assyrian King Nebuchadnezzar. He prophesied that a prince of the lineage of David would humiliate the Gentiles and bring liberation to the Jews. Another outstanding figure was Daniel, a Jewish youth being deported to Babylon in 597 BC. He was to become a Prophet, and a man of great wisdom. The Jews under the oppressive Greek (Seleucid) rule of king Antiochus IV Epiphanes (ca. 175-164 B.C.) suffered severely, and people referred to the Book of Daniel when asking why there was so much suffering. Daniel had taught the Jewish exiles living in Babylon that the coming Messiah would liberate them. He called the Messiah 'Son of Man' while the prophet Isaiah (ca. 750 BC) described the expected Messiah as a king born of the royal house of David.

The Dead Sea Scrolls

A Jewish sect founded in the second century BC, lived in the secluded wilderness at Qumran near the Dead Sea who called themselves the 'Essenes'. Jesus and John the Baptist must have been familiar with their way of life and their teachings. The Essenes were ascetic men of a Jewish sect who rejected worldly involvement and tried to restore the purity of its teachings. The Greek influence, that had influenced the other branches of Judaism, was abhorrent to the Essenes as was close contact with the Roman conquerors. The doctrine and practice of their theory was circulating in the last century before the birth of Christ. The community was highly organized and strictly observed the oral and written law. The aspirants had to prove themselves worthy and live three years of probation within the community before they were fully admitted. Their lives were almost monastic, and property and homes belonged to the community. They also performed ritually immersion in water every morning, and the communal meals were taken in silence.

Some of the Essenes married and lived in towns but the marriage served only to beget offspring. Like the people around them, the Essenes believed in demons and diseases caused by evil spirits, and exhorted to exorcism. The Essenes believed in the immortality of the soul and expected the coming of the Messiah who would establish his Kingdom on Earth. Josephus Flavius (37-100 AD) the Jewish historian, spent in his youth some time as a member of the Essenes

In 1947, Bedouin shepherds searching for a lost goat discovered a number of clay vessels that contained seven ancient scrolls hidden away in 11seperate caves in the Judean desert near Qumran at the north-western side of the Dead Sea. The priceless treasure was sold without anyone knowing their unimaginable value, and occupied their place on the shelves of antique dealers and merchants. After changing hands and spending time on shelves they finally reached their destination. Old Testament scholars were ecstatic at the treasures placed into their care. The scrolls are referred to as the Dead See scrolls contain over fifty texts from the Old Testament including the entire Book of Isaiah, Psalms, prophesies of Daniel, Ezekiel and Jeremiah including non-biblical writings. They were written in three languages, Hebrew, Greek and Aramaic and dated from the periods of 200 BC to 68 AD. Some scholars pointed out that the scrolls may have been part of the Temple library, and were hidden during the Jewish Revolt in the year 70 AD.

The Dead Sea Scrolls are unparalleled in significance and may be the most significant archaeological discovery in centuries. Its study grants a glimpse into the early years of Christianity and the Jewish society of the era.

Some of the writings were apocalyptic and modern scholars regard the source of apocalyptic writings as to the suffering of mankind, and the questions about the existence of good and evil.

The apocalyptic writer and prophet believed that God would overthrow the powers of darkness in a final conflict between them and the powers of light, and afterwards send the Messiah to rule with wisdom and justice. The writer believed that the end of all evil on earth would be eliminated and the Kingdom of God was imminent (see: Revelation of St. John the Divine).

Chapter 2

The Life of Jesus

Little is known about the early years of Jesus' life spent with his family in Egypt until the dead of the Jewish king Herod Antipas. The family felt safe enough to return and settle down in Nazareth.

Yeshuah's (Jesus) lineage was of the Royal house of David but his kingdom was not of the earthly dominion which he avoided to explain until to the last days of his life. (My kingdom is not of this world). He knew that the concept would be too complex to understand.

Jesus inherited the hope of the people to be the long awaited Messiah and a strong military leader who would redeem Israel from the hated Roman joke. Jesus never claimed to be the 'worldly' Messiah. He was a King of the Spirit, the Son of God, co-existing with God since the beginning of the universe (Gospel of John).

Jesus was filled with divine love for mankind and tried to ease the sorrows of their lives and comfort them, not by helping on a material level but by addressing the anguish, the anxieties and daily worries. First and foremost, he firmly believed that the dawn of the Kingdom of God was upon them, and he was chosen to inaugurate it.

Galilee, the home of Jesus, had extensive trade networks with Syria, Egypt, Babylonia and the Hellenistic world. The society was a multi-cultured and cosmopolitan, consisting of Persians, Phoenicians, Greeks and Palestinians. The climate was favourable for agriculture, and the lake provided profitable fishing.

We know very little of the early life and youth of Jesus. He grew up in Galilee and spoke Aramaic but most likely his religious training at the local synagogue included Hebrew. His father Joseph was a carpenter and Jesus learned the honourable trade from him (in ancient Israel, the work 'carpenter' had an expanded meaning, and may have included other media such as leather or metal besides working with wood). Although, Jesus did not receive a formal education, he was very well versed in the Scriptures. When he was twelve years old, he and his family went to the Temple at Jerusalem (perhaps to receive his Bar-Mitzvah) and he surprised and amazed the learned rabbis with his knowledge of the scriptures and his spiritual insight (Luk. 2:41).

John the Baptist, the son of the priest Zacharias and Elizabeth, a very pious couple, was a cousin of Jesus. John was born to his parents when they were advanced in years, and his birth was a miracle. While Zacharias attended to his duties at the temple, an angel appeared to him to pronounce the answering of the couple's prayers for a son. Zacharias, fearful of the radiant angel, lost his speech, and the people realized that he had received a profound revelation. Elizabeth, in due time, gave birth to a son, and they named him John.

We do not have details concerning his childhood. John, the grown man, emerged from the dessert near Qumran, where he had fasted and prayed. He called on the people to repent their sins and accept baptism which was practiced as purification rite, and at times repeated. The prophet Ezekiel regarded it as moral cleansing.

John the Baptist associated the repentance with the cleansing of the heart, and prophesied that the Kingdom of God was near. He was asked if he was the promised Messiah to which he replied that he baptized with water but the one following him would baptize them by water and spirit. John was a powerful preacher and had a very large following.

John baptized Jesus at his request although John hesitated. According the scripture (Matt. 3:14 -15) he expressed his unwillingness to baptize Jesus by stating that he needed to be baptized instead of Jesus who was sinless. Jesus' baptism symbolized an invitation to Mankind to come and join him. He was about thirty years old when he accepted his divine mission for which he had been chosen by God.

John the Baptist was imprisoned at the order of Herod Antipas for criticising his marriage to his wife's half-brother Philip who was still living. While incarcerated, John may have had some doubts about Jesus, and sent two of his disciples to him, "Art thou he that should come, or do we look for another?" (Matt.11:3-6). Jesus replied that the blind received sight, the lame walked, the lepers were cleansed, the dead are raised and the poor have the Gospel preached to them.

During a celebration sponsored by Herod, his step-daughter Salome entertained him and his guests with an alluring dance. Herod, who was pleased with Salome's enthralling performance and granted her the fulfilment of a wish. Salome questioned her mother concerning the reward, and she suggested to request of the head of John the Baptist presented on a platter. Herod was reluctant but obliged to grant Salome's gruesome wish. It is also likely that Herod Antipas felt threatened by John and his followers and feared sedition.

After his baptism, Jesus was full of the Holy Spirit and went for forty days into the dessert to pray. The devil tempted him in various ways and promised power of the kingdoms of the world if Jesus would worship him. Jesus refused by answering him that 'man shall not live by bread alone, but by every word that proceedeth out of the mouth of God.' (Matt.4:4)

Jesus taught in the synagogues and his teaching was stirring and powerful. He went home to Nazareth, and according to custom, went on Sabbath to the local synagogue where he read the scripture from Isaiah 61:1-2. "The Spirit of the Lord is upon me; because the Lord has anointed me to preach good tidings to the meek: he hath sent me to bind up the broken- hearted, to proclaim liberty to the captives, and the opening of the prison to them that are bound: To proclaim the acceptable year of the Lord, and the day of vengeance of our God; to comfort all that mourn."

The worshippers responded with wrath. Jesus had grown up amongst them, and the congregation was amazed at the authority with which he spoke. According their opinion, he was the son of Joseph the carpenter, and Mary, but not a learned Rabbi or a scribe. They rushed out of the synagogue, and tried to push him down the hill but he managed to escape and left. (Mark 4:18-30)

After John the Baptist's imprisonment and later, his death, Jesus continued John's work by urging repentance, and preaching of the coming of the Kingdom of God. Following his return to Galilee, he chose twelve disciples whom he taught and gradually sent away in pairs to teach and bring the joyful message of the dawning Kingdom of God. The twelve disciples were according to Matt 10:1-4: Simon (called Peter, the 'Rock') and his brother Andrew, James the son of Zebedee with his brother John. Philip, Bartholomew, and Matthew, who was the tax collector, became disciples. The chosen disciples left their trade and followed Jesus. James, son of Alphaeus, Thaddaeus, and Simon the Canaanite also became followers. Judas Iscariot, the only disciple not from Galilee, was entrusted with the money. Some of the friends like Martha, Mary and their brother Lazarus welcomed Jesus into their home to offer rest and relaxation.

Jesus loved children and he pointed out to his listeners that their faith in God should be as childlike and trusting as a child's faith is to his or her parents.

He was not ascetic like John the Baptist. He and his mother attended the joyous celebration of a wedding where he performed his first miracle. Like John the Baptist, Jesus strongly emphasized the necessity for repentance to receive God's forgiveness. The repentant heart would bring about a profound change and lead to a god-centred life. The Kingdom of God was near. The rich, Jesus knew, would not accept his teachings but the humble and deprived who put their life into the care of God, would be the receiver of the Kingdom.

The Pharisees and scribes were constantly observing him and asking probing questions to detect contradictions and errors in his teachings. They were the leaders concerning religion who taught submission to God's will, and adhered to the belief of the resurrection of the body. The Pharisees were not fundamentalists nor were they extremely narrow-minded. The synagogues were influenced by them, and also a strong emphasis was put on the teachings. Jesus taught in the synagogues but also preached wherever an audience gathered around him. It gave the Pharisees the opportunity to watch and spy on him. He objected to the Pharisees so-called insincerity, and accused them of lip service, and acting pretentious. Jesus called them 'hypocrites' and the Jews themselves were critical of their dishonesty. Nevertheless, Jesus had sympathizers among the Scribes and Pharisees (like Nicodemus, John 3:3-7).

The scribes were professionals (lawyers) and legal councillors, the interpreters of the Law and were well versed and capable to recite them by memory. Their powerful influence extended to the Council of the Sanhedrin at Jerusalem.

The Temple at Jerusalem was controlled by the conservative Sadducees who paid great attention to ritual and the written word in contrast to the scribes and Pharisees who discussed the interpretations of the scriptures. In contrast to the Pharisees, the Sadducees did not believe in the resurrection of the body and Jesus' redeeming message of the coming Kingdom of God meant nothing to them. The Sadducee's were members of the noble ruling families of Jerusalem, and very influential. At the time of Jesus, Caiaphas officiated as High Priest. He served as the mediator between the population and the Roman occupational authority represented by Pontius Pilate, and collaborated with him. The Sadducees were fearful of a Jewish revolt and knew very well that an uprising would end in bloodshed and defeat and therefore viewed Jesus with distrust and even hostility. His teaching of the coming Kingdom did not interest the Sadducees.

The priestly class did not accept Jesus' teachings because he had not received the required training as Rabbi. Jesus came from Galilee which was regarded as crude and provincial. It was not hard-core Judaic province but had been annexed to Israel about 100 years ago. The population of Galilee was mixed because it was located near the important trade routes. The Galileans spoke Aramaic which was considered as 'coarse.'

The Zeolots, political extremists, hated the Roman domination. Jesus teachings, like the 'Sermon on the Mount', opposed the Zeolot's promotion of military resistance. During the social instability of the first century resulting in social division, banditry and crime, the Zeolots were the catalysts who sparked the First Jewish Revolt against the Roman masters in 66 CE. They banded together with other groups in quest of overthrowing the Roman authority. Some groups of Zeolots went to the Jewish fortress of Masada on the Dead Sea were they committed suicide rather than to become prisoners of the Romans or fought the Romans to their death.

Jesus was renounced for performing miracles but at times he refused. He was requested to show a 'sign' which he rejected. Perhaps he felt that those, who declared to love him and believe on him should do so from the conviction of their hearts and not because he was able to perform miracles.

He stressed the importance of forgiveness, and in the Gospel of Matthew we read that Jesus recommended forgiving not one time only but 'seventy times seven'. (Matt. 18:21) God forgives the repenting wrong-doer and we must forgive also. Jesus added something more that really stirred up trouble: he said that he forgives sins (Mark 2:6-7). Some of the scribes heard Jesus' statement and called him a blasphemer. God only could forgive sins. He ran headlong into trouble by preaching to 'sinners'. People of ill reputation were ignored and frowned at because they were considered as corrupt and unclean. What was Jesus' purpose to eat with people of ill reputation? He wanted to preach to everyone, educated or without learning, rich or poor, about the Kingdom of God. This was his mission, and he was determined to carry it out. He taught the disciples 'the secrets of the Kingdom' and his teaching was more in-dept and profound. When addressing his casual and illiterate listeners, he preferred to speak in the well-known literary style of parables, using examples from the everyday life experiences his listeners could comprehend and relate to. (Matt.13:11)

Jesus loved to preach to the people wherever he happened to find listeners. One of his deep and insightful sermons is the famous "Sermon on the Mount". A large audience gathered around him and requested him to preach, and Jesus sat down on a hillside to deliver his profound and inspiring teaching.

The Beatitudes and the Sermon on the Mount

Matt. 5-7, Luke 6:20-49

"Blessed are the poor in spirit for theirs is the Kingdom of Heaven". The poor in spirit realize that without the loving guidance of God they are like leaves blown by the wind. The 'poor in spirit' do not exercise self-will but put their worries into the hands of God, knowing that through their prayers they shall find the answers, guidance and comfort they need.

"Blessed are they that mourn: for they shall be comforted." We do not only mourn for the loss of a loved one. Sometimes we mourn because our life seems to be filled with injustice and hardship. Life may be very harsh and we may have experienced sorrow and hopelessness but sometimes this is the only way to learn to seek God who is Truth and frees us from sin and limitations. Jesus assures us that we shall find comfort and guidance through Him.

"Blessed are the meek: for they shall inherit the earth" Truly blessed is the one who is anchored in the teachings of Christ which permeates their thoughts and actions. If we put our trust in God, nothing can threaten us.

"Blessed are they which do hunger and thirst for righteousness: for they shall be filled". The righteous are of right thinking which leads to right action. Thoughts are very powerful and we may create the conditions accordingly, either positive or negative. If you wish to be loved, you must emanate love toward your fellow man. 'As you sow so shall you reap' is a spiritual law. It takes strong aspiration for thinking and living right and to overcome negative and unkind thoughts and speech. It is a slow progress to change bad habits but by praying for guidance, and wholehearted search for seeking God and His righteousness we shall succeed.

"Blessed are the merciful: for they shall obtain mercy." Jesus applied the fine and noble emotion of mercy when he spoke of the merciful. We go wrong and are in need of help as much as our brother who is misguided. It is our responsibility to extend our experience and help to our fellow man and be merciful in our attitude toward him.

"Blessed are the pure in heart: for they shall see God". To be pure in heart is to love God first and foremost. God is spirit and an attempt to comprehend God and His truth is to 'worship Him in Spirit and in Truth' (John 4:24). His creation is all around us. We are witnessing His creation since we are immersed in it and we are part of it. This is a wonderful and mind-baffling realization.

The 'pure in heart' have needs and worries but the problems and troubles of daily life does not destroy their hopes and aspirations because they know that at the right time, according to the Lord's reasoning, their problems shall be addressed and resolved. The 'pure in heart' shuns anything that would separate the soul through sin from the beloved Creator who is unconditional love. The 'pure in heart' wishes to be guided by God, and puts his or her trust into God's care.

"Blessed are the peacemakers: for they shall be called the children of God." The peacemaker has overcome pain and tribulations and attained serenity within himself, and strives for justice within the family, the community, or the nation he is a member of. The peacemaker does not shun discomfort or danger but follows single-minded the purpose to bring consolation and peace to the troubled individual or society in trouble and conflict. His attitude is of open-mindedness and non-judgemental opinions. Such a person is a blessing to many.

"Blessed are they which are persecuted for righteousness sake: for theirs is the Kingdom of Heaven. Blessed are ye when men shall revile you, and persecute you, and shall say all manner of evil against you falsely, for my sake. Rejoice, and be exceedingly glad: for great is your reward in Heaven: for so persecuted they the prophets which were before you" The first Christians were subject of persecution because they confessed Christ as their redeemer and Son of God. It also applies to many who have been persecuted during the centuries as well as the twentieth century. The missionaries faced and still do face persecution and put their life in danger to bring the teachings of Christ to other nations. Not only missionaries but individuals faced and still face persecution and discrimination through nations and individuals who are anti-Christian. We do not know how many persons living in foreign countries have to face harassment because they confess to be Christians. Jesus promises those individuals a rich reward: to be united with Him in heaven.

The 'Sermon on the Mount' outlines the teachings of Jesus in short version. He emphasized the realization of our faults and sins and assured us that through repentance we shall attain forgiveness. He warned of judging others and pointed out the importance of honesty in contact with other individuals, and of trust in God whom he called with the loving word 'Father'. Jesus declared that we should love our enemy and pray for the one who had hurt us, and to forgive the person who had a nasty attitude toward us or used our kindness for his own ends. He taught the listeners not to be revengeful and to retaliate, and pointed out that the sincere and heartfelt prayer would bring consolation and answers to our problems. Jesus included the spiritual law of treating others as we want to be treated (the 'Golden Rule). Through the profound change of the repenting heart can we become the children of God, and only then.

Jesus stressed the observances of the first and second Commandments The 'First Commandment' asks us to love God, the Creator of Heaven and Earth, with all our heart, mind and strength, first and foremost. The 'Second Commandment' is of equal significance "love thy neighbour as thyself" He told a scribe (Mark 12:28-34) who was one of his listeners, that all other commandments relate to the first and second Commandment. Jesus meant to say, a person, who loves God, would never try to steal or kill a man. To love God and to love and honour your neighbour (another human being) prevents one from disobeying the other eight commandments His mission in Galilee faltered. The multitude listened, and did not understand what he was attempting to communicate. His popularity dwindled, and his own family failed to recognize the purpose of his mission and tried to bring him home (Mark 3:31-34 'He is besides himself). Some of the parables reflect the frustration of preaching to a crowd as well as his disciples who did not comprehend his message. The downtrodden population lived in abject poverty and struggled paying crushing taxes, and the country was subjugated to a hated foreign and brutal power. Since antiquity, no country ever cherished an occupying army on their soil. Jesus appeared to his listeners as a profound preacher and compassionate healer but the urgency of his message of the coming kingdom did not strike them as realistic and helpful.

Returning to Jerusalem, Jesus tried to explain his teaching to the disciples. He was aware of the short time left to him.

In the Gospel of John 8:13, Jesus gave the saving message, "I am the living bread which came down from heaven: if any man consume of this bread, he shall live forever: and the bread that I will give is my flesh, which I will give for the life of the world. Verily, Verily, I say unto you, except ye eat the flesh of the Son of man, and drink his blood; ye have no life in you."

In Matt. 16:13, we read that Jesus tried to find out in what way his disciples saw him. He asked: "Whom do men say that I the Son of man am?" And they said, "Some say, that thou art John the Baptist: some Elias; and others, Jeremiah, or one of the prophets". But now he asked the probing question: "He saith unto them, but who say ye that I am?" And Simon Peter answered and said, "Thou art the Christ, the Son of the living God." And Jesus answered and said to him, "Blessed art thou, Simon Bar-Jona: for flesh and blood has not revealed unto thee, but my Father which is in heaven. And I say unto thee, that thou art Peter, and upon this rock I will built my church; and the gates of hell shall not prevail against it. And I will give unto thee the keys of the kingdom of heaven: and whatsoever thou shalt bind on earth shall be bound in heaven: and whatsoever thou shalt loose on earth shall be loosed in heaven."

Jesus tried to avoid of calling himself the Messiah or the Son of God. He was the Messenger of God, the Father, who was sent to announce the coming Kingdom of God, He referred to God as of the Father whose work he was appointed to do (John 10:37). Throughout the gospels we find that he commonly referred to himself as 'Son of man' (Luke. 6:24, 8:31 and 9:22 and Mt.12:32) including various references throughout the gospels).

Jesus resurrected Lazarus, the brother of Mary and Martha from the dead. Those who witnessed the miracle and others, who were informed about, were moved and stirred and many believed on him. (John 11:1-44) Some of the Jews went and reported the incident to the Council and the chief priests. The miracles Jesus performed were undeniable, and the priesthood faced a dilemma. The Sanhedrin feared that the people hoped that Jesus was the militant Messiah and free Israel of the Romans. The leaders knew too well that the Romans would brutally retaliate, and an ensuing bloodbath would bring devastation and amplify the sufferings of the population. Caiaphas decided that it was better to let one man die for the people in order to save the whole nation from perishing (John 11:47-53). He and the priests decided on how to take Jesus and put him to death.

Jesus knew of his ending days. He had carried out the mission God had chosen him for: to bring the good tidings of the coming Kingdom of God.

Jesus would under no circumstances compromise his sacred mission. God's will was the thriving force that lead his life and it meant acceptance and submission under His will.

Chapter 3

The Mystery of the Cross

Exodus 12:18-27, Isaiah 53:3-12, Matt. 26-28, Luke 22-23, John 18-20

Jesus and his disciples went a week before the celebration of the Passover to Jerusalem. When he entered the city, riding on a young ass, he was greeted by the population who took branches of palm trees and called: "Hosanna, blessed is the King of Israel that cometh in the name of the Lord". (John 12:13). He tried to emphasize that he was not the Messiah of arms bringing war but that his mission was one of love, peace and salvation. The prophet Zechariah spoke of the redemption of Israel through the king of peace: (Zech. 9:9): "Rejoice greatly, oh, daughter of Zion: shout, oh daughter of Jerusalem: behold, thy king cometh unto thee. He is just, and having salvation; lowly, and riding upon an ass, and upon a colt the foal of an ass".

Jesus was loved by the common people but he was also a man who relentlessly expressed the truth. Occasionally he exhibited anger when he felt that the laws were violated. The Sadducees, in opposition to the Pharisees, did not believe in the resurrection of the body and Jesus' message of the coming Kingdom of God meant nothing to them. The Sanhedrin (judicial court) were opposed to the teachings and miracles performed by Jesus. The Pharisees accused him of blasphemy because he forgave sins, and according to the teachings, only God could forgive sins. He offended the Law by eating without washing his hands, and dined with 'sinners'

When he was asked if he was the Christ, he answered, "If I tell you, ye will not believe". Being asked again, he answered, "Ye say that I am" (Luke 22:67-70). In the eyes of the Pharisees, his reply constituted another blasphemy and enough proof to condemn him. According to them, Jesus was a pretender and blasphemer.

He ran head-on in trouble with the Sadducees when he 'went into the temple, and began to cast out them that sold therein, and them that bought, saying unto them, It is written, my house is the house of prayer: but you have made it a den of thieves.' (Luke 19:45-46) To the Sanhedrin, it was a grave insult and one more reason to get rid of him, and Jesus knew it!

During the week before Passover, Jesus and his disciples went to the Temple where he taught. A few of his friends were members of the Sanhedrin but were afraid of openly supporting him. The Jews hated and feared Pontius Pilate, the Roman governor of Judea. To judge and condemn Jesus, the Sanhedrin needed the agreement of Pontius Pilate. Many of Jesus friends and a great number of the population oppressed and heavily taxed, hoped Jesus to be the promised Messiah especially after his entry to Jerusalem, and longed for an end of the Roman occupation while the leaders feared a Jewish uprising and blood shed.

The Romans declared their Caesars to be God, and demanded adoration as such from their citizens. (The Christian community living in Rome refused to adore Caesar as God and became the victims of persecution).

Jesus and the disciples prepared for the celebration of the Passover, the festivities which commemorated Moses leading the Hebrews out of bondage of Egypt.

The custom required the offering of a one-year old male lamb without blemish according to the Book of Exodus12:5. The blood of the lamb applied to the doorposts of the home according to the law given by Moses, was a sign for the Angel of Death to pass over the dwellings of the Hebrew families. The angel, noticing the unmarked homes of the Egyptians, struck their firstborn son's dead. After the Pharaoh lost his firstborn son, he was horrified, and permitted the Hebrews to leave Egypt.

Jesus arranged to have the Passover with the disciples in a room set aside and arranged. The disciples were saddened and upset. During the last weeks spent with them, he spoke of his approaching trial and death as prophesied. He tried to comfort the disciples, "Let not your heart be troubled: ye believe in God, believe also in me (John 14:1) I am the resurrection and the life: he that believes in me, though he were dead, yet shall he live. And whosoever liveth and believeth in me shall never die. (John 11:25-26) This is my commandment, that ye love one another, as I have loved you" (John 16:12).

Much of Jesus teachings had been difficult for the disciples to understand no matter how much he tried to elucidate and explain a lesson. He assured the disciples that the Heavenly Father would send the Holy Spirit, the 'Comforter' and this would help them to comprehend his teachings.

Jesus mission of the Coming Kingdom had failed because most of his casual listeners did not understand the significance of his teaching of the coming of the Kingdom, and anything else like the daily wants (see: Sermon on the Mount) was to be regarded as of secondary importance. The teaching of the Kingdom of God was a dangerous lesson because it could have been a political statement and an assault to the Roman Empire. Jesus was well-versed in the study of the prophets. According to Isaiah 53, the servant of the Lord is described as suffering for the transgressions of the people. The servant is described as of no violence and deceit. Isaiah's prophecy corresponds with Jesus' personality and his life's mission as of serving God and mankind.

Jesus expressed of how much he had wanted to celebrate the Passover with the disciples (Luke 22:15-20) He told them that this was the last supper he would share with the disciples. During the ensuing meal, he compared himself to the paschal lamb being sacrificed for the Passover. After breaking the bread, blessing it and passing it around, he spoke of it as of his body given up for many. He lifted the chalice filled with wine, blessed it and drank from it and passed the wine around, referring to it as his blood of the new covenant spilled for many for the remission of sins. He told the disciples that in future they should share the supper in such a way, as in remembrance of him.

Since antiquity, blood resembled the symbolism of sacredness and of life. The blood of the immaculate sacrificial lamb covered the altar while the flesh of the lamb was the sacrifice made to God. Bread was the staple diet and accompanied every meal. Wine and bread were served and contained the elements of nourishment. Jesus, the Lamb of God (John 1:29, Peter 1:19) tried to use symbols to explain a more complex spiritual meaning concerning the Last Supper and his eternal unity with the celebrants. He knew of the betrayal of Judas Iscariot who left them after Jesus revealed that one of them was a traitor. He also knew that Peter, influenced by the devil, would deny him three times (Matt. 26:69-75) Peter would never forget his betrayal, and followed the example of the beloved master by accepting his mission and death on the cross.

After the meal was over, Jesus rose to fill a basin with water, and washed and dried the feet of his disciples (John 13:4). Simon Peter, who did not comprehend the deep significance of Jesus' action, argued to get his feet washed by his Master. Jesus explained to Peter without the foot washing he would have 'no part with him.' Jesus explained that he, the 'Lord and Master' washed the feet of his disciples and that they must do the same to each other. He emphasized on the relationship between master and servant and tried to indicate that both must serve each other equally.

Jesus walked with Peter, James and John to the garden of Gethsemane to pray. It was night, and he asked them to stay awake. Jesus was very sorrowful while he prayed asking the Heavenly Father 'if it be possible, let this cup pass from me' but he added as the true and devoted Son of God,' nevertheless not as I will but as thou wilst' (Matt: 26:39).

Judas, who had in the meantime called the guards, escorted them to the garden He indicated with a kiss on Jesus' cheek that he was the wanted one, and they arrested Jesus and lead him away.

Jesus was brought before Caiaphas the High Priest, surrounded by his scribes, priests and elders. They tried to find some evidence to condemn him but the testimony was contradictory. One witness reported of Jesus having said, "Destroy this temple (body) and in three days I will raise it up" (John 2:19) but Jesus referred to his resurrection (Matt. 27:63).When the High priest heard the remark concerning the temple, he rose in anger and demanded an answer from Jesus but he kept silent. He demanded from Jesus to answer the significant statement: "Tell us whether thou be the Christ, the Son of God". Jesus answered, "Thou hast said: nevertheless I say unto you, Hereafter shall ye see the Son of Man sitting on the right hand of Power, and coming in the clouds of Heaven" (Matt:26:60-66 and Luke 22:67-70).

Caiaphas, the High Priest, tore his clothes to demonstrate his deep dismay and shock. Jesus statement was the ultimate blasphemy ever uttered. Caiaphas turned to his audience and asked them, "Do we need more proof?" They agreed that Jesus was a blasphemer and guilty of death.

Jesus was sent to Pontius Pilate and King Herod, who was at that time in Jerusalem Herod interviewed and ridiculed Jesus and arrayed him in a magnificent robe. The soldiers put a crown of thorns on his head, and King Herod sent Jesus back to Pontius Pilate (Luke 22:52- 23:56, John 19:1-23). Pilate's wife had a dream in which she received the affirmation of Jesus' righteousness. She revealed the dream to Pilate with the assurance that Jesus was a good and just man. (Matt.27:19). Pilate addressed Jesus and asked him, "Art thou the King of the Jews?" And Jesus answered, "My kingdom is not of this world; if my kingdom were of this world, then would my servants fight, that I should not be delivered to the Jews: but now is my kingdom not from hence" (John 18:35-36).Pilate told the waiting crowd that he interrogated Jesus but could find no fault in him (Luke 23:13, John 18:38-40). There also was present a bound prisoner called Bar-Abbas who had committed murder. Pilate argued with the crowd whom he should release Bar-Abbas or Jesus. He offered to chastise Jesus and release him but the multitude cried, "Release Bar-Abbas, crucify Jesus" (Mark 16:6-15). The elders and chief priests convinced the crowd to plead for Bar–Abbas and eliminate Jesus (Matt.27:20).

After the interrogation by Pontius Pilate and the ensuing flogging, Jesus was led to the place of crucifixion. Jesus was crucified with two thieves, his cross placed in the centre. A plate was nailed above his head, saying in Greek, Latin and Hebrew, "This is the King of the Jews." His female followers who had shown devotion and faith in him, and his grieving mother witnessed the agonies of her son, accompanied by the disciple John. The crowd watched in the distance while the Roman soldiers, who carried out the sentence, gambled for Jesus robe.

The sky darkened and the earth shook, and the curtain in the temple tore into two pieces. As the end of his suffering arrived, Jesus lifted his head and said, "Father, in Thine hands I commend my spirit" (Luke 23:46) and died.

A wealthy and honourable man, Joseph of Arimathae, went to Pontius Pilate and asked for the body of Jesus to be laid down in a tomb owned by him. Pontius Pilate was surprised that Jesus had died after so short a time (it usually took days for the victim to die) granted the request. Jesus body was covered in linen and put into the cave because it was against the law to have a crucified body on the cross during the Sabbath. The next day, the Pharisees and chief priests went to Pontius Pilate, and requested that the sepulchre be blocked by a large rock and a watch to be placed because they remembered Jesus saying that after three days he would rise again. The priests also took into consideration that the disciples may take the body of Jesus away (Matt.27:62-66).Pontius Pilate granted their request. The sepulchre was sealed and a watch placed next to it to keep anyone away who may want to remove the body.

The next morning, Mary Magdalene and the other Mary went to the tomb to anoint and wrap Jesus body in linen. When the women arrived, the earth shook and an angel appeared and removed the rock that sealed the entry. The guards fled in fear because the angel's radiant appearance frightened them. The angel informed the two women that Jesus had risen from the dead as he had prophesied, and that they should depart and bring the glorious news to the disciples. According to the angel, Jesus would appear in Galilee and be seen and met by the disciples.

The women left in great hurry to bring the glad tidings to the disciples. Jesus showed himself to the disciples who were overjoyed and worshipped him (Matt. 28:1-11).

The guards went into the city and told everything that had happened. The disciples went to Galilee and Jesus again stayed with him He showed them his hands and feet to convince the disciples that it was him, Jesus. He stayed with the eleven disciples for forty days and deepened and increased their understanding of his teachings, and assured them again of the promise given by the Heavenly Father to send the Holy Spirit.

Jesus told the disciples to return to Jerusalem. He walked with them and while he blessed them he was lifted up to heaven (Luke 24: 39-52).

Reflection

The Last Supper – Holy Eucharist – Holy Communion – as it is referred to by various denominations – is introduced to the catholic child when he or she celebrates her first confirmation. It is easier for the adult to understand the significance of the Last Supper considering the historical background that shaped the life of Jesus, and ultimately lead to the cross. The profound spirituality of the Last Supper requires maturity to fully comprehend.

What may have happened if friends would have helped him to escape and hide in a safe place? Jesus had enemies but also friends who would have been very willing to hide him in a safe place. He would have been remembered by those who had the good fortune to know him. Jesus knew that he had to accept the mock trial and gruesome death on the cross because that was the mission given by the Almighty Father. He would never abandon the sacred message of the coming Kingdom of God for bringing himself into safety! Jesus was completely immersed into the love and will of God to the point of accepting the unjust and cruel death.

His disciples realized that he was the Messiah sent by God. In the beginning of their discipleship, they may have hoped Jesus to be the warrior-like Messiah who would free Palestine of the hated Roman occupation.

Appointed by God and announced by the prophets, he accepted the mission of delivering humanity from sin. Those who accept and declare him as their Saviour, and faithfully live by His teachings, shall find salvation and eternal life with Him and through Him.

If we are trying to understand Jesus, we must picture ourselves living in his century in Palestine occupied by the indifferent Romans. Jesus was a devout Jew born into a pious Jewish family. He strongly emphasized to obey the Jewish Law although he showed some leniency towards rituals which was of utmost importance to the Sadducees. Pontius Pilate's attitude was not very sympathetic toward the Jews. He carefully avoided involvement of religious disputes as long as the population paid the requested crushing taxes.

One more point regarding Jesus has to be made: Christianity described Jesus as a single man.

According to Jewish law, a healthy, single man was to marry and raise a family. If he declined marriage as it was his responsibility, he would have to justify his rejection to the inquiring Sanhedrin! It may be that Jesus spent much of his time as a disciple of the Essenes. Would the 'Sermon on the Mount" be different if he was a married man? Peter was married, and his wife accompanied him on his mission including the other female disciples who followed Jesus.

A similar conflict and outrage has been created through Dan Brown's book "The Da Vinci Code" declaring that Leonardo Da Vinci's famous 'Last Supper' depicted Mary Magdalene leaning away from Jesus who is at the centre of the picture. Leonardo posed the disciples in four groups, each of them showing three disciples. If the long-haired, feminine-looking disciple is allegedly Mary Magdalene-where is John, the 'beloved disciple'? To add another (thirteen instead of twelve) disciple would destroy the symmetry of the painting but how can Leonardo dismiss the 'beloved disciple' John? The disciple John was an adolescent and Leonardo painted him as such.

Considerations such as the obligation of a Jewish male to marry and raise a family, did not apply to Jesus because he was of Divine birth, the Son of God. It was impossible to explain this to the common and uneducated people including the members of the Sanhedrin. Jesus knew that his life would soon be sniffed out like a burning candle, and in one of his final statements he revealed his purpose of life and identity:" I have been sent by God, the Father. I and the Father are One."(John 14:10).

Part 2

Part 2

Chapter 4

The teachings of Jesus / The Holy Ghost

The Holy Ghost as spoken of by Jesus puzzles Christians of the modern age as much as it did the disciples of Jesus. What is the Holy Spirit? The Old Testament is vague in describing the Spirit of God but makes mention of it.

Genesis 1:2, states, "And the earth was without form, and void, and darkness was upon the face and deep. And the spirit of God moved upon the face of the waters. And God said, "Let there be light: and there was light".

The prophet Ezekiel reveals a vision in which he found himself in a valley of dry bones, and commanded to summon the life-giving breath or Gods spirit (Eze.37:1-14). Reading the prophet Isaiah: (11:2, and 61:1) "And the spirit of the Lord shall rest upon him, the spirit of wisdom and understanding, the spirit of council and might, the spirit of knowledge and of the fear of the Lord".

The Gospel of John begins with the words, "In the beginning was the Word (logos, the divine word) and the Word was with God, and the Word was God." John 1:4 speaks of Jesus by saying, "In him was life, and the life was the light of men." The 'logos' was manifested in Jesus Christ.

The Hebrew word "ruach" translates as "Breath of the Living God". The Book of Job 33:4, declares, "The spirit of God hath made me, and the breath of the Almighty has given me life". Chapter 37:10, of the same scripture mention the 'breath', "By the breath of God frost is given and the breath of the waters is straightened".

John the Bapist baptized people in the Jordan River, and proclaiming that the Kingdom of God was near. He urged his listeners to repent their sins. He, too, refers to the spirit: the one, who will follow him, will baptize with water and spirit.

God is threefold: God the Father, God the Son, God the Holy Spirit. We refer to the 'Three in One' as to the 'Holy Trinity.' The Gospel of Matt, 12:31-32, Jesus explains the Holy Ghost more clearly by warning against the sin of denying the Holy Ghost, "Wherefore I say unto you, all manner of sin and blasphemy shall be forgiven unto men: but the blasphemy against the Holy Ghost shall not be forgiven unto men. And whosoever speakest a word against the Son of man, it shall be forgiven him:

but whosoever speakest against the Holy Ghost, it shall not be forgiven him, neither in this world, neither in the world to come." The Gospel of Mark 3:28, is even more severe, "Verily I say unto you, all sins shall be forgiven unto the sons of men, and blasphemies wherewith so ever they shall blaspheme: but he that shall blaspheme against the Holy Ghost has never forgiveness, but is in danger of eternal damnation". To deny the evidence and the presence of the Holy Ghost is a greater and graver sin than to deny the teachings of Jesus.

The Holy Spirit is 'the spirit of God' and the third aspect of the Trinity. One may think of it as the essence that sets creation into motion, permeates and sustains it. Jesus was pre-ordained as the Son of God, and was conceived by the Holy Spirit. While John the Baptist performed the baptism of Jesus, the Holy Ghost in the shape of a dove descended on him. John received the assurance from God that Jesus was the 'lamb of God which taketh away the sins of the world.'(John 1:26-33). The Holy Spirit was and is forever imminent in the Son of God. Jesus made the statement according to John 6:63, "It is the spirit that quickenth: the flesh profiteth nothing. The words that I speak unto you, they are spirit, and they are life".

Jesus spoke on various occasions of the Holy Spirit, as in Mark 13:11, "But when they shall lead you, and deliver you up, take no thought beforehand what ye shall speak, neither do ye premeditate: but whatsoever shall be given you in that hour, that speak ye: for it is not ye that speak, but the Holy Spirit." He called the Holy Spirit the "Comforter' and promised the disciples that the 'Comforter' shall be sent to them by the Father to help them understand his teachings (John 14:16-18). Jesus instructed the disciples to baptize in the name of the Father and of the Son and of the Holy Spirit (Matt. 28:19). Jesus appeared after his resurrection to his disciples according to John 20:22. "Peace be unto you: as my Father hath sent me, even so I sent you." And when he had said this, he breathed on them, "Receive ye the Holy Ghost."

Baby Jesus received the Holy Spirit that formed him, at the second of his mother's conception. The Gospels stress the conception by the Holy Spirit but Jesus himself never referred to the virginity of his mother.

The third aspect, or the 'Holy Spirit,' created much controversy within the church of the second century A.D. It was argued that Jesus had two natures, one as the son of Man, and as the divine Son of God, and the opinions were divided. In 428, Nestorius, the bishop of Constantinople, attacked the theory of Theotokos as irreconcilable with the humanity of Jesus and should be referred to as Christotokos, the Christ-bearer. This statement caused resentment among the followers and came to be brought before the Council of Ephesus. Pope Celestine I guided the meeting and it was finally decided that Jesus possessed two natures- one divine and one human but united in the divine being as the Son of God. Since Mary gave birth to Jesus, the divine person, she may rightly be called Theotokos, the Mother of God.

The Holy Spirit is a profound and deep mystery which our limited mind cannot grasp.

Reflection

The Holy Spirit fine-tunes our limited human understanding. We are more sensitive and able to comprehend and interpret the deeper and subtler meanings of spiritual wisdom. The Holy Spirit guided the life and teachings of Jesus, and his words were the expressions of it. A person rejecting his teachings is like a fruitless tree and without spiritual life. Anyone living according to the teachings of Jesus has life. Such an individual expresses guidance, truthfulness, loyalty and love during the various stages of life.

If we are lead by the Holy Spirit, our life is changed. We walk in God's grace, and are guided by Him and through Him, and our life will never be the same again.

Chapter 5

The Golden Rule

Matt. 7:12, Luke 6:31

The 'Golden Rule' teaches to treat our fellow man with respect, consideration and kindness. The politeness one wishes to receive when communicating with friends, neighbours or business relations obliges one to respond with the same courtesy. The 'Golden Rule' sums up correct and right behaviour towards others.

The great teacher of the Law, Hillel (born in 75 B.C.) stated three principles to guide a man's life: love of peace, love of man, the knowledge and love of the Law. He stated also that something that is hateful to one should not be done to another, and added that one must not judge another man until one has been in his place. One may sum it up in one short sentence: be non-judgemental and considerate.

Jesus used the 'Golden Rule' in his famous "Sermon on the Mount" (Matt. 6-7). Anyone being unfamiliar with the teachings of Jesus should read the "Sermon" which summarizes his teachings.

If we were able to conduct yourself according to the "Golden Rule" there would be no crime, deception, lies, cheating and no wars! It would be a world very different from our present society. We create our environment as harmonious or unpleasant. An objective and loving individual knows how to cope with difficulties, and still finds balance and peace.

If a person is of quarrelsome and grumpy nature, he or she perceive any situation negatively, and present an erroneous interpretation. Such individuals are hard to please and tend to be dissatisfied and problematic. Everything 'bad' happens to them and they seem to attract bad luck to them. In fact, evil thoughts and actions return to the sender. One cannot escape the penalty for unkindness and evil acts. If one desires good manners from our fellow man, one must show courtesy and respect. We shall harvest what we have sown, either good or evil. The Apostle Paul knew it very well and recommended in his letter to the Romans, chapter 12:19: "Dearly beloved, avenge not yourselves but rather give place unto wrath: for it is written, 'Vengeance is mine; I will repay, says the Lord'. Therefore, if thine enemy hunger, feed him; if he thirst, give him drink: for in doing so thou shalt heap coals of fire on his head. Be not overcome of evil, but overcome evil with good".

Paul knew that the "Golden Rule" exercises the divine law of justice, and compensates for acts of kindness and love toward our fellow man. It teaches hard lessons if we fail to accept responsibilities, helpfulness, and compassion.

Every person needs and appreciates friendliness and kindness and a kind word or helpful act can change someone's attitude from irritability to a more friendly response. Every action creates a reaction either positive or negative that affects the individual who sent it.

The "Golden Rule" is renowned by other religions besides Christianity. It is one of the spiritual laws ruling the universe. References in the sacred literature of the Hindus, Moslems (Sufi), Chinese and Buddhist literature are stating in different words the same principles as expressed by Hillel.

Jesus lived by the Golden Rule. To follow his teaching, one experiences inner peace because whatever obstacles crosses one's way, one possesses the knowledge and assurance that every problem has a solution, and panic is unnecessary.

Reflection

Many people are not familiar with the "Golden Rule" and do not regard it as a guideline of contact. If we are nasty and unkind to an individual we cannot expect courtesy in return. It is necessary to realize our mistakes instead of blaming the others. Fairness demands correction of behaviour, politeness and consideration. Applying 'eye for eye and tooth for tooth,' has been corrected by Jesus who emphasizes 'love thy enemy as you love thyself'. Retaliation it not the solution to resolve problems but destroys the hope of establishing harmony and peace.

Chapter 6

Prayer

Matt. 6: 9-13, Luke 11:2, 18:9-14

Prayer is a dialog between God and us. When we pray we must pray from the heart to our Heavenly Father. It does not need to be a prayer from the prayer book, and must never be a mechanical and habitual prayer.

We pray for different reasons and some are prayers of adoration and praise, petitions for loved ones or for the country, and so on.

Prayer is the most important part of our spiritual life, and we must also pray for realizing our sins, our shortcomings and faults and pray for the strength to overcome them. Jesus taught a masterful prayer that encompasses the needs of our earthly life, as well as our spiritual ones. He divided the prayer into different sections.

"Our Father who art in Heaven. Hallowed be Thy name", he is holy (hallowed). "Thy kingdom come, Thy will be done on earth as it is in Heaven". God is the supreme ruler and king. Teaching us the Lord's Prayer, Jesus gives an explanation who God is, where He is, and enlightens us about the kingdom that shall come on earth. A difficult clause is the statement that 'thy will be done.' One may pray for God's will to be done without realizing the truth behind it and such mechanically spoken prayers must be carefully avoided. To let God decide our life's path requires a total surrender under His will. He shall show us the right action to take-but many of us have overwhelming egos and want to have their way.

"Give us today our daily bread". In Jesus' time, bread has always been added to the meal which consisted of meat, wine and fruits. We pray for our sustenance, and bread is part of our daily meal. The petition applies for guidance of one's life here on earth, and also for our physical and spiritual needs.

Jesus continues with a very important request: "Forgive us our debts as we forgive our deptors". He does not necessarily refer to monetary debts. Jesus knew how difficult it is to forgive someone who has offended, harmed and betrayed us and earned our wrath. To forgive the offender clears him from guilt and releases him and us because we put the wrongdoing out of our mind and life. It is a spiritual law and must be thoroughly understood and obeyed if one seeks peace of mind and harmony in one's life. Without forgiving the person the (monetary or spiritual) debt we cannot expect God to forgive us our debts, shortcomings and sins.

Jesus continues by praying: "And lead us not into temptation but deliver us from evil". There are strong and subtle temptations. Temptations like lies, stealing, cheating or hiding truth are very common and most individuals think themselves above petty crimes. The subtle temptations are more difficult to recognize and eliminate, and constitute a great hindrance to our spiritual growth. Jesus warned his listeners of spiritual pride when he included the above clause. Meant by it is the arrogant thought of being better than others. He pointed at the Pharisees and scribes who emphasized their righteous lives because of strictly obeying the laws and rituals. They loved to stand on the street corners to pray in the hope that every onlooker sees and regards them as pious. Jesus disliked such a public demonstration of piety and strongly recommended to his listeners 'to go into thy chamber to pray in solitude and God will hear you'.

"Deliver us from evil" the evil-one. He is always cunning and scheming, and tries to divert us from doing God's will. He convinces us that it is all right to tell 'a little white lie' except all lies are black and ugly. The 'evil one' is very subtle and convincing if one is not on guard. We are constantly subject to evil like unkindness in thought and speech as well as carrying out deeds that may bring harm to others including to ourselves. Jesus, who knew the devils destructive and subtle power very well, included the petition of release from the 'evil one' in the Lord's Prayer.

He closed his magnificent and comprehensive prayer by confirming Gods Being and Omnipresence: "For Thine is the Kingdom, and the Power, and the Glory, for ever.

God is the totality, the power, the kingdom and Creator of this magnificent universe. If we pray with such knowledge in our minds, we are able to change our outlook on life. God works in us and through us and this realization grants us strength, inspiration, wisdom and joy.

Reflection

Some people reveal that God never answered their prayers, and they are asking, 'Why do I not receive an answer from God?'

Perhaps we must do some soul – searching: are we self-absorbed and proud? Do we thank Him for guidance, for health and His goodness that embraces us? Are we to sure in our belief to be 'saved' because we are Christians, and others are 'not 'Christians and 'not' saved? Such arrogant attitudes create a wall between us and God who loves the humble heart. When one prays just now and then because our situation in life looks desperate and forget about praying when the dark clouds of problems have vanished, God surely does not like such prayers and attitudes. He does not respond to the 'casual or automatically spoken' prayer but it must come from a devoted heart.

We should ask ourselves the profound question: "What is sin?" Doing something one should not do, telling lies, and so on. People will have a variety of answers and all of them may be correct. Another answer is: sin separates us from God, our Creator, and the source of our salvation, and of righteousness. The awareness of having sinned, and the knowledge of the resulting separation from God creates anguish and torment. The only way of finding joy and peace again is the deeply felt repentance and prayer for forgiveness.

It is a mind-baffling realization that the Creator of the magnificent universe, cares for each individual in the most profound and loving way and is granting free will of choosing or rejecting Him. If we accept God and submit to His loving will and guidance, He will never abandon His children.

1 Kings 3:5, 7, 9, reveals that God appeared to King Solomon in a dream, and asks him what he wished to possess. Solomon answered God that He had shown great mercy to his father David. He reflected on his present situation of being the king of God's chosen people, and admitted that he felt like a child, and insecure. Solomon desired to have 'an understanding heart to judge thy people, that I may discern between good and bad: for who is able to judge this thy so great a people?' God was very pleased and granted him great wisdom and understanding, and promised that if Solomon walks in God's ways and kept His commandments, He would lengthen his days. Perhaps we too, should include this request when praying, "Oh, Lord, grant me a wise and understanding heart that I may become a blessing to others."

In Luke 18:9-14, Jesus distinguishes between two different prayers. One of the prayers was spoken by a Pharisee, who was very proud and self-righteous, and the other man a publican, humble and aware of being a sinner. The Pharisee gave an account of his goodness: He was not 'like other men' and thanked God for it. He was not an extortioner, adulterer or even as this publican, and he continued that he was fasting and giving tithes.

The publican stood alone with his eyes downcast and prayed, "God be merciful to me, a sinner". It is without doubt that God preferred the prayer of the 'sinner'.

Chapter 7

Forgiveness

Matt. 6:12-13, 18: 23-34,

Most people know how hard it is to forgive our offenders. Jesus knew it and tried to explain forgiveness.

Peter came to him and said, "Lord, how often shall my brother sin against me, and I shall forgive him? Till seven times? Jesus said to him, "I say not unto thee until seven times but until seventy times seven (=490). Forgive us our trespasses as we forgive our trespassers. For if, ye forgive men their trespasses our heavenly father will also forgive you. But if ye forgive not men their trespasses, neither will your father forgive your trespasses." The hardness of one's heart, unforgiving and inflexible, is destructive and blocks one's spiritual development. Forgiveness opens the door to kindness, love and compassion.

If someone has hurt another person, he must apologize because it is against spiritual law to offend and upset our fellow man. The transgression is unresolved until the offender asks for heartfelt forgiveness. If the victim kindly accepts the apologies, the offender is free of the wrongdoing. The bill has been paid 'in full.' The great deed of forgiveness cleared the path for both, and peace and joy can return into their lives. It is a profound lesson to be learned and to realize that a forgiving attitude bears in itself the priceless peace of mind. As one forgives the offender who had caused pain, so does God forgive us if we err and repent. An unforgiving person cannot hope for forgiveness.

How do we learn the lesson of forgiveness? The pain of being hurt, insulted or betrayed does not heal overnight, and every time one remembers the distress, the pain re-awakens. At that point, bless the offender and tell him or her, 'I forgive you.' One day, the grief is gone and the soul rejoices in the knowledge of having been able to forgive.

The parable Matt. 18:24-34, explains the spirit of forgiveness. "A king took account and found out that his servant had a dept of ten thousand talents. The king called the servant who declared that he was unable to repay the dept. The king decided to sell the servants wife, children, and belongings. The servant fell to his knees asking for patience and promised to pay the debts. His lord was moved with compassion, and forgave him the debts.

One may sometimes ask why one should forgive while the world in general seems to be indifferent and selfish. If no one would forgive an offender, what kind of world would we live in? It would be intolerable to dwell there (although the world needs much forgiveness and healing).

Jesus gives us a wonderful example of forgiveness in the well-known and beloved parable of the prodigal son.(Luke 15:4-32) Like the father described in the parable, God forgives his repenting children and rejoices in their homecoming. He is patiently waiting for us to learn our lessons and realize His love for us.

Reflection

It is not an easy task to forgive and anyone who says to another person," I forgive you," should think twice about his own words. Forgiveness depends on the deed of another person and some deeds are very difficult to forget and to pardon. Our Heavenly Father forgives a repenting soul and so should we forgive the wrongdoer who threatened our happiness and peace.

There are a few people trying to forgive their erring brothers but many still live by the rule of 'eye for eye and tooth for tooth.' We still have a throat-cutting society, and acts of violence are a daily occurrence and very much on our minds. Forgiveness is by no means a sign of weakness. People fail to realize that it takes courage to admit of having made mistakes, and to ask for forgiveness

There is another thought to be considered: if forgiveness is perceived at as 'altruistic' by some people, why not introduce it again? Someone has to set a good example to be followed.

Chapter 8

The Kingdom of God

Luke 18:20-21, Matt. 4:17, 23, Mark 1:15, John 3:3

Jesus made the concept of God's kingdom the central point of his message, as stated in Luke 4:43:" I must preach the Kingdom of God to other cities also; for therefore I am sent."

He was well acquainted with the writings of the Old Testament, and references concerning the kingdom made in Judges, Psalms, Samuel and Isaiah. What is the definition of the Kingdom of God, and how do we obtain it?

The Gospel of John 4:24 explains that the kingdom of God is of spiritual nature. "God is spirit, and they that worship him must worship him in spirit and in truth."

We worship God in spirit through our prayers and devotions, and by dedicating our actions to Him. By overcoming pride, vanity and self-esteem, we attain a higher spiritual development. The composer Johann Sebastian Bach, who lived from 1685-1750 in Germany, dedicated every composition "To the Glory of God." He humbly realized that God had blessed him and bestowed a great and precious gift on him. Bach's music delights his listeners to this day.

The Gospel of Luke 18:21, tells that the Pharisees approached Jesus questioning about the coming of the kingdom. He answered them, and said, "The kingdom of God cometh not with observation, neither shall they say, lo here, lo there. For behold, the kingdom of God is within you."

"It is not here, it is not there," Jesus explains that the kingdom of God does not have an earthly location. It is not located in a valley or town. If we look for an earthly site, we shall never find God's kingdom. The Kingdom of God is within us and depends on our insight. How can this be? It is possible if our lives are god-centred but still in full anticipation of its daily demands. To realize God's nearness and becoming aware of His guidance helps us to develop a more spiritually oriented way of life. For strength and guidance, we must always return into our inner sanctuary where God dwells.

The Bible tells us to 'abide in God' what means to surrender to His will, and be guided by His loving hand. If we live for Him and express His spirit in our thoughts and actions– then the kingdom is already here. To built walls around our spiritual perception and perceive Him sitting on a throne in an obscured corner of the universe, will not bring us close to Him or reveal Him. If we behold Him everywhere - in the beautiful nature, in a gorgeous sunset, in the love expressed through our loved ones, we shall find Him manifested and close to us, His children.

Mark (12:28-34) describes the story of a scribe who came to Jesus to inquire about the kingdom of God. He asked which of the commandment was most important. Jesus answered him:" The first of all commandments is, "Hear, oh Israel: The Lord our God is one Lord. In addition, thou shall love the Lord with all thy heart, and with all thy soul, and with thy entire mind, and with all thy strength: This is the first commandment and the second is like, namely this, thou shall love thy neighbour as thyself. There is none other commandment greater than these" The scribe agreed that there is one God, and to love him with all the heart, and with all the understanding, and with all the soul, and strength, and to love his neighbour as himself, was more than burned offerings and sacrifices. And Jesus, hearing the scribe's words, said to him:" You are not far from the kingdom of God."

God is the kingdom and His nature is His unconditional love beyond our limited comprehension. Once we realize that and apply it to our lives, we learn to interact with our fellow man. Jesus revealed the secrets of the kingdom to his disciples only He knew them well and specified his teaching. To his casual listeners he spoke in parables since he strove to give his message to his audience according to their life situations and understanding. He talked to the fishermen about fishing. The shepherds understood his parable of the good shepherd who cares for his flock and seeks a lost sheep.

Where Are We Going?

John1:12, speaks of Nicodemus, a Pharisee and member of the Jewish Council and the Sanhedrin, who came to visit Jesus at night-time. He was a religious man and well versed in the scriptures. Nicodemus, inspired by the miracles Jesus had performed, had aroused many questions and wished to discuss them with Jesus.

During the ensuing conversation, Jesus tried to make Nicodemus realize that seeing the kingdom of God required a second (spiritual) birth.

"Unless a man has been born again he cannot see the Kingdom of God" (through baptism and the receiving of the Holy Spirit). Nicodemus applied physical laws to the words of Jesus and failed to realize the spiritual meaning. He asked in confusion," How can a man be born again when he is old? Can he enter a second time into his mother's womb, and be born?"

Jesus attempted to teach Nicodemus that we are born into a material world but our second birth is spiritual, signifying a spiritual awakening to the new life devoted to God and by applying his teachings. Nicodemus faced the same problems as our society today: we seem to have lost the spiritual meaning of Jesus' teachings.

Every sermon Jesus delivered possessed a deeper interpretation but not every person perceived and understood it, and one of them was Nicodemus. Although educated, Nicodemus missed the point Jesus tried to make. It is not enough to live a morally clean life, to help others in time of need, and attend church regularly. God wants our undivided and absolute love and loyalty, in words, deeds and most of all, in spirit. Jesus leads the way. No one can reach the kingdom unless he fully accepts Jesus, the Son of God, as his or her saviour. Jesus stated the message clearly (John 14:6), "I am the way, the truth, and the life: no man cometh unto the Father but by me"

In Matthew 7:21, we read that Jesus warned, "Not every one that saith unto me, Lord, Lord, shall enter into the kingdom of heaven; but he that doeth the will of my Father which is in heaven".

Reflection

Are we not in the same boat with Nicodemus? Some of Jesus lessons are literally interpreted although the spiritual teaching Jesus applied to is quite often not perceived or ignored by the interpreter. Jesus loved to speak metaphorically to his casual listeners to formulate an idea. Take for instance:' turn the other cheek'. Do we have to turn the other cheek to let a spiteful person slap us? It may also mean: let the matter rest, try to forgive, go on with your life and forget about the incident? Jesus taught a passive approach and stressed that physical behaviour and mental attitudes must be non-retaliating. He lived a life that was totally god-entered and of peacefulness although he died an unjust and violent death. His thoughts and words expressed love and forgiveness until to his last breath.

Chapter 9

Baptism

Matt: 3:12, Mark 1:2-6, Luke 3:2-17, John 3:14, 22, 5:24, 8:12, I Cor. 12:13,

"Repent ye, for the Kingdom of Heaven is at hand." John the Baptist, son of Zacharias and Elizabeth, prepared the way for Jesus. John's baptism symbolized penitence, purification and forgiveness of sins. Purification and penitence rites were performed and recommended.

John the Baptist found many followers who asked if he was the awaited Messiah which he denied. He told the people that he baptized with water but someone greater than him would follow him and baptize with water and the Holy Spirit.

Jesus went to see John, who was his relative, after returning from his forty days in the wilderness. He requested to be baptized by John not because to be cleansed from sin (he was without sin). Jesus opened the gates for everyone to follow his example of unity with him and through him. God's salvation, proclaimed by Jesus, is for all of Mankind.

After John the Baptist's death, Jesus travelled through Judea. He preached to the people and baptized followers (John 3:22)

What is the meaning of baptism for us? It is redemption from sins, commitment, identification and obedience to Christ. The wish for baptism reflects the outward sign of the inner development of receiving Jesus as Lord and Saviour. Baptism is the leading to salvation. Many Christians who are not 'twice-born' that is: baptized a second time, or not baptized at all, may ask the question: "How do I find salvation and the Kingdom of Heaven? What must I do?" The answer would be: "Repent and be baptized, and accept Jesus as your Lord and Master. The Holy Spirit will guide you, and you will have a new life that reflects Christ's life on earth". From then on the baptized individual calls himself or herself a 'Christian' and 'reborn'.

Often babies receive baptism weeks or months after birth because it inherited the original sin committed by the first created human couple Adam and Eve. The baptized infant becomes a member of the Christian community, an event important to the parents and relatives. The 'born again' Christians reject baptism of infants because the infant is unable to express the wish for baptism.

Once the older and more mature individual desires baptism to take place, the person must be mentally and spiritually prepared, repent sins and wrongdoings and accept Jesus as one's saviour. Faith in God and the teachings of Jesus take deep roots and determine an individual decide to accept him as the personal saviour.

Paul, who lived among the Gentiles, baptized new members. His teachings employ unity in spirit that permeates and changes the people's viewpoint and conduct. In the first letter to the Corinthians, chapter 12:13, he wrote, "For by one spirit we are all baptized into one body, whether we are Jews or Gentiles, whether we are bound or free, and have been all made to drink into one spirit."

Peter also baptized followers. Cornelius, a Gentile soldier; called on him and asked Peter to baptize him and his household (Acts 10:34-38).

The Churches in Europe, like the Lutheran and Evangelical churches, base their doctrine on the teachings of Paul's letter: "But that no man is justified by the law in the sight of God, it is evident: the just shall live by faith." (Gal.3:11) The person receiving baptism is sprinkled with water on the head and submerging is not necessary.

Reflection

A large number of people coming from different branches of Christianity received second baptism. They affirmed to have had profound experiences that helped them to come closer to Christ and helped them to make fundamental changes in their lives. Good works alone or attending the church every Sunday does not bestow salvation but only through wholeheartedly accepting Jesus as our saviour.

Chapter 10

Rituals

Luke 4:14-30, 11:37-39, Mark 7:2-15, 18-23, Matt. 15:11, 17-20

Jesus was not overly concerned about rituals. He loved to talk under the open sky or whenever he saw a few people gathered around he chose a convenient spot to speak to them.

The Pharisees were eager to set snares for him, as told according to Luke 11:37: "In addition, as he spoke, a certain Pharisee asked him to dine with him and he went in, and sat down to meat and when the Pharisee saw it, he marvelled that he (Jesus) had not first washed before dinner. In addition, the Lord said to him, "Now do ye Pharisees make clean the outside of the cup and the platter; but your inward part is full of wickedness." He tried to point out that clean hands do not change a wicked heart and mind.

The Gospel of Mark (7:21-23) explains even more the grave consequences which can be brought about by not carefully controlling one's thoughts and emotions. "For from within out of the heart of men proceed evil thoughts, adultery, fornication, murder, theft, covetousness, wickedness, deceit, lasciviousness, an evil eye, blasphemy, pride, foolishness. All these evil things come from within, and defile a man."

An outwardly clean person may be harassed with violent thoughts and emotions which need to be controlled and conquered. Emotions must not have the upper hand in our life or they destroy it. Evil stems from within and hateful thoughts that may take control and compel one to act accordingly. One may say that we are what we think. A peaceful and harmonious person emanates friendliness while a violent person creates discord. The Pharisees paid great emphasis to rituals and ritual cleaning. Cleanliness is desirable but does not replace the importance of an inner pure life.

Jesus often bypassed ritual by preaching in the open air. The young Christian church organizing itself over the first few centuries needed order of worship and consequently developed the liturgy to guide the worshippers at prayer, and the holy sacraments, and educational sermons.

Since the worshippers of the early churches were illiterate and did not understand the service spoken in Latin, the church commissioned artists to create murals and paintings. The illustrated events taken from the Bible served as means of education expounding the birth of Jesus, his life and teaching, and the crucifixion, and pictures of Mary and Joseph and the saints describe their lives and sufferings. The art of stained glass enhancing the Gothic cathedral windows created great and stunningly beautiful masterpieces and introduced a new branch of fine art

The first churches built after the decline of the Roman Empire were the Basilicas. They were rectangular with a high central section called the 'nave'. The semicircular section called the 'apse' enclosed the altar. The Basilica of Ravenna in Italy is a fine example of the early Christian architecture and its beautiful mosaics.

The churches of the medieval period tried to were plain, to be replaced to be at the end of the twelfth century in the church. End of the twelfth century, the churches were built in the 'Romanesque' style (called in England the 'Norman' style.) The cathedrals in Worms, Speyer, and Mainz in Germany, Cluny and Arles in France are great exemplars of the Romanesque architecture.

The Romanesque architecture was gradually superseded by the Gothic architecture. The builders of Gothic Cathedrals developed the upward pointed arch instead of the round Romanesque arch. The windows, in contrast to the Romanesque churches, were larger and allowed light to enter. The height of the vaulted ceiling was balanced and supported from the outside through the 'flying buttresses' which enabled the architects to build the cathedrals higher, and to decorate the windows with large and very beautiful stained glass windows.

The interior as well as the exterior of the early Gothic cathedrals were unadorned (Cathedral of Chester, England) in comparison to the later style which became increasingly elaborate and ornamental. The Durham cathedral (England) built in 1093, for example, is a mixture of Romanesque and Gothic architecture.

The style and height of the cathedral and its bell towers changed from country to country. The cathedral at Cologne (Germany) is famous for its beauty while the city of Ulm prides itself for its cathedrals highest and beautifully ornamented bell tower. The cathedrals represent good examples of the ornamental Gothic style used in Europe. France is represented by the famous cathedrals of Notre Dame in Paris, also at Reims, Strasbourg, and Amiens. The towers of the English Gothic Cathedrals like Canterbury, York and Westminster in London are lacking the heights of the Continental cathedrals but are not wanting in majesty and magnificence.

The soaring interiors of the Gothic cathedrals overwhelm the visitor and induce a feeling of otherworldliness and peace. One can very easily forget the bustling world outside of the cathedral, and is, after all, the purpose of going to church and meditate on God.

The churches of the Renaissance (1300–1600) are enhanced with paintings of great artists. An example of such sublime craftsmanship is the Sistine Chapel at St. Peter in Rome decorated with a wonderfully painted ceiling done by the great sculptor and painter Michelangelo. The churches during the Baroque (1600-1700) became very ornamental with gold trimmings and gilded angels.

The Reformation and the break from the Catholic Church did not only change doctrines but also the interiors of the Protestant Churches. There may be only one or two pictures adorning the church. Many of the churches are decorated with a bare cross which indicates the resurrection of Jesus. The sermon contains selections from the Bible lasting approximately forty minutes. Specific Sundays are set aside are for the observation of the Last Supper.

Ritual is part of the service and concerning the Sacraments (baptism, Communion, wedding, confirmation or funeral) the particular ritual is applied. The ritual helps to divert the worshipper from pondering his or her daily problems and attune to the worship. Ritual, therefore, is an aid to achieve concentration and inner stillness but most important is the worship itself. A beautiful church, architecturally beautiful, is uplifting as long as the interior does not distract the worshipper. Ritual and décor of the interior have their place but the most important part of the worship is seeking communion with the Lord.

Reflection

Our society emphasizes cleanliness, and magazines and television advertisements describe soaps and lotions in abundance. It is of course, necessary to pass through the daily ritual of personal cleanliness for reason of self-respect, our contact with other fellow men, and of health.

If one reads the teachings of the Gospels carefully, one discovers that Jesus includes another cleanliness, namely that of a pure heart and clean mind. Jesus pointed out quite clearly that what you say to others is as important as the food you consume because your spoken word, good or violent, determines your actions. The purity and peace of mind is of great importance because it reveals who we really are.

It is not easy to control one's thoughts in our world of cheap advertisement and the wrong attitudes of doing whatever we are fancy to be entitled to do. The thought of self-control is not in favour with most people but it would be a much better world if people would exercise control of action and use restraint in their emotions and speech.

Chapter 11

The Miracle of Healing

Matt.8:5-11, Luk.7:3-9,

Jesus healed many people according to the four Gospels. Healing had been performed by others but his healing was performed through the Holy Spirit.

One of the great writings of the Gospel concerning healing is found in Matthew. Jesus and his disciples came to Capernaum when a centurion approached him. He was a Roman officer, as he introduced himself to Jesus, and he had a very special request: his servant was severely ill and in a lot of pain. Jesus promised to go and see after him but the centurion was a good and modest man. He did not feel himself worthy enough to have the Master enter his house, and therefore he made an astonishing request: "speak the word, and my servant shall be healed." Jesus was surprised and 'marvelled' at the centurion's faith.

If we could have faith like the Roman centurion!

There were instances where Jesus had been unable to perform a healing namely if the person in question half-heartedly approached him. He usually put the questions to the sick person "Do you believe that I can heal you?" The mental state of the individual is very important as any physician may confirm. The trust between the physician and the patient is of great importance.

Jesus knew that a human is not just a body but has also a mind and soul. If the sufferer disbelieved – Jesus could not perform the healing. A physician needs to have the trust of his patient to obtain the best results of his healing labours If one does not trust the physician in charge, the healing hand is hindered to perform well. It takes faith in God and in the ability of the physician as well. Paul knew this very well. He spoke movingly of faith according to his letters to the Hebrews 1:11, "Now faith is the substance of things hoped for, the evidence of things not seen." is the faith expressed by the ailing patient is very important and adds to the healing process. Without faith, the healing cannot be accomplished. The teaching of faith was a concept difficult for the young Greek congregations to understand and to struggle with.

It is not always the body that is sick and in need of the healing art of a physician. Many of the illnesses have their origin in the sufferings of unhappiness, loneliness, lack of love and understanding. The illness has an emotional base, and, if untreated, will take on physical manifestations, as for example: heart condition, stomach ulcers, and so on.

There are many individuals who are of the firm conviction that illness is a way of punishment heaped upon them by the wrathful God. Those people respond with anger, feeling insulted and punished. It is hard to suffer pain and discomfort, and, at the same time keep up the faith and be quiet and self-controlled but illness is not a punishment. Perhaps it is a trial of our love and devotion to God. The Book of Job describes Job's unshaken faith, and praising God in spite of the calamities that beset him and his family. If God gives us a cross, our loving Lord Jesus helps us to carry it.

Reflection

Jennifer had been diagnosed by a cardiologist with Mitral Valve Prolapse. It was not a life-threatening condition but in time an operation would be necessary because the ineffective valve be needed to be replaced. Jennifer lived through a rough time and in seemed to her that she was surrounded by cold und uncompromising people. She was very frustrated and one person in particular gave her much grief. At first, she disliked that individual and later she simply hated him.

Jennifer felt very upset and distraught because she felt that she did not live according to Jesus' teaching who stated: 'Pray for your enemies, pray for those that despitefully use you'.

Jennifer prayed ardently to be able to forgive her tormenter. One night, she dreamed that Lord Jesus stood beside her bed. He touched her heart and removed something that looked like the root of a plant. Then he put the index-and middle fingers on her lips and on her ears, and Jennifer understood what the Lord tried to teach her: speak no evil, hear no evil. After that, Lord Jesus disappeared.

Jennifer pondered her dream. She was scheduled to see her cardiologist who tested her alleged Mitral Valve Prolapse. After the test was completed, Jennifer questioned the cardiologist, 'Well, how is the Mitral Valve Prolapse? Do I need an operation?' The cardiologist answered, 'You have no Mitral Valve Prolapse, but a perfectly healthy heart.'

Jennifer was overwhelmed because she realized that Jesus had performed a miracle. During the next few weeks, she realized a change in her attitude toward the loathed person, and noticed how her destructive hate was gradually replaced by the gentle waves of forgiveness. She felt a great flow of joy and freedom of being released from the dark and evil emotions of repugnance. Her understanding, that Jesus answered her sincere prayers and performed the miracle of healing her spiritual and physical heart, filled her with indescribable delight and new faith. She was able to forgive and be free of her former hateful emotions.

We need healing, not just physical but spiritual healing as well, and free ourselves of emotions that are damaging body, mind and soul. Destructive feelings such as violence, rage, and selfishness need to be recognized as unwanted and harmful. There are injurious to our health, our life and the peace of mind we strife to attain.

Chapter 12

Miriam of Nazareth

A few words must be said about the mother of our Lord Jesus.

The Bible tells of many outstanding and heroic women but none reaches the status of Miriam of Nazareth or more commonly known as Mary, the mother of Jesus. The Catholic Church reveres her in comparison to the Protestant Churches who commemorate her at Christmas as the mother of Jesus. The King James Bible mentions her a few times: at the birth of Jesus spoken of in the four Gospels, the twelve-year old Jesus staying behind in Jerusalem and searched for by his parents, according to Mark 2:41-49. Mary and her family noting the absence of Jesus, and returning to Jerusalem, finding him discussing the scriptures with the Pharisees and scribes, Matt. 12:46-50, and Jesus and his mother attending the wedding at Cana, John 2:10.

Every Christian is familiar with the much-loved story of Christ's wondrous birth and the immaculate life of Mary, his mother.

Mary grew up in a pious Jewish family. According to custom, she was still very young when she became engaged to Joseph, a carpenter. Some sources indicate that she may have been raised and educated at the temple and returned home at the age of fourteen or fifteen to be married. Mary was raised in the Jewish faith, and her belief in God was strong and unshakable. She gave proof of her devotion when she accepted God's will announced to her by the angel Gabriel to become the mother of Jesus, God's Son. Mary accepted it with humility and praise.

The Holy Night of His birth is beautifully described in the Gospels. Announced by the angel and witnessed by the humble shepherds, the Divine baby entered into life in the modest environments of a barn lovingly bedded in a straw-filled manger.

Jesus as a grown man expressed His divine nature through his love, his compassion, his preaching the Kingdom of God and his miraculous healings.

Mary was aware of the danger he exposed himself to. Many of his listeners loved him but he had enemies among the Pharisees and scribes whom he addressed reproachfully, and who tried to set snares to destroy him. Mary must have been in constant fear for her son's life. She attended the mock trial and the crucifixion of him.

Her anguish of seeing her son tortured and dying a cruel and unjust death must have been excruciating and unbearable! Jesus' love to his mother could not be quenched by the horrendous suffering on the cross. He placed Mary into the care of his 'most beloved' disciple John who witnessed the agonies of his much-loved master

. "Woman, behold thy son," and speaking to the disciple, "Son, behold thy mother" (John 19:26). From then on, John cared for Mary, the mother of Jesus

.Through Acts 1:14, we learn that the disciples were praying with the women and Mary, the mother of Jesus, and his brothers. After that, the Bible is silent concerning her. It is believed that John, the son of Zebedee, who lived in Jerusalem, took care of her until her death.

The Catholic Church pays great emphasis on the Virgin Mary, and celebrates special days dedicated to her and to commemorate special events of her life. She is referred to in the early writings of 150 A.D. and of the church fathers of the second century. The Council of Ephesus meeting in 431 proclaimed her Theotokos (God-Bearer). The cult and adoration was based on the above writings, accepted and later added to the Bibles of the Roman-Catholic and Anglican Churches. Many of the churches built during the following centuries were devoted to Mary as the names indicate: St. Mary, Notre Dame, or in Germany, Liebfrauenkirche (Our Lady).

The age of Chivalry and the Troubadours during the eleventh to thirteenth century developed lyric poetry and songs. Some of the recited songs were informing the listeners of important events. The minstrels visited the castles and courts of the gentry and in music and poetry expressed courtly love between the noble knight and his chosen lady. Many songs adoring the Virgin mother of Jesus were recited, accompanied by an instrument.

The Reformation and the split from the Catholic Church changed the attitudes toward Mary as the mediator, and the beneficiary help of the saints. The renowned Catholic scholar and humanist Erasmus (1466-1536) noted that the worship and adoration of the mother of Jesus overshadowed and diminished the life and teachings of her son Jesus. The Reformation and the ensuing split from the Catholic Church changed the outlook. Protestants adore Mary as the mother of Jesus on Christmas. Protestants don't memorialize Mary in special prayers or days or particular events of her life. The Last Supper or Holy Eucharist, as it is referred to, contains the highlight of worship in the Catholic and Episcopal Churches while Protestant Churches have especially appointed Sundays to receive the Last Supper. Catholics to communicate with the Holy Virgin Mary what serves as aid to remember Jesus, his sufferings, the stages of the cross and crucifixion and prayer beads are familiar to worshippers of most of the world religions such as Jewish, Islam, Hindu and Buddhist faiths. Individuals of mentioned religions use the beads for concentration and meditation Protestants insist on praying to God, and to Jesus only, and prayer to any other entity including to the Virgin Mary violates the First Commandment (thou shall not worship any other God besides me).

Mary, the mother of Jesus, deserves our love and admiration regardless of our religious affiliations. She possessed the qualities a woman should strife for: love, loyalty, gentleness, faith and devotion.

Reflection

Isaiah 9:2, 6

"The people that walked in darkness have seen a great light: they that dwell in the land of the shadow of death, upon them has the light shined."

The mother of Jesus steps forward at Christmas when we celebrate the birth of her (firstborn Luke 2:7) son. Do we really celebrate his birth or do we almost forget the reason for festivity, and enter into the now very common shopping craze? The true value of a present is expressed in the thoughtful love of the giver but is not determined by the monetary value.

Our Christmas celebration should become more spiritually oriented because the Son of God enters into our lives. The infant Jesus is and must be the very centre of our attention and the source of joyful celebration.

Part 3

Chapter 13

The early Christian Church

The New Testament consists of 27 books. It includes the four Gospels of Matthew, Mark, Luke and John, followed by the Acts, and describes the lives of the disciples after Jesus' death.

The first three Gospels are referred to as the 'Synoptic' Gospels. Biblical scholars are quite certain that the Gospel of Mark, which is the shortest, was the first one written about 70-100 A.D. after the death of Peter and Paul. It served as base and outline for the Gospels of Matthew and Luke. Mark describes the miracles performed by Jesus. According to Eusebius (260-340) bishop and church historian of Caesarea (260-340?), the writers of the gospels were anonymous but Mark went to Egypt to build a church. Peter, as chief apostle, was involved with the churches established in Jerusalem, Antioch, and Corinth as well as Alexandria.

The bishop Papias of Hierapolis (modern Turkey) about 140 CE) called Mark to be the interpreter of Peter. The bishop credited Matthew for having collected the Sayings of Jesus written in Aramaic, and translated as good as possible, into Greek. Unfortunately, no copy survived. According to scholars, the Gospel Mark was Peter's account and written by a secretary or disciple of Peter. The writers of the Gospels of Matthew and Luke used the Gospel of Mark as their guideline. Luke, the 'beloved physician' wrote his own Gospel and the Acts of the Apostles.

Peter was the 'Rock' (Mt 16:18) on which Jesus laid his foundation of the Church. After Jesus had been arrested and led away, Peter, being asked by bystanders about his association with Jesus denied to be acquainted with him. He remembered that Jesus told him that 'before the cock crow, thou shalt deny me thrice', went away and wept bitterly (Mt 26:34).

The stain of his denial must have pained him for the rest of his life! But Jesus loved and forgave him. The proof is found in John 21:15-18. After Jesus resurrected and spent forty days with the disciples instructing them. It was the third time after his raising from the dead. "So when they had dined, Jesus saith to Simon Peter: Simon, Son of Jonas, lovest thou me more than these? He saith unto him, Yea, Lord; thou knowest that I love thee. He saith unto him, Feed my lambs. Again, Jesus enquired a second time, and Simon Peter confessed his love to him. Jesus told him: Feed my sheep. Jesus asked Simon Peter a third time if he loved him, and Simon Peter was grieved and assured Jesus of his love for him. Jesus told him, "Feed my sheep." (John 21:15-17).Jesus indicated to Simon Peter that he would die glorifying God.

The Apostle Peter made his way to Rome and created the Christian community while Nero still reigned. The scholar Origen reported that Peter was crucified, and his wife, who had accompanied him on his mission, was executed in his presence.

The Gospel of Matthew starts with the genealogy of Jesus. Matthew, the tax collector, was despised by his Jewish countrymen and considered as a traitor because he worked for the Romans, the hated invaders. The Jews did not only loathe him but would refuse to share their meal with a man like him. Jesus met Matthew while he was collecting tax money, and told him, 'Come, follow me.' One may image the shock of the bystanders. The Gospel of Matthew contains the wonderful "Sermon on the Mount" including the 'Lord's Prayer' and speaks of the Kingdom of God. The Gospel reflects the Judaic tradition and teachings of the Law, and its writing strongly indicates Hebraic life and background. The Gospel of Matthew clearly reveals the community to whom the gospel was preached: they were Jews who had accepted the teachings of Jesus.

Except for Luke, there is some doubt about the identity of the Gospel writers. Luke was a Gentile (Greek) but converted to Christianity. He travelled with Paul who referred to him as 'Luke, the beloved physician'. The Gospel of Luke describes Mary's journey to her cousin Elizabeth and includes the 'Magnificat', Mary's praise of God's grace and love for having chosen her to be the mother of the Son of God. He also tells us of eight parables and miracles which are not described in the other gospels He was also the author of the Acts in which he recorded the disciples, their activities and the events that took place after the death and resurrection of Christ.

The Gospel of John is markedly different in tone because of its noticeable philosophical and spiritual writings and almost out of context with the other writers. This is evident when comparing his writings with the other three Gospels who describe parables and miracles performed by Jesus. In John's Gospel, Jesus declares 'to be the light and the way'. In chapter 17, we find the wonderful prayer of Jesus he prayed previous to his arrest and mock trial. Some of the scholars affirmed that John's Gospel contains Gnostic traces. The Gospel was printed about AD 85-125.

The Acts, written by Luke, are followed by the Letters of Paul written to his various established Christian communities. His letters are the oldest of the Christian writings. The Christian scholar Origen (185-254) from Alexandria disputed some of their authenticity and assumed that they were written by his followers.

The last book of the New Testament is the Book of Revelation. It is uncertain who John was. The author of the Revelation, a man named John, wrote the book around

95 A.D. The Greek Orthodox Church did not include it into their Bible. John lived on the Island of Patmos and corresponded with the churches on the mainland of Asia Minor, the cities of Ephesus and Smyrna. He described a profound vision but used coded language because of fear of persecution under the Roman Emperor Domitian. The letters reflect the horrors of the Jewish War and the destruction of the Holy of Holiest, the Temple and the devastation of Jerusalem. Many of his descriptions of the Revelation point at the decedent Roman society and the city of Rome, and correspond as well as our own desperate world situation but Revelation is ending with the manifestation of a 'New Jerusalem'.

The early Church (ca. A.D.) began with Saul from the city of Tarsus, the capital city of the Roman province of Cilicia. He was a Hellenistic Jew and devoted Pharisee (believing in life after death) and a fierce enemy of the Christians. Saul lived in Jerusalem and was feared by the Christians who fled to Damascus. Saul went to follow and persecute them. The teachings of Jesus, declared by his followers as the Messiah and dying a humiliating death on the cross, seemed to be utterly blasphemous, and Saul was determined to stamp it out (Deut. 21:23 quotes: 'Cursed is anyone who hangs on a tree (cross)'. On his way to Damascus, he had a divine revelation that changed not only his life but the lives of millions (Acts 9:14). While he was riding towards the city, a brilliant light blended him, and he heard a voice saying, "Saul, Saul, why persecutest thou me?" Blinded by the light, he fell to the ground, and asked, "Who are you, Lord?" And he heard the respond, "I am Jesus whom you persecuting; but raise up and enter the city and you will be told what to do".

The group, who travelled with him, led him to Damascus to meet with the Christians. The young congregation was suspicious and fearful of him and did not trust his account of events on the road Ananias, who was a Christian, restored his sight and baptized him. After his conversion he is referred to as of Paul. He was also a tentmaker and at times supported himself through his trade. Paul's attitude changed completely because he realized that Jesus had risen from the dead, as he had prophesied, and he, Paul, would bring the message to the Gentiles (Acts 9:1-21).

Paul's life was turbulent. His mission was very difficult and trying because of the totally different Greek culture being contrary to the strict rules of the Hebrew culture he grew up with. His Greek parishioners were often unruly, undisciplined, and tended to drift back to their former pagan lifestyles. His unique letters reflect the troubles with his converted Greeks. He became the pillar of the developing Christian communities which he established along the coast of Asia Minor (modern Turkey) Syria, the Greek mainland, and finally in Rome. He suffered stoning, persecution, beatings, imprisonment and shipwreck but untiringly preached the Gospel of Jesus. Under the Roman Emperor Nero, Paul was arrested and in AD 64, beheaded instead of being crucified (He was a Roman citizen).

Thirteen of the letters addressed to the new and growing congregations in Greece and along today's costal area of Turkey were written by Paul. He is subject to contradicting interpretations because of his complex and controversial character and writings.

In contrast to Peter, who had been fortunate as to walk with Jesus and be directly taught by him, Paul seemed to have paid little emphasis on the life of Jesus but strongly emphasized his death and resurrection. After Jesus death, his brother James called the Just, and members of his family became followers of Jesus. James became the leader and the guiding spirit of the Jerusalem church (Gal 1:19). The congregation were Jewish Christians of the Jesus movement (Acts 1:14). Paul explained in a letter to the Corinthians (Cor.15:7) that the risen Jesus had appeared to his brother James who experienced a change of heart. According to the Jewish historian Josephus, James was a deeply pious and righteous man. He was very much concerned about keeping the Law of Moses and emphasized that the Jewish Christians should live as observant Jews.

About AD 49 James called a Council to meet at Jerusalem to discuss and settle important issues concerning new members who were Gentiles. The dispute centred around the question if the Gentiles were required to become circumcised and accept the dietary laws as subscribed to Jews. Paul had met Peter at Antioch and had observed that Peter had not shared his meals with Gentile Christians (whose food was not kosher) and Paul had been very upset because of it. Paul had insisted that the Jewish dietary and circumcising laws were overcome through Jesus death and resurrection. (Gal.2:11-21) The two were at odds with one another. Peter was a disciple of Jesus and had known and been taught by him. Jesus had proclaimed that Peter was the 'the rock on which Jesus shall built his church' while Paul's brief encounter with Jesus was through a vision. .

Paul' converts were Greek and came from a totally different society than Jesus had ever met. The problems of Paul's Greek parishioners were in many ways unlike of those Peter or Jesus had encountered.

Peter attended the meeting and met Paul who was accompanied by Barnabas. Both witnessed of how much God had granted guidance. Peter revealed that his doubts were resolved through a vision in which God gave him to understand that the food he had refused to consume because he perceived as for unclean was accepted by God as pure (Acts 10:10-16)

Next spoke James and he informed the members of the meeting that the new members did not need to be under the Jewish law and therefore did not need to be circumcised. James quoted the Book of Amos (chapter 9) and pointed out that according to the scripture the Kingdom of God was intended for the Jews as well as the Gentiles. The promise of the Old Testament was fulfilled and the Gentiles united themselves to a Jewish Messianic Sect whose heart and core was Jesus. James disagreed with Paul's outline of teachings. While Paul insisted on the 'person being justified by faith in Jesus Christ' (Gal. 2:16) 'and not by the works of the law' God, James emphasized that 'a person is justified by works, not faith alone' James 2:24 and 2:26) 'Faith without works is dead' (charity, according to Jewish tradition as performed by Abraham, must be accomplished). Paul freed the Gentiles from the Mosaic Law while James felt that this approach violated the Mosaic Law and turned the Jews away.

Paul insisted the Mosaic Law was an added blessing but not an obligation to obey to which James disagreed. James ministry was long and successful and he was highly respected even amongst non-Christian Jews.

The years 52-68 A.D. were turbulent and the Roman procurator Felix added fuel to the unrest. Felix executed the Jewish messianic disturbers what resulted in more violence among the Jews. The Church of Jerusalem felt the pressure as well. Herod Agrippa II was on bad terms with the Temple. Through the Jewish historian Josephus, we learn about the death of James (The New Testament gives no report on it). Ananias was the High Priest, adopting the school of Sadducees. The new procurator was on his way to Jerusalem when the Sanhedrin brought charges against James 'the Just', the brother of Jesus. He was accused of blasphemy, troublemaking, false teachings and seducer of the Jews. The Jews felt that injustice was done to him but he was stoned to death.

A relative of Jesus, named Symeon, son of Clopas became the head of the Jerusalem Church.

Chapter 14

The Destruction of Jerusalem

The destruction of Jerusalem and in particular of the Temple, was prophesied by Jesus (Luke 21: 5-6, 20, 23-24) "And as some spake of the temple, how it was adorned with goodly stones and gifts, he said, As for these things which ye behold, the days will come, in which there shall not be left one stone upon another, that shall not be thrown down".

The 'Jewish War' of 66-70 A.D. is one of the most brutal, bloody and pitiless events in history. The population protested ever more against the Romans. Quarrels between the extremist and the moderate parties broke out and the dead and wounded stayed untended. The Zealots and the rebels banded together and demanded the removal of the hated foreign power. Encroachment by the Roman procurator increased the tension as well as the number of the radicals.

The stress reached its breaking point when the procurator Florus demanded 17 talents from the Temple treasury. The Roman garrison was overrun, and Jerusalem fell into the hands of the rebels. Rebellion flared up in the whole country. Florus was no longer in control of the situation, and Cestius Gallus, governor of the province of Syria, marched with a legion and auxiliary troops towards Jerusalem. He suffered heavy losses and had to retreat. The rebels were in control of the country. .

The rebels knew that Rome would retaliate and they hastened to fortify the cities. Joseph, later knows as Josephus the historian, became commander-in-chief of Galilee. The Roman general Titus Flavius Vespanius, accompanied by his son Titus, was appointed by Emperor Nero to put down the rebellion. The legions attacked Galilee from the north and the province was restrained by October 67. Six thousand Jews went as slaves, and Josephus, the commander in-chief, was captures and brought to Vespasian's headquarters. In the spring, the campaign against the rebellions was continued. News of Nero's suicide and of civil war in Rome reached Vespasian. Three of the following emperors lost their power until Vespasian was declared Caesar, and he left for Rome and gave the command to his son Titus to finish the Jewish War.

Jerusalem was teaming with pilgrims who had arrived from far to celebrate the Passover. Titus appeared with an army of around 80 000 men before the gates of Jerusalem. The Romans called on the population to surrender which was answered with contemptuous laughter. The Roman army was equipped with heavy stone throwers which cracked the heavily fortified northern side of the fortress. An incessant rain of heavy stones came hurtling into the city. In early May the throwers and battering rams had managed to make a large hole into the northerly wall. The defenders managed to regain the wall, and it took the Romans several days to recapture it.

Titus felt confident that this was warning enough for the beleaguered Jews and pompously paraded the army outside of the city. They may have saved themselves the trouble because the population of Jerusalem did not surrender. Titus tried one more time to change their minds by sending his prisoner Josephus, the Jewish Commander-in-Chief, to berate them Josephus tried in heart-rending words to change the mind of the Jewish leaders within the walls but failed. The battle continued and raged within the Temple area and the upper part of the city but the Romans were held back because the defenders tried to upset their efforts.

Under the cover of darkness, some of the beleaguered people slipped out. Titus gave orders to capture and crucify them. According to Josephus' reports, thousands of starving Jews were captured and slowly, a forest of crosses with crucified bodies sprung up until there was no more wood available. Dead within the city took its toll, and hunger drove the population to extremes.

Titus was in hurry to end the dreadful war. The battle turned now against the Temple which was extremely well fortified. He opposed the wish of his commanders to treat the Temple like a fortress because he wanted to spare the famous sanctuary. Rams and siege engines, rains of arrows and stones showered upon its precincts. The Jews fought angrily and unyielding. Titus tried to force an entry into the temple and set fire to the wooden gates. He gave the order to spare the sanctuary but the fire quickly reached the inner court and reached the "Holy of Holies" which went up in flames fed by jars of holy oil. Titus ordered the flames to be put out but the fire spread and went out of control.

In August, 70 A.D. half of Jerusalem was in the hands of the Romans but the Zealots did not surrender. In September, after Titus deployed his military skill, the resistance was finally broken. The loss among the population was extremely high. Josephus estimated the number of prisoners as many as 1,197, 000 not numbering the crucified subjects. Within three months 116,000 corpses were removed and thrown over the city walls.

In 71, Titus paraded 700 Jewish prisoners in a triumphal procession through Rome. One of the highlights of the procession was the seven-branched candlestick made of pure gold and the table of the showbread, both items from the Temple of Jerusalem. Both items were placed into the Temple of Peace in Rome.

At the final assault about 73 or 73, about 960 Jews had fled to the fortress of Masada near the western shore of the Dead Sea. This was the palace built by King Herod the Great, and the refugees held out in spite of starvation und hardship until to the final assault in the spring of 73 or 74.When the Romans finally entered the fortress, they were shocked to find that the besieged Jews had committed suicide.

After the destruction of the Temple, the Jewish High Priesthood lost its authority. There was still the hope to rebuild the Temple.

Sixty-two years later, the Emperor Hadrian forbade anyone, either Jew or Christian, to set food on the ruins of Jerusalem. He built a Roman colony Aelia Capitolina, a race course, baths, a theatre and a statue of Jupiter. It triggered a new rebellion among the population not being massacred in the war of 66-70. The new leader of the rebellion was Simeon Bar Kochba. For three years, the region was back under Jewish control. In 135 A.D, Emperor Hadrian and his Roman troops stamped out the uprising. The remnant of the Jewish population was sold into slavery.

Chapter 15

Development of the Greek Orthodox Church

Maximinus Caius Julius (240-310), commander was claimed as Roman emperor by his legions. He ruled three years but never visited Rome and preferred his camps on the Rhine or Danube instead. He increased the taxes to support his campaigns and the wealthy upper classes revolted The Roman Senate declared him an outlaw and chose Balbinus and Maximus as emperors. Maximus led an army against Maximinus and besieged him. The soldiers hated Maximinus and killed him in his tent.

The Roman Emperor Diolectian (245-313) divided the empire into eastern and western sections. The Empire was threatened by the infiltration of Germanic and Slavs tribes. The kingdom of Palmyra (Tadmor) tried to break away from the Roman rule. Diocletian and Constantine tried to counterbalance and reorganize the government. Diocletian made Galerius (Caius Galerius Valerius 250-311) the Caesar of the Danube Valley while Italy and Africa were under the rule of Maximian (240-310). Two emperors received the title Augustus supported by minor emperors with the title of Caesar. Under Diocletian's rule the Christians endured for eight years horrible persecution documented by the Christian scholar Eusebius After Diocletian and Maximian abdicated, the Empire witnessed chaos and anarchy.

Constantine was born (272) in today's Serbia, the son of a Roman officer. His mother Helena was a devout Christian. The young Constantine fought in Egypt and on the Danube. He joined his father, and in 305, fought together in Britain. His father died in 306, and the army acknowledged him as his father's heir and acclaimed him as Augustus (emperor).In Rome, Maxentius, the son of Maximian, was hailed by the Praetorian Guards as emperor. The competition for the title 'emperor' was keen because there were several other debutants viewing each other with envy. Constantine lived in Gaul in 310-311 when in the spring of 312 Maxentius threatened an invasion

The aging Roman Emperor Galerius appointed Licinius as emperor. Maximian plotted with Maxentius, who had been hailed as emperor by the Praetorian Guards, to overthrow the Roman Emperor Licinius, and Constantine. Both crossed the Alps and advanced upon Rome. Constantin met the forces of Maxentius north of Rome, and according to Eusebius, Constantine saw a flaming cross imprinted with Greek words meaning 'in this sign conquer' Constantine won the battle of the Mulvian Bridge. Maxentius and his troops drowned in the Tiber River while crossing.

In 313, Emperor Licinius and Constantine met at Milan, and issued an 'Edict of Milan'. The Edict confirmed religious tolerance. Constantine returned to Gaul and Licinius went to Thrace to defeated Maximian, who died in the same year. Licinius protested Constantine's entrance into Thrace (Byzantium) and they engaged in battle. Constantine won and Licinius became his prisoner. Licinius plotted intrigues and Constantine ordered his execution. He was the sole emperor and granted freedom of worship.

Emperor Constantine noticed that the pagan majority were separated among their many creeds while the minority of Christians were united. The Christians impressed him because of their orderly conduct, their devotion to their clergy and the morality and acceptance of their lives.

In 325, Constantine called the First Ecumenical Council of the Church held in Bithynian Nicaea, because of the existing controversies concerning the divinity of Christ. The imperial palace was the chosen meeting place of the emperor and the bishops, and the emotions were running high. Constantine presided over the meeting and appealed to the clergy to restore harmony and unity within the Church. The controversial questions concerning the divine and human nature of Jesus lead to great controversy and dissent among the Council members. They also argued the relationship between Jesus, God and the Holy Spirit. Arius, a priest of Alexandria, held the belief that Jesus was not fully divine, begotten by the Logos, and subordinate to God. He postulated that Christ did not participate in the divinity with God the Father but as his son was chosen to be the instrument of salvation of mankind. According to Arius, Jesus was not God or redeemer but there was only one true God. Bishop Alexander of Alexandria protested and persuaded the Egyptian bishops to excommunicate Arius and his group. Arius had a great following and the Council feared that his teaching may endanger the structure of Christian belief and threatened to destroy the authority and unity of the Church. Arius was exiled by the Emperor and sent to a far away province Illyria on the Danube River where he converted the Ostrogoths. Constantine was the driving force that supported a unifying doctrine and a unifying Creed. The Council was in charge of the meeting and, requested by the emperor, to settle the existing differences besides composing the wording of the Nicene Creed. The gathered clergy approved of the belief as to Jesus as the Son of God and eternally one with the Heavenly Father. Both were One, and of the same substance. The Council, including the Emperor, finally agreed to the wording of the Statement of belief (it differed from the Nicene Creed of today.)

Athanasius, born in Alexandria and attendant of Bishop Alexander the Council of Nicaea, a scholar became bishop in 328. Athanasius was a strong supporter of the divinity of Jesus Christ. He defined and approved in his thirty-ninth festal letter the outline of the New Testament. In his letter, written in 367, he insisted that the twenty-seven books should be acknowledged in the canon of Scripture. Though the existing and debated books were written by early Christians, the Gospel of Thomas, Peter, Philip, Mary Magdalene and various other writers were banned. The disputes were not completely resolved as various churches debated admittance or exclusion of various existing writings. The battles between 'heretic' and 'orthodox' documents lasted more than three hundred years. Since some of them had been labelled as forgery, it became a major challenge to sift through the myriads of writings. The arguments concerning the validity of the documents were finally settled around the end of the forth century.

A year later, Constantine built a new city what came down as Constantinople. In 330, he returned from Rome to make his permanent home in the newly established city. He founded a new university where Greek and Latin, philosophy, law, rhetoric and literature were taught. The professors were paid by the state. Christianity was declared as the official religion although the pagan rites were tolerated for some more years before they were banned.

Constantine's mother Helena went to Jerusalem and ordered the Roman Temple of Aphrodite that had been built over the Jesus' tomb, to be levelled and, according to Eusebius, the Holy Sepulchre, and the Cross, on which Jesus died, were exposed. Constantine ordered the Church of the Holy Sepulchre to be built over Jesus' tomb and the relics to be kept in a special shrine. Constantine died at the age of sixty-four after receiving his long deferred baptism.

Antagonism between the East and the West between pro-Nicene and Arian-leaning churches lingered on. The various interpretations were accepted or condemned. The church at Antioch split up into three congregations. Emperor Theodosius, who was pro-Nicene, decreed in 380 that Christianity in its Nicene description to be the official faith, and he summoned a Council in Constantinople. The 'Nicene Creed' was reaffirmed and revised to the wording as we know it today.

The Greek Orthodox Church allowed the clergy to marry and raise a family in contrast to the Roman Catholic Church where the priest had to exercise celibacy. The Roman and Greek theologians were both moving apart in religious issues as well as in secular power. (In 392, Christianity became the official religion of the Roman Empire.)

See: Development of the Roman Catholic Church.

The Byzantine Empire (527-1054) under Emperor Justinian I 'the Great' (483-565) kept Greek learning alive. Justinian was of humble birth and through his uncle, who usurped the throne, served him first in the army and later as aide and ruler. At forty-five, (527) Justinian and his beautiful wife Theodora ascended the throne.

He wished to restore the rule of the Roman Empire in the west. The Vandal kingdom in North Africa was in decline, and Justinian sent in 533 his general Belisarius and a large army against them. Belisarius overwhelmed the Vandals and ruined their state. General Belisarius fought against the Ostrogoths in Italy but it turned into a long and costly war that lasted for eighteen years and devastated the country. Belisarius tried to fight the Visigoths in Spain but his army never managed to conquer more than the coastal areas while northern Europe remained in the power of the Germanic kingdoms.

Justinian's most noteworthy accomplishment was the 'Body of Civil Law' (Corpus Juris Civilis). The existing laws had been modified over time but proved to be contradictory and confusing.

Justinian appointed jurists to organize the legal structure into a single code In 533 the Corpus Juris Civilis was published. The Roman laws outline the rights of each individual although harsh in some instances but adjusted to the needs of the sixth century.

Justinian commissioned the building of the magnificent church of "Hagia Sophia" (Holy Wisdom) in 537.He built the church upon the foundation of the former church built by the Emperor Constantinus in 360 and ruined by fire in 404. Emperor Theodosius II rebuilt the church in 415 which was destroyed by a fire a hundred years later Justinian personally supervised the construction. Anthemius, the architect, employed 10 000 men to create the masterpiece of architecture and mosaics. It was the finest example of Byzantine architecture with its display of splendour of decoration and particularly beautiful mosaics.

Justinian never accomplished the reunification of the Eastern Roman Empire with Western Europe. The separation was permanent and gradually deepened.

The Byzantine Empire suffered from frequent attacks of the invading Slavs, Avars and Bulgars who conquered large areas of the Balkan Peninsula and made frequent attacks on Constantinople. The Byzantine army fought bravely, and in 591, the invaders were driven back north of the river Danube.

After the fall of the Roman Empire in the fifth century, the Byzantine Empire with its capital city of Constantinople developed into a centre of trade and magnificence. Greek learning was fostered and, separated from the influence of Rome the Byzantine Empire developed independent ideas in theology and politics. The deep-seated differences between the Roman and the Byzantine Churches caused disagreements and the split between the two. The Byzantine Emperor Leo III (714-741) strongly opposed the worship of Christian icons. He feared that it would lead to paganism and idolatrous worship (forbidden according to the First Commandment) and outlawed them (referred to as Iconoclastic Controversy). Leo ordered the destruction of the icons in the monasteries and churches. The theologian and monk John of Damascus championed for the icons. He declared that the icons must not be adored but their purpose was to serve as contemplation and deeper reflection of God and Jesus. Empress Irena restored the icons in 780 and Emperor Michael III (842-867) allowed them to be erected in the churches. The usage of Latin had been discontinued, and Greek was spoken throughout. The Greeks hated the Roman Catholic Church and the Romans did not feel great love for them, either.

The Sassanid Shah Chosroes Parviz and his army came from Persia. They worshipped the religion of Zoroaster (about 1200 BC) the prophet who taught Mithras, son of the God of Light, to ne the God of light, purity and truth. The Zoroastrian worshipped the fire that expressed the light and image of Ahura Mazda. His adversary was an evil and dark god called Ariman, Prince of Darkness and both echoed the conflict of good and evil. The Zoroastrian religion was the dominant religion of the Persian Empire (550 BC-AD651).

The Persians invaded parts of the Byzantine lands of the eastern Mediterranean. Emperor Justinian could hardly contain them. After Justinians death, the Empire lost its significance. The Persians seized Egypt and Jerusalem and marched close to the Bosporus across Constantinople. They were driven back by Emperor Heraclius in 627. A new and even greater threat came from the Arabian Peninsula. The successors of the Prophet Muhammad, founder of the religion of Islam, conquered Egypt in 642. The Arab Muslims overran the Byzantine lands in the Middle East and North Africa and controlled the Mediterranean. In 717, they laid siege to Constantinople but were unable to conquer the city. Byzantine armies under their Macedonian kings in 863 and 976 were able to regain some of their territory and drove the Arabs back.

Byzantine missionaries went in 863 into (Rus) Russia to convert the Slavs to Christianity. In 987, Prince Vladimir of Kiev became converted. He strengthened is alliance with Byzantine through his marriage to Princess Anna, a sister of the Byzantine Emperor Basil. Prince Vladimir fostered Christianity and sent monks into Russia to Christianize the population. The Cyrillic alphabet was adopted, and Vladimir ordered Greek craftsmen to built a magnificent church at Kiev. Christianity found fertile ground, and churches and monasteries were established.

The schism between the Roman Catholic Church and the Eastern Byzantine Church occurred in 1054. The disputed issues concerned God, Jesus and the Holy Spirit. The Patriarch Michael Seruliarus of Constantinople denounced the Roman Catholic Church and closed the Latin schools. Both were moving apart in religious as well as secular issues. The Patriarch refused to accept the delegation sent from the pope who excommunicated him. The Greek synod in turn excommunicated the pope, and the final split between the Roman Catholic Church and the Greek Orthodox Church took place.

In 1448, the Russian Church repudiating the merging of Greek Christianity with Roman Christianity at the Council of Florence and affirmed their independence from the Byzantine Patriarch and called themselves from then on the "Russian Orthodox Church'

Constantinople was conquered in 1453. The last Byzantine Emperor Constantine XI Paleolgus led the defence against the Turks who were led by Sultan Mehmet. Constantine's army consisted of 7000 soldiers equipped with rudimentary firearms, bows and arrows, torches and cannons. On May, 29, 1453, the Turks fought their way over the walls of the city. The Emperor removed his royal garments and put on the outfit of a common soldier. Surrounded by his nobles, he fought heroically in the streets of his city. Constantine knew that he was totally outnumbered but defended Constantinople and his Empire with his own body and blood. His rule as monarch was not outstanding but his hopeless fight and valiant death indicate that he was a man of courage and of noble character.

The magnificent Hagia Sophia, the church of the emperor and the patriarch, became a Mosque and was re-named as 'Aya Sofya'.

Following the fall of Constantinople, Moscow assumed the position of former Constantinople as the centre of the Orthodox faith. Moscow was viewed as the 'Rome of the East'. The split between the two Christian beliefs remained.

Chapter 16

Development of the Roman Catholic Church

The Nag Hammadi Library

In 1945, a group of Egyptian farm labourers, who were digging around limestone caves to contrive fertilizer, unearthed a jar near the town of Nag Hammadi near Luxor. The jar was sealed and the men smashed it open. Inside the jar were thirteen papyrus codices (manuscripts bound as a book) containing some fifty-two texts written in Coptic language, and were most likely translated from the Greek. The writings were written by the Early Christians of the second century and are referred to as the Gnostic Gospels. Some of them were formerly unknown and not included in the New Testament as for example the Gospel of Thomas (sayings of Christ) and Philip, the Book of James, the secret Book of John, and of Mary Magdalene who was one of the disciples. Some of Jesus Sayings were collected and found in Q (for 'Quelle – Source) but was not a narrative gospel. The Secret Book of John is in the least a relating account to the teachings of the historical Jesus, and rather mythological in its content. According to the later Gnostics, it seems to be apparent that Jesus taught the disciples sacred knowledge that was not meant to be written down. The collection was used during the early part of the Coptic Church. The Gnostic Gospels were regarded as 'heretic' and according to authorities like Athanasius, not included into the canon. Instead of destroying the rejected manuscripts, someone hid them safely away.

The scrolls passed from antique dealers to storekeepers until they reached the Coptic Museum of Cairo. The resident of religious history realized the immense importance of the fund, and referred to the fund in an article in 1948. The papyri changed hands several times until they were translated and available to scholars versed in religion, language and editing. It was an important fund and added much information concerning the writings of early Christianity. The collection is now known as the 'Nag Hammadi Library'.

The earliest assemblies of Christians gathered in the catacombs below the city of Rome. Slaves were welcomed and their number increased. Around 64, the Romans persecuted the Christians under the alleged reason of arson. The Christians suffered persecution and death but the numbers of adherents grew steadily. The Romans who attended the circus and witnessed how courageous the Christians faced their horrendous deaths, were profoundly moved. It stirred the audience so deeply as to learn more about those despised Christians, and they themselves became converted. Persecution of Christians raged for centuries throughout the Roman Empire.

At the end of the first century, the Roman authorities became aware of the Christian communities. Pliny the Younger, the Roman governor of Bithynia (northern Turkey) investigated the new religion. Informers gave horrible accounts of the Christians like performing acts of cannibalism. The charges of such accusations resulted because of the informer's ignorance concerning the Communion and the consuming of the 'bread' and 'blood' (wine). Pliny put the Christians to trial, and some of them denied their religion

Emperor Trajan commanded to leave the Christians alone as long as they were returning to the worship of the Roman gods

In 107 AD, Ignatius, Bishop of Antioch, was brought to Rome to be slain by the animals in the Coliseum. Ignatius, much loved and respected, wished for nothing more but to be with Jesus Christ. Pliny observed very correctly that Ignatius' death served to increase the curiosity about the Christian faith, its moral code and charity.

Gnosticism (Greek-meaning gnosis – knowledge) developed as a heresy within Christianity during the early years of the first century AD. Gnosticism may be considered as a mystery religion based on the knowledge and existence of God, Agnosticism is the absence of such knowledge. The roots of Gnosticism may be found in Zoroastrianism (about 600 BC) who thought that the world was a battlefield of the two gods, Ahura Mazda, the god of light. Christian Gnosticism is just a branch of much older schools of religion similar to the Dionysian cult and the cult of Orpheus, Gnosticism is based on very ancient beliefs reaching far back to the sixth century BC at a time when various types of magic were performed. Much of Greek mythology was incorporated into Gnosticism.

Valentinus (about 136 AD) was a prominent Egyptian priest baptized a Christian and educated in Alexandria, at that time a centre of learning. He taught the creation myth of Sophia (wisdom) was an emanation of the transcended God and mistakenly created the Demiurge. The fall of the world was due to the fault of Sophia who was charged to correct her mistake.

Valentinus, who was labelled as heretic, tried to explain human nature and the distinction between the loyal God of love and the so-called Demiurge, the revengeful God of the Old Testament who tried to keep mankind in slavery. It described the material body encasing the spark of divine light who attempted to become free as taught by

Plato. According to Gnosticism, Jesus was the true son of the loving and compassionate God who was sent by Him to deliver mankind of the vindictive Demiurge.

Valentinus desired to hold the position of Bishop of Rome but lost the vote He lived in Rome as a priest, and attempted to reunite the dogma of Christianity and Gnosticism He denied Christ's divinity and declared that Jesus was the true son of Joseph and Mary and at baptism received the spirit in the form of a dove descending on him. Valentius declared that this was the true virgin birth and rebirth from the death. He and his contemporary, Marcion, a wealthy Roman who held that Christ's teaching was the Gospel of love, agreed that mankind was created by the cruel Demiurge of the Old Testament, the God who appeared to Moses, and crucified Jesus. Marcion preached the existence of two Gods, one of mercy and of the God of revenge and punishment. He strongly emphasized the Letters of Paul revealing Jesus' true message. He pointed out so as to renounce the Demiurge, and trusting the true and gracious God and his crucified son who had shown love, one would find salvation. In 144, Marcion was excommunicated but continued to preach in Rome

Irenaeus (178) bishop of Lyons and a great Catholic theologian strongly opposed Gnostic belief. He recorded a 'Rule of Truth' which was a forerunner of the Nicene Creed. Irenaeus attacked the Gnostic writers in his book 'Against Heresies' and described their teachings as sacrilege and madness directed at Jesus. Gnosticism faded out in the West during the third century but survived longer in the East. The cult of Mary appeared about 150 in the Infancy Gospel of James where her holiness was stressed. During the following centuries, literature developed about her life and her intercessions for the damned. The writings were condemned as heresy in the fifth century though still considered as authentic in later centuries (the cult of the Goddess is found in the mystery cults as well as in Eastern religions.) Some individuals regard the adoration of the Virgin Mary as idol worship which is forbidden according to the Ten Commandments – Thou shalt not have other Gods before me. Thou shalt not make unto thee any graven image or any likeness of any thing that is in heaven above --- Ex. 20:3-4).

By 180, many churches were established between Syria and Rome. Carthage and Alexandria as well as modern Algeria and to the borders of Persia and India, churches were established. The Emperor Septimius Severus (146-211) was shocked by the increased Christian community in Egypt. He closed the established Christian school in Alexandria and forbade conversion. The Coptic Church in Egypt in 211 was lead by twenty bishops. The Coptic monks penetrated slowly through the southern regions into Nubia and Ethiopia.

A very important Christian scholar was Origen (185-254) born in Alexandria and of Greek ancestry. Some of his fragmentary writings survived and were incorporated in the diverse articles of faith. He wrote commentaries on various books of the Old

Testament but his greatest contribution was his writing On First Principle. According to Origen, God the Father, Christ the Logos (see Gospel of John who described Christ as the Logos) and the Holy Spirit represent the Godhead. Three persons become the Trinity, presenting Christianity according to the philosophical Platonic explanation.

The regular Sunday collections at the established churches aimed to help the poor. Individuals like the centurion Cornelius, noted for his charity (Acts 10:2) helped the destitute. By 251, the Church of Rome supported a large number of poor people and widows. In Carthage, the plaque struck and Bishop Cyprian sent his deacons to help and to nurse the sick.

A very important Christian scholar was Origen (185-254) born in Alexandria and of Greek ancestry. Some of his fragmentary writings survived and were incorporated in the diverse articles of faith. He wrote commentaries on various books of the Old Testament but his greatest contribution was his writing 'On First Principle'. According to Origen, God the Father, Christ the Logos (See: Gospel of John who described Christ as the Logos) and the Holy Spirit represent the Godhead. Three persons become the Trinity, presenting Christianity according to the philosophical explanation.

After Nero's death, four emperors, Domitian (51-96), Decius Marcus Aurelius (the philosopher, (200-251), Valerian (?-260) and Diocletian (245-313) continued the persecutions and ghastly tortures. The Christians refused to worship the Roman emperor as god, and were put to death in the most cruel and atrocious method possible. The last wave of terror against the Christians, known as the 'Great Persecution' was in 284. The Emperor Diocletian realized the decline of paganism and the rise of Christianity at court and among his soldiers. Some of his officers refused to fight, and bravely declared themselves as 'Soldiers of Christ'. Diocletian issued on February 23, 303, forbade holding of Christian services and ordered the priests to be tortured. In 304, a verdict demanded Christians to worship pagan gods. The fury swept through Syria, Egypt, Palestine, and included North Africa. The philosopher Plotinus (203-270) a Coptic Egyptian, who's Neo-Platonism, linked the gap between Greece, and Christianity. He emphasized on the plurality of the various levels of being of which the lowest level was comprised by the physical universe. In comparison, the highest level derived from the final principle which, as he postulated, was without boundaries and completely transcended comprehension.

The "Dark Ages" A.D. 300-650

In the Third century, the Roman Empire was fragmented. Diocletian split the Empire and made Augustus Galerius Caisus 250-311) Caesar of the Danube Valley while Italy and Africa were under the rule of Ceasar Maximian.(240-310)

Young Constantine was sent to the East to serve with Constantinus, his father. See: Development of the Greek-Orthodox Church

There was a huge amount of literature produced by early Christian writers. In 334, the Church fathers established the teachings of the church and decided which of the writings should be included into the canon. The Gnostic writings were banned because there were believed to be 'heretic' and of magical source, witchcraft and mythology.

The Eastern Christians commemorated the birth of Christ on January sixth. In 354, the Western Christians celebrated the Nativity on December 25th. The date was erroneously calculated as the winter solstice on which Mithraism celebrated the birthday of the invincible sun. Many of the Romans adhered to the religion of Zoroaster's theology of Mithras, the son of Ahura Mazda, who was the God of Light. The Christian community decided to celebrate the birth of Christ at the time of the Mithras celebration because they were sure to be undisturbed. A number of other pagan celebrations (Isis/Osiris) were celebrated at that time which made a Christian celebration inconspicuous.

The Christian Church produced men of great intellect and true love for Christ. One of them, who profoundly influenced Christian thought, was Augustine of Hippo (354-430) a Berber from today's Algeria. Augustine was a brilliant student, but undisciplined and frequently punished at school. He described his unruly youth in his book "Confessions". His mother Monica was a devoted Christian while his father was of violent temper. He lived with a lowborn girl who bore him a son when he was about eighteen years of age.

At that time, Augustine developed an interest for philosophy that lead him to read Cicero's dialogue 'Hortensius' The book had a profound influence on him. He had abandoned his faith taught by his pious mother but Augustine was a seeker. At twenty, he became familiar with the teaching of Mani (240 AD), a Persian mystic who proclaimed himself of a Messiah. Mani adopted the teachings of Zoroaster and his teachings of the realms of light and darkness. His philosophy included suggestion of Gnosticism and Judaism as well. Mani taught his doctrine successfully for thirty years until he was overwhelmed by his enemies, and crucified.

Augustine had to provide of his young family and taught rhetoric at Thagaste and later Carthage. He was displeased with his students whom he declared as lazy and undisciplined. Disgusted with them, he left for Italy, and after teaching in Rome, accepted a position as professor of Rhetoric in Milan. The post gave access to influential administrators at the court. The Western Emperor, Valentinian, was thirteen years old, and Augustine was chosen as educator to the boy King. He began to doubts the Manchean teachings and found some of their viewpoints too fantastic. Augustine lived through a time of depression. Because of his brilliant mind, he had opportunities of becoming governor in one of the provinces but his mother realized that he needed a suitable wife. She found a girl who fulfilled the requirements but Augustine showed no interest. He sent his mistress back to Carthage but felt very unhappy especially because he considered himself not capable to rid himself of his physical desires. His book 'Confessions' gives a clear indication of his seeking of God, and the awareness of his inadequacies which tormented him.

Augustine and his son received their baptism together. He loved his son who was highly intelligent. His mother, being very happy about her son's conversion, died soon afterwards followed by his young son. Augustine was ordained at thirty-seven years of age at Hippo, and became later bishop. In 386, Augustine had an experience what he described as finding God. In the year 388, Augustine returned to Thagaste to set up a monastery. He trained his monks to oppose the pagans, the Donatists and the Manichaens and stressed the power of the Catholic Church. A crisis developed because the Donatists refused to accept a bishop of Carthage. His consecrator was a traitor who sacrificed to the old gods and tried to avoid martyrdom. He stressed the authority of the church during the crisis. Augustine was not against war but insisted that it was a Christian's duty to fight a just war for the sake of peace.

Augustine lived during the era of the collapse of the Roman Empire. The Vandals and Alans under the leadership of Gaiseric conquered Africa. The Vandals destroyed and ransacked buildings and churches and did not spare the lives of civilians or clergy. In 429, Gaiseric with his band of Vandals entered the city of Hippo when Augustine died. Augustine's philosophy is still widely read. God is according to his teaching, the centre of wisdom and of the supreme level of Reality. The next level is the soul, experiencing, understanding, memory, and will. Augustine believed that humans have free will of choosing good or evil. He agreed with Paul on the teaching of Original Sin, and only God's grace can grant us salvation. He, too, believed that God elected souls that will receive divine grace and be pre-destined to be saved. His book "The City of God" compares Christianity and the world. Augustine declared the "City of God" as the truly eternal life while life on earth consists of violence and injustice

A wave of invading Huns who came from north-western Asia and being driven away by the Chinese, appeared in 355 at the river Volga and the river Oxus. The Sarmatians and the Ostrogoths (eastern Goths) being harassed by the Huns, moved across the Danube. The Romans used the Ostrogoths as their soldiers and put them into the front of the raging battle to be killed. The Ostrogoths learned warfare from their abusing Roman masters, and possessing weapons, turned against them. In 378, the Ostrogoths defeated the Roman army at Adrianople. The Ostrogoths were already Christians converted by Ulfila the 'Apostle of the Goths' and followers of Arius.

Patrick, the son of a Roman decurion, was born around 389 most likely in western England or southern Scotland. At age sixteen, he was captured by Irish raiders on

Britain and sold as slave to Meliuc, a Druicic high priest In Ireland. He served as shepherd (near Ballymena) and tended his sheep while incessantly praying.

Patrick learned the pagan language and rituals of his captors. After six years of captivity, he was told in a dream that his ship had arrived. He managed to escape and travelled south where he boarded a ship that brought him to Britain, and from there he managed to return to his family.

Patrick's heartfelt wish was to return to Ireland as missionary, and therefore studied for the priesthood. Between the years 412-415, Patrick studied at the monastery of Lerins near the Cote d'Azur and the monastery of Auxerre. Bishop St. Germanus, his guide, ordained him in 417. Patrick spent fifteen more years as his disciple.

In 431, the Bishop Palladius of Ireland died and Patrick was chosen to replace him. He was called to Rome, and in 432, Pope Celestine consecrated him as bishop and received the name of 'Patritius'.

Patrick and twenty-five followers travelled to Ireland. He and his entourage arrived at Slane in the winter of 432-433. He settled in the north at Armagh under the protection of the local King Dichiu where he established an important church and monastery. King Dichiu became one of Patrick's first converts.

Patrick travelled widely through Ireland, preaching and teaching. He established churches, monasteries and schools, converting the population. He died on March 17, 461, at Saul, County Down. During his tireless life, he consecrated 350 bishops and established Christianity in Ireland.

In 392, Christianity was recognized as the official religion of the Roman Empire. The young church inspired men to live as hermits in the wilderness and seeking God and Christ. The hermits spent their prayerful days and nights in caves wearing animal skins and mortifying themselves. After time, they established small communities which gradually developed into monasteries and cloisters. Not only men but women also entered the seclusion of a convent to meditate, praying and seeking God. Education became more widespread, and monks taught reading and writing, and some of them copied Bibles and sacred scriptures. The Bibles and manuscripts produced and decorated by unknown monks are extremely valuable because of their age and craftsmanship, and are kept as special collections in museums and libraries.

Christ's nature his aspects of Man and of God were the cause of widely different views and opinions: the Armenians, Syrians and Copts (Egypt) believed in the single divine nature of Christ while the Nestorians insisted on two distinct natures of Christ – one human, one divine (hypostases). Nestorius was an eloquent preacher at Antioch who in 428 became bishop of Constantinople. Even though being orthodox, he attacked the concept of 'Theotokos' which declared Mary as the God-Bearer (Jesus). He argued that Jesus possessed two natures, and believed that the two could merge but did not share the same essence. His presbyter (Elder of the church) Anastasius unsettled devotees of Mary by declaring that she had been human and God could not be born of a human mother. Both of the opinions were condemned as heretic and the believers of the doctrine were harassed by the kingdom.

Cyril, the patriarch of Alexandria, insisted that Christ had 'one personified nature'. Nestorius dualism annoyed Cyril who was brilliant and a hunter of heretics. Cyril defended the teaching of 'Theotokos' in his paschal letters directed to Constantinople, his clergy, and to Pope Celestine in Rome. The pope summoned a Roman synod and the use of 'Theotokos' was accepted. Nestorius was ordered to renounce his views or face excommunication to which he submitted himself. In 431, Emperor Theodosius called a meeting at Ephesus which was held in the newly-built church of St. Mary. The assembly discussed theological issues and sprinkled with strong political overtones. The Romans were jealous of the influence which Patriarch Cyril exercised on the patriarch of Constantinople. The Council created a lasting schism between the Roman Catholic and the Greek Orthodox churches.

Alaric, the leader of the Ostrogoths was of noble birth. In 400, he led the army of the Ostrogoths across the Alps into Italy and in 410, conquered and sacked Rome. Alacic died of a fever in southern Italy. He had been admired and loved by his people, and according to legend, the Ostrogoths buried him in the riverbed of the Busento River in southern Italy.

In 406, the Vandals, another Germanic tribe, moved through Gaul and continued their conquest of Spain and North Africa. Attila, the leader of the Huns, in 451 directed attacks on Gaul and Italy. He was defeated at Chalons but conquered Lombardy In northern Italy. In 472, a general chose his son Orestes as emperor and named him Romulus Augustulus. He was the last Western Roman emperor and witnessed the collapse of the Roman Empire in 476.

Emperor Augustulus was killed by the Germanic chieftain Odovacar who in the same year established his kingdom of Italy. He acknowledged the Roman Emperor Zeno who was residing at Constantinople. Odovacar was accepted by him as vassal king. Odovacar made his overlord, the Eastern Roman Emperor, his enemy, and the Roman emperor Zeno asked Theodoric, king of the Ostrogoths, to restrain the insubordinate Odovacar. King Theodoric invaded Italy in 489, and in a five year war, finally killed Odovacar. Theodoric established his Ostrogoths kingdom and Ravenna became his capital city. The Ostrogoths were Christians but Theodoric tolerated the various existing religious beliefs

King Theodoric was a wise ruler and loved by the populace. After his death, his successors broke up his kingdom and quarrelled among themselves. The Ostrogoths were gradually absorbed into the populace and ceased to exist as an independent tribe.

The huge expansion of the Roman Empire proved to be impossible to keep under central control and this may have been an added factor considering the fall of Rome in 476. The empire began to decline and its government became increasingly less effective. Internal conflicts, combined with the inability to ward off the various invaders, administered the final blows. After the last Roman emperors were disposed of, Europe was in a state of political turmoil and the Western Roman Empire ceased to exist. The time of the 'Fall of Rome' is in history labelled as the 'Dark Age'. Five centuries followed the collapse which were marked by poverty and uncertainty, and are referred to as the 'Early Middle Age'(A.D. 650-1000). Slowly but gradually, Europe found its way to express new ideas and thoughts. The Eastern Empire, who had developed independent from the Western Empire, continued until to the fall of Constantinople in 1453.

The Saxons and the Picts (Scots) drove the Roman legions from northern England at the beginning of the Fifth century. Germanic tribes like the Angles and the Jutes invaded the island and pushed the indigenous Celtic population back into the mountains of the northern and western parts.

Christianity was introduced to Scotland around 560 by St. Columbanus who built a monastery at Iona near the coast of Mull in Scotland. Iona became renowned as one of the most important centres in Europe. Columbanus and his companions converted the Picts and Angles. The magnificent manuscript 'Book of Kells' is believed to have been produced by the monks of Iona. In 806, raiding Vikings massacred 68 monks. Columbanus' monks returned to Ireland while others fled to the Continent and established monasteries in France, Belgium and Switzerland.

The chieftain Clovis (481-511) son of Childerich, (descendant of the mythical Merovech) founded the Frankish kingdom. His tribe was referred to as Salic Franks. Clovis conquered and annexed the arguing neighbouring tribes and dominated northern France while being still young. In 493 he married Clotilde, a Christian princess of Burgundy, and after subduing the Alemanni in 495, converted to Christianity and helped to spread Christianity throughout his realm. King Clovis entered into an Allegiance with the Roman Catholic Church and the title "New Constantine" was passed to him and his descendants (Later on, the title was changed to 'Roman Emperor'). His dynasty became known as the Merovingian's, the 'long-haired kings'. King Clovis was fascinated by the Romans and their law. He attempted to write a law code for his subjects called 'Sallic Law'. After his death in 511, his sons conquered large areas in France and his Neustria extended north to the Normandy. Paris, Reims, and Aquitaine, including the western part of the Rhine River to the border of Thuringia became Austrasia. Dagobert I, born in 603, annexed Burgundy and large parts of western Germany into his kingdom, as did Sigibert who included Switzerland into the realm. There was much quarrel and strife among the members of the dynasty, and the kings were reputed as inactive (Rois Fainéants). The kingdom was divided among the sons of the royal house until Clotaire II in 613 reunited the Frankish territory. His son, Dagobert I who died in 639, was one of the last powerful Merovingian kings.

The frequent wars had weakened the royal house but the aristocracy had made great gains by supporting the kings were rewarded with land. Chilperic II, son of Sigibert III, was assassinated in 675.His young son Dagobert (II) kidnapped at the age of five by the Palace Mayor Grimoald wanted the throne for his son. Dagobert was brought to Ireland but in 671, returned to claim his right to the throne. He married Giselle de Razes, the niece of the king of the Visigoths (western Goths) to ally the Merovingian dynasty with the Visigoths Royal House. He lived for some time at Rennes le Chateau in southern France. Dagobert was murdered in December of 679 while hunting. The Church canonized him in 872.

The Frankish state grew poor while the church grew rich from the gifts of the pious and those who had become poverty stricken and turned their land to the church while remaining as tenants. The kingdom became divided into three large duchies and the royal government fell into the care of a prime minister, sometimes a duke of one of the duchies without royal status. Duke Pepin II appointed a member of the royal family to control a rebellion. Peppin detained two of the duties and became mayor of the palace. His son, Charles Martel (the Hammer, 714-741) defeated the invading Muslim at the battle of Tours in 733, and extended Charles power in south-western France and Germany. In 751, Pope Zachary gave Peppin III (the Short) the permission to depose of the last Merovingian king Chilperic III. He was placed in a monastery, and tonsured. Peppin, blessed by Pope Zachary, began the rule of the great Frankish Empire which reached its climax under his son, the Emperor Charlemagne (768-814). Charlemagne married a Merovingian princess.

Gregory (the Great) was born about 540 to a pious and distinguished Roman family. He witnessed the last years of Justinian's rule and the Gothic War. As a young man he served as a senior municipal official but he resigned and sold his estates. He founded six monasteries in Sicily and became a monk. The Church called him for administrative duty and he went first to Rome and later became papal envoy to the court of Emperor Maurice at Constantinople. Gregory was a responsive diplomat but the opulence of the imperial court did not change his love for the pallid glory of Rome. On his return to Rome in 590 he half-heartedly accepted the papacy. Rome was ravished by the Ostrogoths and in the north overran by the Arian Germanic Lombards (Langobardi) who captured Milan in 569. Pope Gregory made peace with the Lombards and tried to convert the Spanish Visigoth to Christianity.

Pope Gregory was a humble and modest man. He kept a record of the poor and ensured that they received a weekly ration of foods, and shared his daily meal with twelve paupers. Gregory was a good politician and tried to be tolerant towards the ruling kings and Emperor Maurice. Britain was no longer administrated by the Romans, and some of the population was still pagans worshipping Wotan and Thor. Gregory sent out a mission to England under the leadership of Augustine, the prior of Rome, who landed in 597 in the south-eastern part of England and converted the Kingdom of Kent to Christianity.

He realized it would take generations to wean the pagans from sacrificing to nature spirits and offerings to idols. He knew that the pagan habits would exist alongside introduced Christianity for centuries. He allowed Augustine to destroy the idols and instructed him not to raze the temples but built altars and sprinkles them with holy water.

Christianity spread in England and the missionaries converted King Ethelbert who was married to Bertha, a Christian princess. In the year 598, approximately 10.000 Englishmen converted to Christianity. The Anglo-Saxons became exposed to Roman culture and English priests undertook the difficult pilgrimage to Rome. The pope was esteemed and created the desire for learning and knowledge of the church.

Pope Gregory kept up an extensive correspondence that ranged from practical counsel to the care of the Church-owned land. His 'Regulae Pastoralis' was a most cherished handbook for music and supported to develop the Latin plainsong or plainchant (singing without accompanying instruments) referred to as the "Gregorian Chants". The 'plainchant' is a form of monophonic liturgical music as performed at the Roman Catholic Church during the service. In later medieval, one or more voices were added to the plainchant, and became the basis of the polyphonic western music.

Pope Gregory longed for the solitude of the monastery. He accepted his involvement with politics and power but his mission of bringing Christianity to the pagans of the North was his lives work successfully achieved. In 589, the Visigoths in Spain converted to Catholicism.

The Persians took advantage of the weakened Byzantine Empire. Between 603 and 620, the Persian army was guided by a Sassanid Shah who conquered Syria and Palestine. Persians who were adherence of Zoroaster's teachings of his God Ahura Mazda and the polarization of good and evil, and worshipped the fire (light) as God officiated by the Magi. Zoroaster lived about 600 BC.

In 613, the Persian army conquered Damascus. Many citizens were massacred and sold into slavery. In 619, the Persians subjugated Egypt and moved towards the Bosporus. The empire fought desperately the invading groups of Slavs who fled to escape the Avars, an Asiatic tribe. The Bulgars, coming out of Asia, made various attacks on Constantinople. In 627, the Byzantine Emperor Heraclius (610-641) drove the attacking Sassanids, coming from Persia, successfully back. Sergius, the Patriarch of Constantinople, handed the church treasures to the emperor to pay for auxiliaries, and to fight the Persians. Heraclius regained the lost territories and in 627, he drove the Sassanids back to their homeland.

Soon, an even more formidable opponent would be at the gates of Constantinople

Chapter 17

The Rise of Islam

The prophet Muhammad 'the last of the Prophets' was born about 570 in Mecca. He was an orphaned boy and brought up by his uncle who trained him a camel-driver. Muhammad was a thoughtful and religiously inclined boy, and through his travels with his uncle to Yemen and Syria, exposed to other societies. The Arabs respected the Jews and Christians and called them 'The people of the Book' (meaning the Torah and the Bible.) The Arab tribes fought among themselves and there was no unity. Muhammad felt that the Jewish Ten Commandments gave the Jewish population the necessary guidelines of proper conduct the Arabs severely lacked.

Muhammad married the wealthy widow Khadija who was fifteen years his senior, and lived in comfort. About the age of forty, he went through various religious experiences and visions and gradually accepted the confirmation that Archangel Gabriel appeared to him to reveal divine messages while in a trance. After some time of receiving divine communications, Muhammad and Khadija believed him to be divinely appointed as God's prophet.

Muhammad called his religion 'Islam' (submission to God). His teaching was based on the Old Testament. He declared Abraham (Ibrahim) and Ishmael, son of Abraham and his maid Hagar, as the ancestors of the Arab tribes. Muhammad accepted the concept of monotheism as taught by the Jews and Christians alike, and began to preach about 616. He demanded that the rich should support the poor, and the ancient idols of the Arabian Mother Goddess at the shrine in Mecca should be destroyed. The privileged classes in Mecca did not cherish his opinions because the idols brought a good income. They decided to get rid of the troublesome prophet, and kill him. Muhammad learned just in time of the plan, and he and his followers fled to Yathrip (Medina), the 'City of the Prophet'. The flight (Hegira) on July 16, 622 is commemorated by the Muslims and regarded as the first of the Muslim year 1, and as the month of Ramadan observed through fasting and prayer.

Mecca housed the Ka'ba (cube) a sacred black stone Abraham had supposedly received from the Archangel Gabriel. The Ka'ba was enshrined and members of Muhammad's Quaraysh tribe were the guardians. Mecca was a holy city and annually visited by pilgrims.

Muhammad gained a large number of followers, and in 629, he and his Arabs conquered Mecca. In 632, he made a pilgrimage to Mecca (hajj) the Holy City and centre of the Muslims. He granted the non-Muslim citizens four months to convert or to be forced to accept Islam. Muhammad united the warring Arabic tribes and sat as supreme judge and commander of the army. He also incorporated property rights and laws for widows to improve their and their children's lives.

He refrained from forcibly converting Christians and Jews as long as they paid a heavy land tax and poll tax. Muhammad accepted much of the Old Testaments teachings, and believed that Jesus was a great prophet and inspired teacher but not the Son of God.

When Muhammad died in 632, Arabia was under Muslim control. His father- in-law Abu Bakr, member of the Quaraysh clan, became heir and first Caliph (successor of God's Prophet) the spiritual and political leader of the Faithful, from 632-634. He was followed by Omar bin Khattab (634-44).Under his leadership the Muslims won victories against Byzantine and Persia, and took Damascus in 635, and in 638, conquered Jerusalem. Omar was succeeded by Othman ibn Affan, also a member of the Quaraysh tribe of Mecca. Othman was murdered in 656. Two rivals tried to replace him. Mu'awiyah, a member pf the Umayyad tribe and Ali, who was a cousin of the Prophet and married to Fatima, the daughter of Muhammad, was regarded as the legal authority of Muhammad's line of decent and accepted as the first Shi'ite Imam (party of Ali). Both of them were assassinated. Ali's second son Hussein claimed the khalifat (succession) but he to, was assassinated. The split between the Shi'ite and the Sunni derived from this power struggle. Shi'ite's declared that Ali had inherited the spiritual testimony of the Prophet, and his descendants should carry on the leadership. The Sunni were the traditionalist and emphasized on the descendants of the Umayyad caliphs as the leaders of Islam. Sunni's accepted the chosen caliph though not of Ali's descent as long as he followed the prophet's laws and customs. The division within Islam still exists.

Islam gained over the centuries millions of followers. The Qur'an (Koran), Book of Allah, consisting of 114 chapters (suras) presents an instruction book of philosophy, law and morality. The 'Five pillars of Islam" are: the first Pillar demands affirmation of belief in God (Allah) the second Pillar stresses to pray five times a day while facing towards Mecca. The third Pillar demands to give alms to the poor. The forth Pillar demands to fast from dawn to dusk during the Holy Month of Ramadan, and the fifth Pillar instructs Muslims to make the hajj (pilgrimage) to Mecca at least once in a lifetime. "Jihad" (Holy War) was justified as sacred duty to fight the enemies of Islam, and spread the faith. This was included in the Koran, and practiced by the Prophet.

The Muslims subjugated the nomadic tribes of Iraq where many of Christian Nestorians dwelled. They forbade the Christians to build new churches and to demonstrate the cross or publicly celebrate Easter Monday. Arab rule was very cumbersome but the Nestorians were able to send missions to far-away China. Slowly, the population under the second Caliph Omar (685) converted to Islam. The Jewish population had been expelled under Omar's rule and many Christians, who had been forbidden to baptize their children and suffered restrictions of practicing their faith, left their Arabian homeland.

The collapse of the Persian Empire inspired the Arabs to turn toward Syria and Palestine. The cities of Antioch, Damascus Gaza and Jerusalem were at first not conquered. Heraclius' backup was destroyed before it could reach him and the loss of manpower was great. In August 636,Heraclius and his Byzantine soldiers fought the Arabs at Yarmuk and lost the battle. Antioch surrendered, and in 637 the Moslems set up camp at Bethlehem. Patriarch Sophronius tried to avoid bloodshed and surrendered. Caliph Omar conquered Syria and Jerusalem in 637, and the Patriarch rode to the Mount of Olives to meet him. Caliph Omar negotiated his terms of surrender with the Patriarch, and he had no other options but to accept them. There was no slaughter. The grief-stricken Patriarch died a few weeks later.

The destroyed Jewish Temple became the site of the Dome of the Rock. The Foundation Stone where Abraham prepared to sacrifice his only son Isaac is one of the holiest sites in Judaism. The Muslims claim to be sons of Abraham (and Hagar, his maid) and both religions recognize the sanctity of the Foundation Stone. According to Muslim belief, Mohammed ascended from there to Heaven attended by the Archangel Gabriel. Muslim historians recorded that when Caliph Omar visited the Temple Mount, he was shocked to observe that the site of the former Second Temple had become the city dump. The Dome of the Rock, launched by the Umayyad Caliph Abd al-Malik ibn Marwan and built around 689-691, is a Holy Site in Sunni Islam and renowned as one of the great achievements of Islamic art.

The Muslims ruled that Christian churches were not permitted to be higher than the buildings of Muslims. Wine and pigs were forbidden, and Christians were required to respect Islam and the Koran. Very few conversions were committed by the Muslims. Muslims were approved to marry a Christian girl but not vice versa.

The other cities, who offered resistance to the conquering Arabs, did not fare so well. Caesarea fell and many inhabitants where slaughtered. Women and children became captive and sold into slavery. Constantinople struggled under the repeated raids of the Arabs and Christianity and Islam were trying each others strength and endurance

Egypt was next to be conquered by Caliph Omar's General Amr ibn al-As in 639.The Byzantine army surrendered in northern Egypt being outnumbered and betrayed by the Copts who hated the bickering Byzantines. The Byzantine Emperor Heraclius died in 641.

In 642, the great city of Alexandria fell mainly due to treachery. The city walls were torn downand many Greeks fled. The remaining Christians were heavily taxed. The Arabs took possession of northern and southern Egypt, Libya and Morocco, and were part of the large Umayyad Caliphate. Southern Italy and Sicily were conquered by them, and in 711, they crossed the Strait of Gibraltar, and subjugated the Visigothic kingdom of Spain to their rule, and continued to cross the Pyrenees and into the kingdom of the Franks. In 733 the Arab conquest was defeated by the Frankish leader Charles Martel at the battle of Tours. (Charles Martel was the son of Duke Pepin II and grandfather of Charlemagne). The beaten Muslims withdrew across the Pyrenees into Spain.

The Umayyad Caliphs (descendents of Umar) (661-750) capital city was Damascus. In 750, the Umayyads were defeated and overthrown by the Abbasites (descendents of al-Abbas), the most distinguished of Islamic dynasties that founded Baghdad as their capital, and ruled from there 749-1258.

The wealth of the Umayyads, a merchant class from Damascus in Syria, created envy and the Umayyads broke away. In 756, an Umayyad ruler declared himself Emir of Cordoba in Spain. There were now two caliphates: the Abbasites, descendents of Abu al-Abbas and residing in Baghdad, and the Umayyads, the conquerors, who governed the southern part of the Iberian Peninsula including large sections of North Africa. The Islamic part of Al-Andalus professed Islam as religion but was politically independent from the Abbasids in Iraq. Commerce thrived and the production of ceramic objects, jewellery and crystal made the area prosperous. The Muslims of Spain and Portugal prided themselves of large libraries and mosques. The Emirate of Cordoba acquired a period of high culture, art and science flourished as nowhere else in Europe. Caliph Abd al-Rahman III cherished learning and invited poets, scientists and scholars to his court. Cordoba was a splendid city with paved and lit streets and provided with water. The language of the scholarly was Arabic.

The Spanish Jewish culture reached its pike during the tenth to the twelfth century. On of the most brilliant minds was Moses ben Maimonid (Maimonides), born in Cordoba. He was physician, philosopher and scientist and wrote in Arabic on the subject of medicine which was translated and widely studied in Europe. Maimonides contributed to mathematics, astronomy and his philosophy and his writings influenced Christians, as well as Muslims. Under the rule of the Umayyads, Jews, Christians and Muslims lived peacefully together especially those of higher education who where bilingual and in the case of Jews, trilingual

By the early eight century, Arab conquest had reached the borders of Persia, Afghanistan, areas of India, Morocco, and North Africa, including Egypt. The Abbasid Caliph al-Mansur moved the administration to Iraq. He founded in 762 the circular-built city of Baghdad located between the banks of the Tigris Rivers. Baghdad was by the early ninth century one of the major cities. Both, the Umayyad in Al-Andalus and the Abbasids concentrated on the development of the arts, education, astronomy, scholarships, and commerce. Muhammad ibn Musa al-Khwarazmi (780-850) who was an Arab mathematician, wrote the first book on algebra.

Islam readily adapted and absorbed from the culture of its conquered peoples. The Arabs were originally nomadic people but being exposed to the culture and learning of their conquered subjects influenced and educated them. Cosmopolitan civilisation with intellectual centres in Spain, the Middle East and North Africa, witnessed a flourishing of science, astronomy as well as literature. 'A Thousand and One Nights' are among the priced treasures of literature. One of the heroes of the stories was the famous Abbasid Caliph of Baghdad, Harun-al Rashid who reigned from 786-809 and transformed Baghdad into an intellectual centre of learning and art. According to history, the caliph loved to garb of a commoner, and mingle with the crowd of Baghdad to learn about their grievances and complains which he tried to remedy as a wise and just ruler.

The teaching of Islam developed about the ninth century the mystical branch of Islam, Sufism. It is rooted in Islam and supporting the Five Pillars. Sufism teaches that essential truth is contained in all religions. Those who love God shall receive three sublime blessings: submission, faith and awareness (of God).

The Sufis regard Jesus as the greatest prophet sent by God, and call him the 'Spirit of God'. Sufism was introduced from Persia and gradually spread into Turkey and India. Sufism describes the path to God through self-purification, inner examination, and mystical practice.

The fifteenth century Persian Sufi poets like Omar Khayam, the author of the "Rubiyat", the poets Rumi, al Ghazzali, Hazrat Inayat Khan and Hafiz tried to describe the unspeakable bliss of spiritual union with the 'Divine Beloved'. The poetry, clothed in metaphors, was understand only by the initiates. Sufis were at times subjected to persecution by Fundamentalist Muslims because of the preference of spirit over the strict adherence of the letter (Koran). Sufi poets have been poorly comprehended by Westerners because of its metaphors. Wine symbolizes the intoxication of the soul with divine love. To become drunk means losing oneself in that celestial love. Body and mind are represented by the cup, and the cupbearer is the Grace bestowed by God on the soul.

One historian, al-Masudi (d. 956) wrote a comprehensive history of the world. Mathematic and science studies, including pharmaceutical studies flourished.

Arithmetic and algebra books were written by the mathematician al-Khwarizmi (780-850). Arabic mosques were patterned according to the floor plan of the Hagia Sophia with slim minarets (towers) from which the people were called to prayer.

The Arabs increased the commerce and their ships dominated the Mediterranean and being superb navigators, they ventured to the Far East, and trade increased. The religious fervour which had been the foundation of its power gradually declined and various discords developed among the Arabs to become the cause of the splitting within Islam. By the end of the tenth century, Al Andalus (Arabic Spain) had divided into three caliphates, and political unity was never established. The commerce failed to expand over a long period of time. Some parts of their arid land that lacked good farming conditions, and was unproductive. Christians and Muslims faced each other with distrust and affected the trade with European countries.

After 929, the Caliphate of Cordoba encountered internal breakdown, and by 1002, it had broken up into thirty small arguing kingdoms. The Muslims were never accepted by the Spaniards and their status as 'invaders' made them unwanted and despicable. By 1055, the Spaniards regained Toledo and central Spain. Berber warriors from North Africa came to the aid of the Moors (descendents from Berber and Arab ancestors, the Spaniards called the Berbers 'moros') and during the eleventh century, Spain was the scene of heavy warfare.

Rodrigo Diaz de Vivar, called the 'Cid' (Master) first fought for the Moorish king al-Mu'tamin and later for the Spanish King Alfonso. Rodrigo Diaz captured the Moorish kingdom of Valencia and ruled there until his death in 1099. The city was re-captured by the Almoravids.

King Alfonso VI of Leon declared himself emperor of Spain in 1077, and united his kingdom with Castile until his death in 1109. The small northern kingdoms of Spain united and with the assistance of the Knights Templar began a series of raids against the Moors. In 1095, Pope Urban II urged the Spaniards to fight the Muslims in Spain rather than to join the Crusaders in Palestine. The crusaders from Scotland, England, the Normandy and Germany en route to Palestine stopped in Spain and Portugal to recapture Lisbon while Alfonso VII of Castile and Ramon Berenguer IV of Barcelona took Almeria.

In 1212, Pope Innocent III declared a crusade against the Berber Almorhad caliphs from Morocco (Muslim Fundamentalists) who had ousted the Almoravid predecessors and overpowered the kingdom of Castile in 1195. There was much bloodshed between the Muslims because the Amorhad Muslims were suspicious of the Moors still loyal to the Almoravids. Jews and Christians alike were forcibly converted to Islam They taught their children their beliefs in the safety of their homes though it caused the parents uneasiness and distress. Some of the Jews managed to flee to northern

Christian Spain where they were welcomed because of their expertise as physicians, bankers, diplomats, and in commerce.

The United Spanish kingdoms of Navarre and Aragon, including crusaders from France, under the leadership of King Alfonso VIII of Castile, won a victory over the Almohad Muslims. In 1212, King Alfonso and his Christian military inflicted another severe blow to the Almohads and their caliph, al-Nasir, fled to Marrakech.

The magnificent Alhambra – Al-Hamra, the Moorish palace overlooking Granada, is one of the most superb buildings of Moorish architecture. It was built by the Nasrid dynasty in the late thirteenth century. The Alhambra consists of several palaces which functioned as the Royal place: for guests (Mexuar) and foreign dignitaries (Serallo). The famous and incredible beautiful Lions court is the centre, and connected to the Harem. There are the lovely Gardens of Generalife with water fountains, and the Fortress of Alcazaba, which is partly in ruins.

In the following years, the leadership of the Almohad Empire considerably weakened due to dynastic quarrels, and one city after another fell into the hands of the Christian kings and nobles.

The first part of the fifteenth century witnessed more strife of the Christian kingdoms against the Moorish rulers. King Ferdinand II of Aragon and his wife Queen Isabella of Castile and Leon expelled the Jews from Spain and entered into a religious war. The crusaders captured Malaga in 1489 and laid siege to Granada. Sultan Boabdil surrendered and the royal couple made a formal entry into the captured city on 2 January, 1492. The Moors were finally ousted and gone from the Spanish soil.

Europe in Transition

The venerable Bede (673-735) was a Benedictine monk. His most existing writings comprised rhetoric, astronomy, philosophy and other branches of knowledge. He chronicled the history of the English Church and people, and was regarded the greatest scholar of his time.

Christianity spread throughout Europe. The French King Charlemagne (768-814), son of Peppin III, conquered large areas of territory in France, Germany, the Netherlands and Italy. He forced his new subjects to accept Christianity and executed 4500 people who resisted conversion. The Byzantine Empire rejected him because they supposed that only one emperor should rule, and Byzantine was the chosen one.

Charlemagne was crowned as Holy Roman Emperor by Pope Leo III in Rome on Christmas Day, 800. Byzantine recognized Charlemagne as Emperor on 812. Charlemagne crowned his son Louis as emperor in 813, and died in 814. The Holy Roman Empire lasted until 1648.

Alfred the Great of Wessex (871-899) ruled the Anglo-Saxon kingdom of Wessex. He drove the Danes into northern England and forced them to accept Christianity. During his wise reign, he promoted education and reforms. The English translation of the Church History of England based on the script by the Benedict monk Bede, may have been made by King Alfred of Wessex.

From 780-880, waves of Vikings (Norseman) from Scandinavia and Denmark terrorized the population. They killed, plundered and raided the shores of Scotland and England. Alfred built great fortresses to protect the land from the raiding Danes.

The large invasion of Vikings terrified the British Ills, Ireland, Germany, France and Spain. They raided and burned monasteries and towns alike and terrorized the population. Perhaps the Vikings faced an increase of overpopulation and were forced to discover new land to settle. According to the Norse law, the oldest son inherited the land and the younger sons became traders or went to sea to conquer new territories. After the Vikings settled down in a place to become farmers or traders they accepted Christianity. The medieval warm period encouraged the Vikings to explore unknown waters. They ventured to discover new farm land, to establish new settlements, and to free themselves of the harsh Norwegian ruler, Harold Fairhair

Between 780-1200, Vikings in their longboats expanded their conquest of the Orkney, Shetland and Faroe Islands. In 862, Swedish Vikings traded along the rivers of Russia selling amber, whalebone and sealskin, and established outposts in Novgorod and Kiev, which became the capital city of the state of Rus. The Vikings reached in 870. Eirik the Red settled there but he was later banned from Iceland for killing two men. He sailed west and reached land which he called 'Greenland'. Eirik and his fellow Vikings settled along the west coast of Greenland.

In 911, the French King Charles III gave land to the Norman king Hrolf (Norsemen,Vikings) in exchange of protecting the Franks, and to submit to the king as overlord. Their land became known as 'Normandy'.

Christianity was established in the Scandinavian countries around 966, when the King Harold 'Bluetooth' Christianized his subjects.

In 985, Vikings sailed along the coast of North America but were forbidden by their leader to go on land. Vineland (Newfoundland) was discovered in 998, and Leif Erickson tried to establish settlements along the coast at Epaves Bay but according to Thorfinn Karlefni, Icelandic trader Leif Erickson abandoned the attempts because of constant Indian attacks. After three years of struggle, Leif and his Vikings returned to Greenland.

King Olaf Tyrggvason of Norway reigned around 995-1000. King Olaf Haroldson (1015-1030) and King Olaf II had been baptized while away from Norway. King Olaf II encouraged English missionaries to come to Norway and convert the population from the Norse religion to Christianity. The traditional shamanic practices were banned and persecuted. The population of Iceland adopted Christianity around 1000 through the efforts of tribal chief Borgeir Ljoretninggagodi.

The High Middle Ages (1000-1300) was affected by the short-time mediaeval warm period that lasted until approximately until 1300. Europe witnessed a population increase since the milder weather conditions yielded better and more various crops, and an increase in prosperity. Life for the average person was more organized and the Christian church regulated the church year and its various celebrations. There was in increase of inventions like the iron cannon which changed warfare. The ruling royal houses of France and the Holy Roman Empire of Germany consolidated their feudal states under central control.

Sweden accepted Christianity around 1066. The population was split between the practice of the indigenous religion and the advocates of Christ. By the mid-twelfth century, Christianity was well-established in Sweden and in 1164 Uppsala became the seat of the Swedish Archbishop.

The Reformation was fully accepted and supported in Scandinavia as early as 1530, and became the stronghold of Lutheranism.

Around 1350, a period of increasingly cooling temperatures ushered in the 'Little Ice Age' which made farming over time almost impossible, and affected the lives of millions. The Greenland icecaps, the Alps, and Scandinavia experienced advancements of their glaciers. The farmers of Greenland and of the northern hemisphere were faced with continuously poor harvests due to the cold and damp summers. The crop in the fields rotted before it was ripe for harvest, and the animals died of starvation. The fishers noted a dramatic decline on cod fish. Drift ice along the East Coast of Greenland prevented ships from Iceland and Norway to reach the Greenland settlers on the West coast, and bring supply of goods like wood and other necessities to be bartered for Greenland's fur, woven goods, highly prized wool, walrus tusk and dairy products. The settlers refused to fraternize with their 'heathen' Eskimo settlers who could have shown them of how to adjust to the changing climate and living conditions.

Incessant outbreaks of illnesses among the Greenland settlers were the consequences of severe malnutrition, and the patients suffered of convulsions, hallucinations, gangrene and finally death. The symptoms were referred to as St. Antony's Fire.

According to scientific research, the climate change was caused by a decrease of solar activity which reduced westerly winds by means of cooling the northern hemisphere during winter. The decreased output of solar energy and little or no sunspot activity lasted until 1850.

Chapter 18

Thomas Becket, Church vs. State

William, Duke of Normandy 'the Conqueror" defeated in 1066 the Saxon King Harold at the Battle of Hastings. William became crowned as William I of England.

Thomas Becket was born in Cheapside, a lovely piece of property of the city of London, on December 21, 1120(?) to Matilda and Gilbert Becket. Gilbert and his family belonged to the English middle-class as Gilbert was a prosperous merchant and sheriff of London. Both of them were of Norman ancestry. Thomas had three sisters of whom one, Mary, became a nun. The two other daughters Agnes and Roheise married and raised a family. At Thomas' birth, Henry I, the youngest son of William the Conqueror, reigned in his twenty-first year. Thomas was most likely bilingual with French spoken at home and English picked up from the society he grew up in. He attended a boarding school at Merton in Surrey that had been established by a religious order known as the canon regular. It is most likely that he attended London grammar schools to be taught the basics of Latin, and went to complete his studies in Paris. The death of his mother at the age of twenty two made him to return to England. The father's fortune had declined and Thomas accepted a job at the business office of a relative. He was a very handsome man, slender and tall. Thomas loved the outdoors and was skilled in hunting and hawking.

After a few years (about 1143) he gained a position in the household of Theobald, Archbishop of Christ Church at Canterbury (Kent). It was his first step towards the priesthood. Thomas impressed the Archbishop who employed him with diplomatic missions with the papal curia. Theobald promoted him to Archdeacon and consulted him over difficult matters. There was much tension between the monks and the archbishop who sometimes used hurtful language and was hot tempered. Thomas' charm smoothened out and glossed over Theobald's harshness. In 1150, Theobald was appointed papal legate. Thomas learnt the subtle points of the archiepiscopal administration and diplomacy while serving the archbishop. He granted Thomas leave of absence for a year to study law at Auxerre, and Bologna. It is quite possible that Thomas took the minor orders and had been consecrated a deacon while serving the archbishop. This would exclude him from marrying, bearing arms, and other unsuitable activities.

In 1154, the young Henry, Duke of Normandy, Count of Anjou, Duke of Aquitaine (through his marriage to Eleanor of Aquitaine) grandson of William I (the Conqueror) was crowned at Westminster as King Henry II of England by Theobald, Archbishop of Canterbury.

Thomas became acquainted with King Henry II, and a strong friendship developed between them. In 1155, Henry appointed Thomas as Lord Chancellor, the highest position next to the king. Thomas was now a rich man and had a large household of servants. He lived a flamboyant lifestyle with limitless credit. One a visit to the French court of King Louis VII, Thomas had a retinue of 200 servants, including musicians, hounds, and wagonloads of presents. The chancellor travelled with the court and frequently met the king. His obligations concerning the royal household were many as he was in charge of the church services at court, the archives and secretariat. Thomas excelled as Lord Chancellor and performed his duties with efficiency and competence, and had the authority to issue payments from the royal assets. Though being rich, he did not neglect his religious duties of fasting and prayer, and lived a chaste life.

After the death of Theobald, the Archbishop in 1161, Henry II wanted Thomas to assume the position of archbishop but Thomas was reluctant to accept. He warned the king that the occasion may arise where he had to oppose him. Henry ignored the warning. Thomas, archdeacon of Canterbury and royal chancellor, was powerful and admired, but also envied by his enemies. At the request of his royal lord and friend, he was ordained as priest and in 1162, appointed as Archbishop of Canterbury.

There was an immediate and noticeable change in the new archbishop's lifestyle. He omitted the appearance of wealth and wore a simple gown and surplice. Thomas' days were occupied with work, prayer, worship and reading. He took personal interest concerning appointments and choices of candidates for the priesthood. As archbishop, he had to grow into his new responsibilities, and a way of life with many different set of duties. The church owed much property which was available to the archbishop.

Herbert of Bosham, whom Thomas had known during his years as royal chancellor, was Hebraist, theologian, and regarded as a distinguished scholar. Thomas' household consisted of knights and officials as well as of clerks some of which were experts in secular law. Herbert was counsellor and advisor in spiritual matters, and aided the archbishop in the study of the Bible.

One of the archbishop's responsibilities consisted in his employment as judge serving as barons and ecclesiastical magistrates in which he had to attend to the various cases. Thomas proved himself to be just and morally upright, and to uproot unfair fees and bribes.

Woodstock, near Oxford, and Clarendon were Henry's favourite hunting lodges were some of the meeting were held. The social environment at the court was filled with envy, intrigue and deceptiveness Even though the king had been tolerant of his newly appointed archbishop but Thomas, finally independent, had made some serious mistakes caused by his pride and his inexperience. Both he and the king realized that their former friendship began to shatter.

His obligations were very demanding, and Thomas approached the king to appoint a deputy to carry out the duties of chancellor but the king was annoyed. There were disputes regarding land and estates that belonged to the cathedral of Canterbury. Thomas may have been ill advised by his lawyers to claim the property which was claimed by the Earl of Harford, a man of importance. It developed into a nasty case, and the king, on business across the channel, was informed about. Thomas had enemies within his diocese who accused him of pride. King Henry himself seemed to be untouched by the accusations. The king and his family returned to England in January of 1163, and he greeted his archbishop with warmth and joy.

The tide changed when Henry demanded a new tax to be levied to which the archbishop declared that no money should be paid from the lands held by the church or the estates. The king was furious. There were particular grievances he wanted to be addressed. One of the important aspects was the merging of church, of branches of the government and law coming together and supporting each other. The archbishop dealt with cases concerning the application of punishment concerning 'criminal clerks' employed in his service. The fact that Thomas in his capacity as archbishop ruled over the outcome of a criminal case concerning any individual connected to the church, exasperated the king. Thomas excommunicated a landowner to which the king angrily responded with the order to grant absolution. Thomas replied that excommunication was for him to issue, and was not one of the king's duties. Henry pointed out that it was his royal privilege, and the archbishop was unable to pronounce excommunication without the king's consent. Thomas had to proclaim absolution to the landowner.

The king gained support of some of the bishops, and called a council at Northhampton. He stated three grievances against the archbishop: he engaged in liberties without consulting the king who was his superior. The archbishop disregarded the ancient customs concerning relations between ecclesiastical and royal authorities. The king also accused Thomas of protecting the clerical criminals from their proper punishment, and of irregular and inordinate persecution of laity for moral offences.

In October 1163, King Henry summoned an assembly to the church of Westminster. He opened the meeting with asking the bishops of they were willing to observe the ancient customs of the realm. There were sixteen ancient customs and were repugnant and contrary to the canon, and the bishops would not give their consent of acceptation without being tested against the laws of God. Henry demanded of the bishops and dignitaries to unconditionally give their assent to the privileges and customs having been observed by his ancestor, Henry I. The king wanted complete control of church and state. The demand created dismay among the bishops who supported their archbishop's determination of not agreeing to customs that opposed canon law. Henry was angered and accused his archbishop of ingratitude while he defended the rights of the church against abuses and injustice through secular court.

The king demonstrated his indignation by removing his son, Prince Henry, who lived with other noble boys at the archbishop's household, from Thomas' tutorship. The young prince liked Thomas what aroused his father's jealousy. Henry also cancelled the former honours and custodies Thomas had received as chancellor. Both parties were involved in secret correspondence with Pope Alexander III to describe their grievance and Thomas kept up correspondence also with King Louis VII of France who was sympathetic to his cause.

At the Council of Clarendon held in October 1164, King Henry ordered that some of the barons and Royal clerks should make a summary of the sixteen ancient customs to determine the usages they had promised to acknowledge. The customs possessed only a few dignities concerning the king, and the barons. They dealt with current matters between church and secular powers. It declared that clerks that were in charge of lands of the king owed him all services such as attendance at court. The barons and royal officials were immune from sentences of excommunication without royal permission. The clause 3 in question caused much controversy, regulated the procedures concerning the trials of criminal clerks accused of felony. The dispute centred around the question if the person was judged by the royal court or, if found guilty, to be judged in the ecclesial court. Double punishment had been exercised in the past but the archbishop ruled that the guilty suffered punishment of degrading by being unfrocked, and, if he should cause offence again, to be judged as a lay person.

While the judicial and administrative proceedings were read, Thomas interrupted the reading and declared that it was impossible for him to know the ancient customs since he was just recently made archbishop. He left the meeting with the promise to study a copy of the Constitution. He may not have realized that to read and study the copy at his office was interpreted as his acceptance. He later on declared in good faith that he just accepted them to study and reject any clause that would be detrimental and contrary to canon law and the church.

The Council at Clarendon ended and Thomas felt torn whether to conform and seal the Constitutions, or not. The king and bishop of Rouen travelled together to Woodstock to visit the archbishop with the request that Thomas write to Pope Alexander to have the English customs confirmed. The pope neither confirmed nor condemned the customs. Henry's attitude toward his archbishop became resentful. The archbishop's disdain for the oath taken at Clarendon to observe the ancient customs aggravated the king, and he searched for discrepancies to vent his anger. He tried to charge Thomas with a series of grievance of failing the royal retinues and royal loans while being chancellor. The archbishop asserted himself by declaring that the profits and business had been done in the king's interest and with Henry's approval. During the meeting, he refused to render the requested account for a large sum of money for the custodies he had been responsible for as chancellor. Henry tried to humiliate him and planned his ruin, and everyone was aware of it. A number of bishops suggested to Thomas to offer his resignation for the sake of the Church of England. His humiliation would satisfy the king who was very angry and impatient. Thomas rejected the suggestion though he was warned that he may face imprisonment or death. It may have been simply threat because no bishop had ever been imprisoned but Thomas decided to fight it out. Another meeting was scheduled when Thomas met with the dispirited bishops who warned him that he was charged with perjury and treachery for violating the royal customs. During the winter of 1163 Thomas negotiated through the moderate John of Salisbury, who left for France and posed as a scholar in Paris while being on the secret mission of agent for the archbishop.

There was a suit against the archbishop concerning a parcel of land belonging to the archbishop's manor of Pagham. The land was claimed by William, Earl of Pembroke, one of the greatest magnates in England. William appealed to the king, and Thomas, when summoned, did not attend. The Marshall, John fitzGilbert complained and Thomas received through the sheriff a summons to meet at Northampton but not as royal chancellor or archbishop but as baron of wrongful conduct Thomas was tried on various charges at the council held in Northampton Thomas acted in defiance while celebrating Mass dedicated to St. Stephen. Afterwards, he planned to attend court while still vested and attired with gird and pallium but some attending Knights Templar discouraged him. He took the cross and approached the castle to the dismay of the bishops who accepted the symbol as provocative and tried to take the cross from him.

The king, who was informed of the event, reminded his archbishop that he was his liege vassal who had sworn fealty. He reminded his archbishop that he had sworn the dignities and royal rights. The king requested to render the accounts while being chancellor, and accept the courts decision. Thomas refused the king's demands and retorted that he had accepted nothing that was against his conscience, and had acted in the interest of the king. He concluded by adding that the church of Canterbury and he, its archbishop, were under the protection of God and the pope.

The bishops were ready to plea to the pope against Thomas concerning his perjury and tried to persuade the pope to remove him. The king was convinced that Thomas was a thief. The bishops agreed to charge the archbishop for financial embezzlement while in the service of the king, for refusing to produce the requested accounts, and for violating his vow to obey the (outdated) Constitutions.

When Thomas left the room, some of the attendance shouted 'traitor' and 'perjurer'. He was exceedingly annoyed and outraged because of the humiliation he had suffered, and being judged and condemned by his appointed parishioners while he tried to protect the liberty of the church. After the trial was over, Henry pronounced that no harm be done to the archbishop but the situation was stressed. The bishops from London and Chichester approached the archbishop with the proposal of offering the king two manors of Oxford and Wingham as payment for fines but Thomas reacted with resentment and declared that both manors belonged to Canterbury.

All of these events may have strengthened the archbishop's decision to leave for France, and consult his case with Pope Alexander III who stayed at Sens in France. In May of 1164, the anti-pope Victor IV had died. He tried to have an interview with the king who refused to see him. Thomas decided to see Reginald, archdeacon of Salisbury, his clerk, who had left for France, and seek advice from Pope Alexander. He left his manor at Aldington and took some of his companions to hire a boat at the coast of Kent. The wind was not favourable and the sailor had second thoughts. Thomas had to return and was summoned to Woodstock. King Henry who had been informed of the unsuccessful departure, ask him if the country was not large enough to hold both of them Thomas by leaving the country without the king's permission, had had violated one of the ancient customs, and was at the mercy of the king.

On October 14, 1164, Thomas left Northampton accompanied by a servant Roger de Bray and two lay brothers. He wore the disguise as a Gilbertine lay brother, and on November 2, the small group landed at Oye in the country of Flanders. The Royalist bishops including the King maintained that the archbishop had never been in danger.

The party hid themselves in the marshlands until they reached St. Bertin and were friendly received by Abbot Godescal. A small group of clerks supported by Herbert of Bosham, joined them there as well. Thomas addressed his situation to the Pope Alexander and curia whom he met at Sens. He presented his case and the Constitution of Clarendon, and declared that the (evil) laws were the reason for his exile. The pope read the Constitution and decided that the laws were not good though some were tolerable. Others were in contrary to canon law and condemnable. William of Pavia represented King Henry and defended the customs while Thomas took his own defence. The pope's judgement was never written down, and he had refused to grant judgement against the bishops. Thomas retained his office and title but he could not return. He did not want to renounce his position because he saw it as his duty to protect the rights of the church from exploitation. The discussion with Alexander and curia ended with the decision that he stay at the Cistercian Order at Pontigny situated in the duchy of Burgundy. Herbert of Bosham disliked the monastery located in the midst of a dense forest, and far away from a town.

In December of 1164, King Henry confiscated all of the revenues of Thomas clerks and the possessions of the churches. The benefices were placed into the care of numerous diocesans except for Canterbury which was given into the custody of the bishop of London.

The exiled archbishop settled down to a life of studying law and the Bible, religious observances, and the prosecution of his case through diplomatic and ensuing correspondence. The household in exile was small. Thomas employed clerks highly skilled in the fine art of writing elaborate letters in Latin besides some chaplains, clerks for copying, and servants. Thomas studied with Herbert of Bosham and John of Salisbury the Epistles, the Psalms, and books on church law. He stayed at Pontigny for nearly two years under the protection of Pope Alexander III and King Louis VII of France but his exile was an embarrassment to them

During spring 1165, Thomas felt that he was in a hopeless position, and sent his complaints of ill-treatment and messages for help to his English acquaintance in power. Communications with the pope were extremely slow, and the pope encouraged the impatient archbishop to lay low. In early 1166, Thomas sent a letter to King Henry and stated that he was looking forward to a just resolution in the argument. The king showed no hurry to make amendments with his archbishop. He had appointed Gilbert Foliot as near leader of the English church, and none of the two felt motivated to recall Thomas.

In May of 1166, Thomas broke his silence that had been imposed on him by Alexander. He wrote to King Henry and requested a meeting with him. In two other letters, he spoke more forceful and prophesied that God would incur His anger on the king.

In a letter to the archbishop of Canterbury, the pope confirmed primacy to him. He also empowered him to punish those persons who had done violence and injury in respect of the possessions of the church though the king was excluded. Thomas was to become appointed papal legate. He went on different pilgrimages within his area of residence.

King Henry fell seriously ill and had to cancel his meeting with King Louis of France. Thomas accepted the invitation of Abbot William de Mello at Vezeley, to celebrate the Mass on Whitsunday. The archbishop preached to the congregation and described the reason of his quarrel with the king, his condemnation of the Constitution of Clarendon, and his sufferings. He emphasized in particular the clauses which comprise relationship with the curia and reduce ecclesiastical jurisdiction.

He continued excommunicating the various members of the church hierarchy who had been involved of causing the church much grief and be usurping possessions and goods of the Church of Canterbury. Thomas pointed out that he had not yet pronounced a sentence on the king, and hoped that he would change his behaviour.

During 1167, correspondence between the archbishop and the English bishops were exchanged about new grievances against Thomas concerning failures of duties and misdemeanours. Gilbert Foliot, bishop of London, sent letters signed by the bishops to the pope defending the king and accusing the archbishop of impertinent and unwarranted behaviour. Foliot denied the accusations of coveting the archbishopric but insisted on the incapability of the archbishop. Thomas issued a letter in which he described the conditions for reconciliation, and outlined the relationship between the liberties and rights of the English church. According to the archbishop's view, the king would restore to Canterbury and its archbishops the rights, possessions and liberties which were presently revoked. The king would surrender on all matters in question, and relating to the church, the archbishop of Canterbury would serve God under the king.

In a letter written by John of Salisbury to Baldwin, archdeacon of Totnes, John defended the archbishop.

The unyielding King Henry complained to the General Council and threatened that unless Thomas was banned from Pontigny he would expel the Cistercian Order from his dominions. Thomas, after consulting his advisers, accepted and declared to remove himself. The abbot of Pontigny, Guerin de Galardun, and the brethren were very distressed. Herbert of Bosham was sent to King Louis to negotiate, and Thomas accepted the offer of St. Columba's abbey close to the city of Sens at the River Yonne. They left Pontigny about November 1166 to move to the ancient Benedictine abbey of St. Columba. In spite of the warm reception, the archbishop was in low spirits as he left behind well meaning friends. He too, was distraught concerning a dream in which he was murdered by four knights. All of this was the assault made on his enemies at Vezelay.

Robert, canon of Merton, Thomas chaplain and personal attendant, witnessed the archbishop's life in the monastery. He passed his nights in prayer and barely slept in his bed. He ate sparingly, and resorted to mortifying his body through scourging until his bare back was bleeding.

Between 1163 and 1170, King Henry tried to modify some of the disputed ancient customs inherited from his ancestor, King Henry I. Some of the concessions seemed to be reasonable but the archbishop knew the king too well and refused to accept the modified version. Some of his former predecessors had opposed them and had been exiled as well.

On November 18, 1167, the legates invited Thomas to a meeting to Trie. He was accompanied by his clerks Herbert of Bosham, John of Salisbury, his chaplain Robert of Merton and Gilbert of Chicksands. The legates opened the meeting by recalling Henry's grievances against the archbishop. Thomas answered the charges and declared that he would humiliate himself only saving the liberty of the church, the possession of the church, the honour of God and his good name. He was not inclined to make any concessions. The legates questioned Thomas if he would accept the king's offer to be satisfied with the arrangement as had existed before the death of King Henry I, (1135). He turned the offer down as too impossible to accept the evil practices. The negotiations came to a standstill.

Henry sent a report through his legates to the Pope Alexander and requested to pursue him to rid him of his disloyal archbishop. The appeals were forwarded to Thomas. The pope was showered with letters of protest from the parties involved, and he replied to encourage Thomas to continue the great effort of not to make peace at the expense of the church.

During the winter of 1169 was hope for reconciliation and reinstatement to Canterbury. The French King Louis and his councillors, and Thomas advisers held distressed discussions with the French commissioners and advisors concerning the clause 'saving the honour of God' which the archbishop intended to include when submitting himself in the presence of the French king to King Henry. The mediators tried to convince him to keep to the simple formalities of reconciliation, and omit the phrase. When Thomas met King Henry, he fell on his knees and was raised by the king. He declared his submission to the king and requested to place the whole situation to the king's judgement. The archbishop finished to the dismay and shock of the attendants with the disputed clause 'saving the honour of God'. He had fulfilled the required conditions but using the unwanted phrase, broken the conditions on which the settlement had been decided upon. King Henry fumed because he misinterpreted the phrase as only the archbishop but not he, Henry, honoured God. He fell into a rage and shocked King Louis, the commissioners and advisors with his excessive and extreme language.

Henry continued by emphasizing the ancient customs of the realm, and demanding that Thomas swear to observe them without reservation which the archbishop refused. Louis declared them acceptable but Thomas explained that he could accept it only in accordance to God's law. He explained that in order of establishing peace for the church, the king, and himself would accept those customs which his predecessors had observed as long as they were in unity with God's law and his order. King Louis attempted to make Thomas submit without reservation to which the archbishop replied that his former predecessors had not been requested to give additional oaths. Henry refused to accept Thomas' offer and brought the meeting to an end. The commissioners tried to intervene and approached Henry to make peace with the archbishop and restore him to Canterbury. Thomas refused to return in disgrace but wrote to Henry to asking him to seek an agreeable way out.

In May 1169, Pope Alexander advised Thomas to withhold any sentences on the prelates of the realm or the king before the mission was completed. He also added that if such sentences had been issued he would suspend it. Thomas excommunicated ten persons whose offences he considered as dishonourable. His action caused a great stir among the clergy. King Henry protested to the pope and requested for cancellation of the sentences. In order to put pressure on him, Henry intrigued with the Italian city states and the king of Sicily to get the archbishop transferred to another see. The pope requested in a letter to Thomas to suspend the sentences he may have issued on his enemies. The papal letter to Henry stated that Thomas must be restored to full dignity to the Christ Church of Canterbury including the possessions he held as archbishop. In return, Thomas would serve King Henry in honour of God and the Order. Thomas himself would regard the 'evil customs' as abolished and no longer a source of debate.

Henry realized that it was in his own interest to make peace with his archbishop. The conflict was harmful to his reputation, and the excommunications of the royal clerks and bishops very oppressive. He assembled a large ecclesiastical council to advice him. The practical details concerning the financial issues became complicated because Thomas requested that the king should compensate for all possessions which had been in his possession as archbishop, benefits and full restoration of property. Henry dropped his demands for the accounts of Thomas chancellorship and cancelled the repayments of debts incurred during that period. The form of reconciliation had to be considered because Henry wanted an unimportant change of the wordings of the document like his 'heirs' for 'sons' including the insertion 'saving the dignity of the kingdom'. The nuncios refused the change of the clause. Thomas suspected that the 'dignities of the kingdom' were replacing the 'customs' and it was a question of which dignities or customs Henry was referring to. He was furious and left the meeting. Thomas instructed the English bishops to suspend the denunciations of excommunications on individuals while the negotiations were in progress. The nuncios proposed to Henry that the clause 'saving the liberty of the church' should replace his suggested clause but Henry refused to accept any compromise.

On November 18, 1169, Thomas, King Henry and King Louis were scheduled to meet at the abbey at St. Denis in Paris. Thomas and his group appeared to meet the two kings and the dignitaries of the church. The archiepiscopal and papal conditions which were in dispute were presented to Henry. Thomas did not like the procedure for the restoration of his property but both parties compromised. Henry dropped the 'evil customs' which hurt the English Church and the saving clauses, and agreed to respect each others rights. Thomas would return to England to be fully installed as archbishop. He asked Henry for the customary kiss of peace as the pope had assured him would be sufficient to seal the agreements. Henry refused to comply because he had sworn in public that he would not give Thomas the kiss of peace and the negotiations were broken off and Thomas had been unable to meet Henry in person. Everything had been cleared but the kiss of peace had been denied.

In early 1170, the pressure on King Henry to settle the dispute with the archbishop became strong. The ecclesiastical sentences against him and his lands were intense and Thomas was reluctant to return to England without guaranties. Henry considered the possibility of joining a crusade. His bishops advised him that an initial settlement with Thomas was necessary. Henry called upon a council of ecclesiastics and nobles and announced that he invited Thomas to return to England. He pledged that he had banished from his heart his anger and complains against his archbishop and his staff. The possessions were to be returned in concord and safety. He just requested that Thomas should perform the services required to serve him, his king. Henry sent his bishops to invite Thomas to a meeting in Normandy and he accepted. When Thomas and his staff arrived at Pontoise to have initial talks with the bishop of Rouen at Chaumont, he was informed to continue no farther as the king was about to leave for England. Gilbert Foliot, bishop of London, right away left for the curia. The clerks and Geoffrey Ridel, the archdeacon of Canterbury, had conspired to prevent the meeting between Thomas and King Henry. Henry received a warning by the nuncios that he had to carry out the peace treaty by the first of May or he would be censured.

In a papal letter dated January 19, 1170, Pope Alexander released Henry's from his oath to give the archbishop the kiss of peace. He suggested that Henry may substitute his son of giving Thomas the 'Kiss of Peace'. The pope requested that Henry resolve the situation to bring about the desired conclusion. The persons who had been excommunicated by the archbishop would receive absolution though peace was not established the absolution would be annulled.

King Henry wished to crown his young son Henry. The pope instructed Thomas and the English bishops on no account to perform the coronation and the anointment unless the prince took the traditional coronation oath and the promise of liberty to the church especially the Church of Canterbury. The bishops were informed that no participation could take place until all conditions were observed and honoured. Pope Alexander in a letter to Roger of York forbade him and all bishops to crown the prince while the archbishop was still in exile.

Henry had to option to accept Thomas re-instalment and use the coronation as an act of resolution. He and the bishop Roger of York still had the papal privilege of June 1161, and Henry decided to arrange the coronation to be conducted by the archbishop of York.

The pope sent a sharp message to Henry and threatened him with excommunication if the terms of reconciliation of had not been carried out within forty days. Rumours spread concerning the coronation of the young prince, and Thomas sent letters of advice to the bishops of Winchester and Exeter to support papal prohibition and defending Canterbury's privileges, and a very carefully worded and respectful letter to Bishop Roger of York. Henry went ahead with the coronation plans and limited the crossings of the Channel. Prince Henry's wife Margaret, the daughter of the French king, stayed behind. Prince Henry was crowned at Westminster Abbey by Roger of York. It was one of Canterbury's primary privileges to crown a prince. The coronation was violating the tradition and a devastating shock for the exiled archbishop. The prince did not hold fast to the established coronation oath but promised instead that he would observe the ancestral customs of the kingdom (the Constitution of Clarendon). It was later denied by Arnulf, bishop of Liseux, and others.

Ten days after the coronation, King Henry crossed the Channel to Barfleur. He was greeted by the papal commission who presented the papal provocation to which Henry agreed except of giving the kiss of peace. Afterwards he and his suite visited Thomas at Sens and tried to convince him to attend the conference between him and King Louis, held at a little border town of Fredeval. Thomas was reluctant to be there but William of Sens convinced him to attend and travelled with Thomas and two commissioners.

King Louis had been a friend to Thomas, and had worked in his favour. Henry promised him to re-install the archbishop to full compensation and peace but without the kiss of peace which he would give in his country and at the time and place of his choice. In a conversation held between the two kings Henry and Louis, Henry told Louis that tomorrow he would met his thief, and `promised to grant him peace'. King Louis was startled, and enquired what thief Henry referred to. Henry explained he spoke of the archbishop of Canterbury. King Louis was very upset at Henry's reply and declared that he wished Thomas would be his archbishop.

On July 22, 1170, Henry and his suite met with Thomas outside of Freteval. The king rode to Thomas and they shook hands. Both dismissed their entourage and discussed existing problems especially the invalid coronation. Henry suggested tore-crown the young royal couple at Canterbury, and renounced his ill will. He expressed his intentions to be a more charitable lord. Thomas was overwhelmed and returned to his party, and the bishops negotiated the settlement of all unsolved matters. In a letter to the pope, the archbishop expressed precautions as to wait in France for the nuncio's report that the confiscated assets had been restored. King Louis advised Thomas not to trust King Henry before he did not receive the kiss of peace. It took months of negotiations between the parties involved until the promises were honoured and carried out. End of October 1170, papal letters arrived. Some of them were addressed to the various bishops of London, Chester, Exeter, Salisbury, Rochester and York. The letters accused the prelates for a whole series of faulty offences against the archbishop and the church. The worst offence committed was the participation in the coronation and the relapse to observe the wicked customs. They were suspended from their Episcopal formalities, and the bishops of London and Salisbury relapsed into excommunication.

In November, 1170, Thomas tried to keep up his spirits though nothing went to well. Henry sent message to encourage his archbishop to return to England as soon as possible. The pope's correspondence expressed his joy at the settlement at Freteval. He reminded Thomas to show patience and mercy. His legation in England was established according to the terms agreed at Freteval. Any clergy who disregarded the injunction should be detained and receive lifelong imprisonment in a monastery. Thomas expected to be protected, and equipped with two portfolios of papal letters, travelled with John of Oxford north to take the ships. While they waited for favourable winds, bad news and rumours reached them. The Count of Boulogne sent a messenger to warn the travellers that the English ports were guarded, and it could be dangerous for the archbishop to cross but Thomas decided to cross the channel as soon as the ships were ready. The more worrisome report related to the resentment of his return expressed by the archbishop of York and the bishops of Salisbury and London who allied themselves with the sheriff of Kent, Gervase of Cornhill. Randolf de Broc, and Reginald Warrene. Thomas realized that they planned to arrest him, and seek for the papal letters in his holdings.

End of November, Thomas sent his baggage ahead and dispatched Osborn, his servant, with the papal letters imposing sentences on the two bishops, Salisbury, London, and York. Osborn avoided the watch and delivered the letters to the church at Dover. He managed to fade away before he could be arrested and killed. Thomas and Herbert of Bosham rejoiced when the learned that the risky letters handed over.

About November 30.1170, they crossed and landed at Sandwich (Kent) to stay at an Episcopal manor and hoped to be safe from the incensed bishops. The archbishop's cross had been raised in the prow of the ship. When the party entered into the harbour, a crowd of people cheered, and prostrated themselves to receive the returning archbishop's blessings. They had hardly embarked when the principal royal officers in Kent rode up with their troops who wore mail under their coats and were armed. John of Oxford confronted them and insisted that they disarm before he allowed them to meet the archbishop. The officers were Gervase of Cornhill, Sheriff Arnulf de Broc and Reginald of Warenne. .

Gervase of Cornhill argued with Thomas that he did not establish peace but discord. Furthermore he planned to undo the coronation besides punish the bishops for serving their king. Thomas explained that he did not intend to cancel the coronation but punished the bishops for performing it contrary to the dignity of Canterbury and to God. King Henry had authorized the punishment, and the sentences were issued by the pope. He promised the officers to give consideration to the issues and answer them the following day.

Thomas and his suite arrived at Canterbury the following day. Each village they passed through welcomed him with a joyful procession led by the priest. When they approached Christ Church, the archbishop removed his boots and completed the journey barefooted. The church bells rung and he greeted the monks with the kiss of peace.

The following day, the returned archbishop received the royal officials, accompanied by the clerks of the bishops of London and Salisbury, and of the archbishop of York. The officials declared that the bishops had appealed to the pope and requested that he withdrew them because they were opposing the peace made at Freteval. The officials pointed that the sentences were opposing the Constitution of Clarendon and were in disapproval of the king. Thomas replied that the pope had pronounced the sentences, and he had no authority to intercede. He was in a difficult position because his answers or actions could be misinterpreted.

Thomas wished to pay his respects to the new fifteen-year old king, and visit his diocese. The young king Henry, who had been in his household, was surrounded by guardians, and the archbishop's contact with Henry was controlled and limited. Some false rumours were reported to the senior king that Thomas rode with a large army in full armour to capture towns and dispose of the young king In reality, the archbishop and Herbert of Bosham were, on their return from London to Canterbury, accompanied by five knights to ensure protection. Thomas sent a request to see the senior king but the audience was denied. His friend Simon, abbot of St. Albans, tried to intervene but King Henry refused to see him. Thomas regretted at not been able to attend Christmas at the court. The situation was grave, and the monk William of Canterbury (later ordained as deacon) went to the archbishop to warn him that he and John of Salisbury, John the Cantor, Gunter and Alexander of Wales, were in great danger. He advised Thomas to be very careful for they may be slain.

Thomas dismissed the five knights who had accompanied his party to Canterbury. He attended to his spiritual and pastoral duties by confirming children and distributing alms. The de Broc family kept up the blockade and stationed troops at crossroads and bridges in the hope that the archbishop may break the royal edict, and they may catch him.

On Christmas Evening, Thomas celebrated Mass at night, and on the next day preached to the parishioners gathered in the cathedral. After the customary prayers, the archbishop excommunicated all violators of the rights of his church. He named Robert and his nephew Ranulf de Broc and those excommunicated in 1169. He included the vicars who had intruded into Harrow and Chilwood (Canterbury church property) were possessions and goods had been seized by the vice-archdeacon Robert, and Nigel de Sacquenville.

After Christmas, Thomas sent his clerks on missions. Herbert of Bosham, his devoted clerk and friend, and Alexander of Wales were sent to the archbishop of Sens and the King of France, and Gilbert de Glanville to the pope. The chaplain Richard and John Planeta went to the bishop of Norwich to grant pardons some of the priests. Thomas' purpose of sending messengers was the insistence that the promises of peace made at Freteval were not performed in England. Herbert of Bosham left reluctantly, believing that the archbishop wanted to keep him out of danger. The mild-tempered John of Salisbury stayed at Canterbury.

The senior king and his court, which stayed at Bur-le Roi, were visited by Roger of York, Jocelin of Salisbury, and Gilbert of London, to complain, and discuss the measures to be taken to restrain the archbishop of Canterbury. While listening to the complaints of the bishops, Henry made an awful remark leading to dire consequences. He expressed the regret of having nourished the miserable traitors and drones, and to accept the contempt of a low-born clerk. The promises made at Freteval were forgotten. Henry's emotional outcry was the signal to plan a secret plot carried out by four of his knights, William de Tracy, Hugh de Morville, Reginald fitzUrse, and Richard de Bret. They had been Thomas vassals at the time of his chancellorship, and acted within.

An official mission was planned by Henry to restrain the archbishop. He ordered William de Mandeville, Earl of Essex, Saher de Quincy, Lord of Bourn, and the Constable Richard de Humet to travel to Canterbury and present an ultimatum to Thomas. If he would refuse the conditions, the messengers should arrest him. Both parties tried to negotiate but when William de Mandeville and his escort arrived in Canterbury, the archbishop was already dead. William explained to the shocked monks that he tried to get the archbishop's agreement concerning matters which pertained to Henry's dignity. Thomas would have been left in peace. In case of his refusal, William de Mandeville would have compelled him to yield.

The unfavourable weather made the crossing from France to Essex or Dover very difficult. Ranulf de Broc and his group finally managed to sail, and arrived on December 28 at Saltwood castle where they spent the night. They planned to surround the cathedral to prevent the archbishop to escape, and pressure him to absolute the excommunicated bishops. Furthermore, they wanted him to pledge to act in a quiet manner, and inform Thomas to prepare himself to stand trial. Ranulf de Broc mobilized the garrisons of Rochester, Dover and Blechingley to join him at

Canterbury. On arrival, they informed the citizens to take up arms and proceed to the archiepiscopal palace but the population was reluctant to obey.

On December 29, 1170, the last day of his life, the Archbishop of Canterbury, Legate of the Holy See and Primate of all of England, was surrounded by his clerks John of Salisbury, William fitzStephen, sub-deacon and drafter, the monk William of Canterbury, and Benedict of Petersborough, including Edward Grim who was on visit. Thomas celebrated Mass and afterwards went to the different altars to pray to the saints. He made his confession to a monk, Thomas of Maidstone, and was scourged by Robert of Merton. During the afternoon, Thomas was informed of the arrival of messengers from the king who was still in France. The archbishop was in his chamber in conversation with a monk when Reginald fitzUrse, Robert de Broc, Hugh de Morville and an archer entered, and seated themselves. After some time had elapsed, Thomas greeted Hugh de Morville. Reginald fitzUrse acted as the messenger of the king with a significant message, and asked Thomas if he wanted to receive it private or public. Thomas chose the latter but as soon as he realized the hostility displayed by his visitors, he recalled the clerks back. Reginald asked in the name of the king that the archbishop should see the young king to give him satisfaction because he had transgressed. Thomas asserted himself by explaining that he would like to visit his young king but had been prevented by the king's guardians. The barons charged him of breaking the peace after his return, excommunicating the bishops and royal servants, and attempting to uncrown the young king.

A heated dispute developed between the archbishop and Reginald de Broc. Thomas pointed out that the sentences had been issued by the pope to punish the wrongs done to the Canterbury church. He did not attempt to rescind the coronation of the young king. He had offered lenient conditions which the bishops had the opportunity to accept according to the permission granted by the king. The barons complained that they had to put up with the archbishop long enough. Thomas recounted the sufferings he had endured while in exile. The dispute developed into shouting and drew the archiepiscopal household to crowd into the chambers. Both parties resorted to treats until Reginald declared that Thomas was no longer under the king's protection. Reginald ordered the assembled people to leave (perhaps he attempted to arrest the archbishop) but as no one moved, he arrested to two archiepiscopal knights and left the shocked and bewildered party.

The clerks expressed their regret that Herbert of Bosham was absent because he would have been able to calm the archbishop while their efforts had failed.

The four barons placed their men on the different points of the palace to hinder any escape and managed to open the palace, and control the entrances. The ensuing noise frightened the servants except for the archbishop who remained calm. He decided so as to celebrate Vespers, one for the monks and the second Vesper for the clerks and the townsfolk. The little group with the cross bearer Henry of Auxerre managed to by-pass the guarded doors by going through the cellars, and entered the cathedral. The monks tried to close the door but the archbishop gave order to open it because, as he emphasized, this was a church and not a castle.

Thomas approached the staircase when Reginald de Broc entered. His group had searched the palace for the archbishop and not finding him, entered the church. The barons wore mail, carrying their unsheathed swords, and axes, to break the doors open. The shouts 'traitor' and 'traitor of kingdom and king' sounded through the cathedral. Thomas descended the steps and stood in the centre near a column. He called, "'Here I am, a servant of God but not a traitor'. The clerks fled except for Robert, canon of Merton and the visitor Edward Grim. The archbishop had the opportunity to escape into the crypt which had provided plenty of hiding places but he deliberately refused to do so. The following events have never been completely established partly because at that time of day the cathedral became dark and because the eye witnesses had fled.

According to the recount of Edward Grim who stayed at the side of the archbishop, the barons caught up with Thomas and demanded to invalidate the sentences on the bishops which he refused as their response was not satisfactory. The barons threatened him with death to which the archbishop replied that he was willing to die but ask them not to harm his men be it clerks or laymen. They tried to arrest him and shouted that he should flee. Thomas refused, and Reginald fitzUrse threatened him with the sword and removed his cap. One of the barons, probably Reginald, grabbed the archbishop by his robe and the barons pulled and pushed him while Edward Grim held on to him. Thomas was furious for being attacked and shoved around. He was God's anointed, and it was blasphemous to treat him like a criminal. He was a tall and strong man, and with Edward holding on to him, Thomas shook Reginald with such force that he nearly fell down. Edward Grim suggested later that the barons tried to remove the archbishop out of the church either to arrest him or kill him away from the sacred environment of the church. Thomas' resistance and the presence of the shaken townspeople who witnessed the horrific scene made the barons determined to move him outside and away from the building. Hugh de Morville tried to keep the shocked people at a distance.

When the archbishop realized that his death was imminent, he bowed his head, and joining the hands in prayer, committed himself to God, the Blessed Mary, and the patron saints of the Church of Canterbury.

Edward Grim believed that Reginald had administered the first blow which cut Thomas head and nearly severed Edward's arm who tried to protect him. Thomas fell to his knees and hands. One of the barons, probably Richard de Bret, gave the dying archbishop the coup de grace. The only one who had tried to protect the archbishop and stayed at his side at the hour of his death was the visiting stranger, Edward Grim.

The barons returned to the archiepiscopal palace to pillage and search for the papal letters and privileges, documents and books to give to the king. Everything of value, including horses, was taken away, and the servants beaten before they retreated to Saltwood castle. The horrified city was declared to by under martial law. .

In the meantime, the frightened monks cleared and closed the doors of the church. The monks placed the body of the slain archbishop on a bier, and found Richard de Bret's broken sword, an iron hammer, and an axe. Thomas' face was almost without a trace of blood except for a fine line running across his face to the left cheek. The monks bandaged his head and put a cap on what may have been his cap that was removed by Reginald fitzUrse, and the body was placed before the High altar.

The monks kept their night vigil over the archbishop's body when Robert de Broc reappeared, accompanied by soldiers. He justified the killing and declared that Thomas had been a traitor. Robert threatened the monks that, unless they bury the body immediately in an undetermined place, he would snatch the corpse and drag it on a horse's tail through the city, and subject the remains to more indignities.

Richard of Dover, an associate and friend of the archbishop, arrived and took care of the situation. It was decided to bury the archbishop immediately in the Trinity chapel of the cathedral. When his soiled and blood-stained garments were removed, some blood dripped on the floor and was collected by the monks. The monks and clerks, who were present, discovered that the archbishop had worn monastic clothes beneath his outer attire. It created a stir and a wave of sympathy as it proved that he had secretly been one of them. The archbishop had not been much loved by the monks but this revelation changed their opinion of him. The final preparations were done in haste as there was no time for the customary washing of the body. The monks reflected later that he was washed in his blood. The body was clothed with his archiepiscopal vestments, mitre and pastoral staff, and placed in a marble sarcophagus. Funeral Mass or public services were not held because of the murder committed within the sacred walls of the cathedral had polluted the church.

The sheep had lost their good shepherd who died while fighting for them and for the freedom of their church.

The news of the murder created a great shockwave. The young king expressed his deep and genuine sorrow, and also relief that none of his men had been involved. The report arrived at the papal court a month later and Pope Alexander went for a week into deep mourning.

The French Church, represented by William of Sens, sent a Carthusian monk to King Henry to investigate the case. According to William, Henry admitted that his callous words had provided the basis of Thomas death. He sent a letter to the pope to protest the late archbishop's sentences against his bishops. He complained about Thomas of having broken the peace, excommunicated royal servants and questioning the validity of the coronation. In his reply, Pope Alexander excommunicated the murderers and all of those who had participated in the plot. An interdict, issued by the archbishop of Sens on Henry's Continental lands, was pronounced, and also excommunication and suspension forced by Thomas on the English bishops, was confirmed. The pope ruled that King Henry was forbidden to enter a church.

The murderers went into hiding at the royal castle of Knaresborough in Yorkshire. After William de Tracy had received counselling by his diocesan bishop who in turn consulted the pope concerning the proper punishment for the murderers. The four were advised to confer with the pope in person, and accept his judgement. One of the penances imposed on them was to crusade in the Holy Land for the time of fourteen years. William of Tracy reached Cosenza in Calabria where he fell ill and supposedly died. It was widely believed that all four of the archbishop's murderers died soon on their way to the Holy Land

In summer of 1171, the archbishop of York and most of the bishops were under ecclesiastical censure. London, Salisbury and York were accused of spurning the prohibition of the coronation, issued by the pope, and of participation of Thomas' murder. After Easter 1171, the pope absolved the two bishops, York and Salisbury, from excommunication but not from postponement from office. Robert Foliot, bishop of London and enemy of the archbishop, was released later in the year. Pope Alexander sent his legates to clear up the penalties caused by the archbishop's exile and death.

King Henry declared that his remarks caused the death of Thomas though he never wished for or had ordered the killing. The legate informed him of the various conditions he had to meet in order to make amends to the church. He was obliged to pay for the duration of one year the expenses for two hundred Templar Knights defending Jerusalem. Henry also had the option of fighting the Saracens (Moslems) in Spain. He had to abolish all customs introduced during his reign that may be detrimental to the churches, and restore the possessions that had belonged to the Canterbury church. The king was urged to restore peace and grace including their possessions to the clerks and laity. Henry agreed to the circumstances, and the young king promised under oath to carry out the conditions except those who applied to his royal father alone.

The legates went with King Henry to Canterbury. He knelt down at the door and the legates entered the church with him. It was remarked that Henry neither removed any part of his garments nor was he scourged before he received his absolution.

The obligations Henry had to accept as to make amends to the archbishop's victims and co-exiles where most likely Herbert of Bosham's influence expressed in his letters to the pope

During the Easter week 1171, the Canterbury cathedral was reopened. Robert de Broc's brother, William, was cured at the archbishop's tomb. John of Salisbury proclaimed Thomas Becket to be a martyr, and requested, with papal authority, the slain archbishop should be remembered and honoured as such. There were signs of healings, and pilgrims started to come in great numbers to Canterbury and to pray at the tomb. The monks, some of them fearful, disapproved of the developing cult, and tried to keep the doors of the cathedral closed. The reason for their resistance was the spilled and collected blood of the martyr that was subject to deterioration and developed smell and evil taste. The monks had another reason for being reluctant to see the pilgrims drinking the martyr's blood which was a theological problem. During the Holy Eucharist, the blood of Christ was being offered and drank by the worshipper. Thomas Becket, the slain archbishop, had not been officially declared a martyr or saint, and to accept his blood seemed wrong.

One of the pilgrims, a woman, applied a blood-soaked shred of the archbishop's garment to her eyes, and recovered her eyesight. There were many reports of healings coming from distant places like Sussex, Essex, Kent, Gloucestershire and Berkshire, and the church was reopened to allow pilgrims to pray at the tomb of St. Thomas

The de Broc's planned to snatch the body, but the monks were warned in time and transferred it from the sarcophagus into a wooden coffin which they hid. After the danger was over, the monks surrounded and reinforced the sarcophagus with substantial stonewalls in which two windows were inserted to see and kiss the tomb.

In May, 1171, the cathedral was filled with sick people, and about ten healings per day were reported. The water mixed with blood called St. Thomas or Canterbury water was sold in a phial hanging from the neck of the pilgrim.

Pope Alexander III issued the bull of canonization. Most likely, the driving forces came not from King Henry but from the devoted clerks of the archbishop, Herbert of Bosham and John of Salisbury. Canonization emphasize on three vital elements: the martyrdom (poena), the reasons the martyr had died for (causa) and the confirmed miracles (signa). The pope referred to the third element, and investigated the validity of the reported miracles, and, receiving agreeable confirmations, canonized the Archbishop Thomas Becket on February 21, 1171 (Ash Wednsday).

In 1172, the young king made his pilgrimage to the martyr's tomb. The following year, King Henry undertook his pilgrimage to his former slain friend. The rebellion, instigated by his wife Eleanor of Aquitaine and older sons including the kings of Scotland and France labelled him as a king of ill reputation. The pope and the English and Norman churches rallied behind him.

It was July 1173, when King Henry arrived at Canterbury. As the cathedral came into sight, Henry removed his boots and continued barefoot until he reached the steps of the cathedral. He prostrated himself at the tomb and in the presence of his men, bishops and monks, confessed his sins and deeply mourned of being the cause of Thomas death. Henry requested to be punished and ask the brethren to keep him in their prayers. He removed his outer garments, and the prelates including Gilbert Foliot, each of them delivered five strokes of the rod, followed by the eighty monks who each administered three strokes. After the scourge, Henry made an offering of four marks in pure gold. He allocated land to the convent, and promised to reinstate the rights the archbishop had demanded. Henry promised to build a monastery in honour of St. Thomas. He spent the rest of the day and the following night lying on the floor next to the tomb without taking food or water. The pilgrims were allowed to enter the church. The next morning, after attending Mass and praying at the altars, the king drank some of the 'Canterbury water' and received a phial to wear around his neck before riding back to London. He fell ill but continued his acts of piety. In autumn, his situation improved, his enemies had submitted or had been defeated.

Thomas Becket, son of a merchant who rose to the high ranks of Royal Chancellor and Archbishop of Canterbury, achieved in death was he had stood and fought for in life. By resisting King Henry's demands of obedience to the arcane laws, Thomas brought them to the attention and scrutiny of the pope and the canon lawyers who studied and abolished some or reformed them. Thomas Becket, archbishop of Canterbury, with the help of the pope and the French King Louis VII, sped up the process and helped to defend the rights of the church and men against tyrannical rulers.

Thomas Becket, Archbishop of Canterbury, had agreed and fully accepted the responsibilities of the spiritual welfare for his flock. King Henry, crowned king of England, was accountable for the welfare of the subjects of his kingdom. The same thoughts are expressed in the Gospel of Matthew: 22:17-21 "The Pharisees were trying to set a snare for Jesus, and approached him with the question 'Is it lawful to give tribute unto Caesar, or not?' Jesus answered, "Render under Caesar the things which are Caesar's, and unto God the things that are God's."

Chapter 19

The Crusades

Palestine, the land where Jesus had lived, taught and died, was for the Medieval Christians the Holy Land. The Muslims took Palestine during the seventh century but allowed Christian pilgrims to visit the holy sites. The 'Holy Lance' which had pierced the side of Jesus, had been found in Jerusalem and seen by Christian pilgrims around the fifth and sixth century (by the time of the Crusades the spear was kept in Constantinople.)

In the mid-eleventh century, a new threat advanced from the steppes between the Aral and Caspian Seas. The Seljuq Turks, newly converted to Islam, were Sunni Muslims. On their westward conquest, they subjugated Baghdad in 1055, and fought the Byzantines in 1071. The Seljuqs gained control over large areas of Asia Minor. Pilgrimage routes to Jerusalem were threatened, and became the reason of the Crusades.

The destruction of the Holy Sepulchre in Jerusalem by the Fatimid caliphs of North Africa and the mistreatment of Christian pilgrims prompted Pope Urban II at the Council of Clermont (1096) to call for a Holy War to regain Palestine and the city of Jerusalem. It launched the first of the Crusades, and more than 50 000 Europeans, knights and common people gathered to free the Holy Land from the Turks. Jerusalem was sacred to the Christians because Jesus died there. The Jews held it sacred because Abraham was buried there, and it was sacred to the Muslims because Muhammad ascended from the spot of today's 'Mosque of the Rock' to Heaven.

During the summer of 1096, the princes and nobles split into five armies and travelled by different routes to reach Constantinople. The first army was led by Hugh of Vermandois, a younger brother of King Philip I of France. Robert of Flanders, Godfrey of Bouillon, his brothers Baldwin and Eustace III, led the Belgium and northern France armies. The Normans from southern Italy were lead by Bohemont of Taranto and made up the third army. Raymond, Count of Toulouse, who was the first of the knights to respond to the pope's call, guided the forth army and was joined by Duke Robert of Normandy and the fifth army to join up with the combined force of the People's Crusade at Constantinople.

In 1098, the Crusaders elected Bohemond of Taranto as commander-in-chief. He proved himself to be an excellent leader, and after fierce fighting's between the crusaders and Sultan Kerbogha' army, Bohemond captured Byzantine Antioch. Raymond of Toulouse insisted that the city to be returned to the Byzantine Emperor Alexius but Bohemont claimed the city and declared himself Prince of Antioch.

In July of 1099, Jerusalem was captured by Raymond of Toulouse, Tancred de Hauteville, Robert of Normandy and Godfrey of Bouillon. The French knight Robert of Flanders distinguished himself during the capture of Jerusalem. The three-day customary looting turned into slaughter of Muslims who took shelter in the Al Aqsa Mosque. The synagogue, filled with Jewish men, women and children, was burned to the ground. Tancred was unable to protect the population.

On July 22, Godfrey de Bouillon, who reclined to accept the title of king and preferred to call himself as 'the Defender of the Holy Sepulchre', was elected by the crusaders to rule Jerusalem. Arnolf of Choques, who was the chaplain of Robert of Normandy's army, was elected Latin Patriarch of Jerusalem. The Egyptian (Fatimid) army, lead by Vizier al-Afdal Shahanshah, was on the march toward Ascalon, an important port east of Jerusalem. The Fatimids fled at the sight of the approaching crusaders and the battle was won.

In 1107, King Sigurd I of Norway joined the crusaders. Baldwin I of Edessa, the brother of Godfrey of Bouillon, was crowned King of Jerusalem in 1100, and he and King Sigurd I of Norway captured Sidon. In 1110, Tancred of Hauteville became Prince of Galilee and regent in Antioch. He captured the fortress Krak des Chevaliers and King Raymond gave the fortress to the Knight Hospitallers. Baldwin I died in 1118, and was succeeded by his cousin Baldwin II of Le Burg. The Crusaders expanded the territory with the captures of Caesarea, Acre, Tripoli and Beirut.

The settlers who remained created a Christian outpost called Outremer (overseas). It encompassed the crusader-states: the county of Tripoly and Edessa, the Principality of Antioch and the Kingdom of Jerusalem.

King Baldwin II died in 1131 and was succeeded by his daughter Melisande and her husband Fulk of Anjou.

The First Crusade provoked anti-Jewish riots and violence in Germany, stirred up by an anti- Jewish monk named Rudolf. Abbot Bernard managed to end the outburst of violence and ordered Rudolf to return to his monastery.

Ilgahzi, who was a gifted Muslim general, recaptured the cities of Antioch and Aleppo in 1119, followed by the recapture of the crusader state and capital of Edessa in 1144 by the Turkish General Imad Ed-Din Zengi.

In 1145, Pope Eugenius III called the Christians to arms, supported by Bernard of Clairvaux (1091-1153) who was the spiritual leader of the Cistercians. When he was informed of the fall of Edessa, he left his monastery to preach the Second Crusade.

Bernard enforced strictest religious discipline. He was renounced for his holiness and his preaching, and exercised a great influence in matters of the church and of secular connections.

The Second Crusade (1147) was fought by Nur-ed-Din, son of a distinguished Sunni Muslim general. The French King Louis VII and his wife, Eleanor of Aquitaine (after divorcing King Louis VII, Eleanor married King Henry II of England in 1154) and the Holy Roman Emperor Conrad III arrived in Constantinople. In 1153, King Baldwin III became King of Jerusalem and in 1162 was succeeded by Amalric I.

Both armies looted Byzantine cities while on their way to the Holy Land. The Byzantine Emperor Manuel I Comnenus retaliated. He secretly stalled the crusaders progress in Anatolia (Turkey) and commanded the Turks to beat them. King Louis and Emperor Conrad reached Jerusalem with the remnants of their armies, and in 1148, participated on the attack on Damascus. Nur ed-Din attacked the Crusaders at Antioch and in1150-1154, captured Damascus. Emperor Conrad III was defeated by the Turks at Dorylaeum in Anatolia. In 1157, Nur ed-Din besieged the Knights Hospitallers at the Castle of Banias, and captured Reynald de Chatillon, then Prince of Antioch. The Kurdish general Salah ed-Din (Saladin) a military genius, marched against the Kingdom of Jerusalem. In 1174, King Baldwin IV, son of King Almaric I, installed himself with knights at Ascalon but General Saladin encircled the city. Baldwin and his knights managed to break through the circle and inflicted a shattering defeat on the Muslims at Montgisard in 1177.

In 1185, Baldwin IV died and his nephew Baldwin V and Raymond of Tripoly acted as regents. A year later, Baldwin V died and was succeeded by his mother Sybilla who ruled as queen with King Guy de Lusignan as her consort. The city of Acre surrendered to Saladin, and he took Ascalon.

July 4, 1187, marked the battle of the Horns of Hattin, the beginning of defeat for the crusaders. King Guy ignored the advice from Raymond of Tripoly not to risk a battle in the desert without shelter or water but the king ignored the warning and advanced toward Tiberius. The army of 1200 knights and 20 000 infantry men marched for hours in the blazing sun without water or food and harassed by Saladins advancing army. At evening, the army advanced towards the two hills known as the Horns of Hattin. In the morning, they found themselves surrounded by Saladins army who set fire to the dry grass and the smog and stung in the eyes made the exhausted crusaders coughing and wretched. The Templars and Hospitallers fought bravely and desperately while the Bishop of Acre was robbed of his Holy relic, a piece of the original and true cross which he carried into the battle. The crusaders were defeated, and the captured crusaders executed by their captives.

Saladin recaptured the cities of Acre and Ascalon, and continued his march towards Jerusalem. On October 2, 1187, Saladin recaptured the city. He demanded unconditional surrender, forbade any looting, and opened the Church of the Holy Sepulchre for pilgrims.

The second Crusade was a great victory for the Muslims and a sad failure for the Crusaders. It culminated in the fall of Jerusalem, and to the Third Crusade.

The Third Crusade (1189-1192) was launched by Richard I (Coeur de Lion) son of Henry II of England who fought Saladin. The participation of King Richard I, King Philip of France, and the aged and beloved Holy Roman Emperor Frederick I (Barbarossa) made the Third Crusade the most glamorous of them. Frederick Barbarossa drowned while trying to cross a stream.

The two kings, Richard and Philip, conquered in 1191 the city of Acre. Richard ordered 2700 Muslim prisoners, soldiers, including women and children, to be beheaded because Saladin was slow to accept the agreed terms of surrender.

King Philip returned to France while Saladin and Richard fought for two years. Richard came within twelve miles of Jerusalem but was unable to recapture the city. In 1192, King Richard and Saladin signed a truce that permitted the travellers safe journey to Jerusalem, and granted the Crusaders some costal towns. Saladin died a year later.

On his way home, Richard was disrespectful and to travel through the lands of his enemy, Leopold of Austria, who captured him and held him prisoner until a handsome ransom was paid.

In 1198 the newly elected Pope Innocent III called for the Fourth Crusade. The envoys of Count Theobald, the elected leader and brother of Henry of Champagne, King of Jerusalem, approached Venice for negotiations to make travel arrangements per sea, but the crusaders were short of money. The envoys commissioned a fleet large enough to transport the army including horses, fodder and food. Venice demanded money and was agreed that half the plunder gained through looting by land or sea to be granted to Venice, including with the payment. Venice hoped to gain control over the eastern Mediterranean.

The huge crusade fleet arrived at Constantinople in 1203. Emperor Alexius III sent an envoy with the offer of providing supplies and money if the fleet would move on to Jerusalem. The offer was rejected.

The Crusader's diversion of Constantinople was to restore the deposed Emperor Isaac II to the imperial throne. The Crusaders besieged Constantinople, looted the city, captured the displaced Emperor Isaac II, and installed the usurper Alexius III as co-emperor. The following year, the Byzantines disposed of their unwanted rulers. The promise for help and money had vanished and the Venetians and Crusaders besieged the city a second time. Seven days later, on April 13, 1204 during the Easter week Constantinople was taken. The army was allowed to loot for three days and they committed murder, stealing and robbing. During that rampage the altar of Hagia

Sofia was damaged in order to remove the gold and precious stones. Byzantine art treasures were smashed or stolen. Pope Innocent was upset and appalled by the armies disrespect and greed.

On May 16, 1204, Count Baldwin of Flanders was crowned emperor of the Latin Empire of Constantinople, in the Church of Haghia Sophia. The Crusaders and Venetians divided the Byzantine Empire. Venice seized parts of Greece and the islands of the Aegean Sea.' Latin Byzantium' was recaptured in 1261 by the Byzantines, and Orthodox Christianity was re-established.

The only ones who profited from the Fourth Crusade were the Venetian merchants who gained control of the eastern Mediterranean.

The following crusades during the thirteenth century did not achieve much but were pathetic attempts to regain Jerusalem.

The Fifth Crusade, proclaimed by Pope Innocent III in 1212, called the ill-fated 'Children Campaign' where children joined the Crusaders. The alarmed monks tried in vain to persuade them to return, but the boys stayed firm in their decision to free the Holy Land. The children were from France and Germany and mostly under the age of 15. Many of them died of exhaustion or illness. A sizable number of French youth boarded ships but drowned when the ships capsized during a storm. The surviving children were sold into slavery while the German children boarded ships in Pisa but were never heard of again.

Holy Roman Emperor Frederick II, grandson of Frederick I, Barbarossa, was crowned King of Germany, and just nineteen years old when he responded to Pope Innocent's call in 1213 to take up arms and embark on the Fifth Crusade. In 1220, he was crowned Holy Roman Emperor by Pope Honorius III. Frederick II was ambitious, brilliant and very talented but meddled in the affairs of the church, and a ban of excommunication had been placed on him. It took Frederick eight years until the pope lifted the ban and he was able to embark to the Holy Land.

In 1218, John of Brienne, King of Jerusalem, and crusaders sailed to Egypt and beleaguered the town and port of Damietta with the hope to sail from there to take Cairo. The army was ill organized, bad weather and an epidemic hampered their efforts to conquer Damietta. Sultan al - Kamil tried to negotiate and offered Jerusalem and the Kingdom if the crusaders would lift the siege of Damietta, and leave Egypt. The proposal met the opposition of the Spanish cardinal Pelagius of Albano who argued that the Holy City could not be bargained for with a Muslim. The knights were unhappy at the suggestion because they would lose their castles of Krak and Montreal. St. Francis of Assissi arrived, and pleated for non-violence. Sultan al-Kamil granted him an audience and was so deeply impressed by his saintly visitor that he allowed him to preach to his subjects. In November 1219, the crusaders conquered Damietta, and sacked and looted the city.

In 1221, Sultan al-Kamil repeated his offer again, and was met with Pegalius refusal. He ordered the army to march towards Cairo. The sultan went with his army to meet the crusaders when the Nile began to rise and cut off their ships by the sultan's ships. Pelagius ordered retreat but Sultan al-Kamil ordered the flood controls to be destroyed. The crusaders were trapped in the thick mud and suffered heavy losses. Pelagius signed a humiliating peace treaty which included his promise to leave Egypt.

In 1225, Frederick II married Isabella (or Yolande) Queen of Jerusalem. She was the daughter of Maria Montferrat and King John of Brienne, former King of Jerusalem. Holy Roman Emperor Frederick II was now King of Jerusalem as well.

The Sixth Crusade brought triumph for the Crusaders when in March 1229, Frederick II re-entered Jerusalem. The city was to be under Latin control, and a treaty was signed by Sultan al-Kamil and the Crusaders. The knights were dissatisfied because they reasoned that the Kingdom of Jerusalem should have been conquered with the sword and not through diplomacy. Frederick II left Jerusalem to return to Italy. The position of Outremer was strengthened.

In 1242, the French King Louis IX declared his intentions of leading the seventh Crusade in 1245. It took four years of preparation and recruitment of the French knights to embark from Marseilles. There were disputes and disagreements between the Knights Templar and the Knight Hospitallers but the differences were calmed down when in 1244 the Khwarismian Turks recaptured Jerusalem. The city was looted, churches were burned down and only about 300 Christians survived to tell the story of their horror.

In 1242, the French King Louis IX declared his intentions of leading the Seventh Crusade in 1245. It took four years of preparations and recruitment of the French knights to embark from Marseilles for the Seventh Crusade. In May 1248, the crusaders sailed to Cyprus were other participants from Italy, Scotland and England waited for them. The leaders decided that they should target Egypt, and in the battle of Damietta, defeat Sultan al-Salih Ayyub.

Damietta was recaptured in 1249, and the Sultan of Egypt al-Salih Ayyub offered to exchange the town for the possession of Jerusalem like his predecessor Sultan al-Kamil had done in 1219 and 1221. King Louis declined, and hoped that with God's help the French army would take possession of Egypt, Syria, and Jerusalem. He stayed in Damietta because the Nile had risen in the meantime, and military movements were impossible.

End of November, King Louis lead the French army southwards towards Cairo. The Ayyubid army camped at the fortress of al-Mansourah and the crusaders were unable to find a way of crossing the river al-Bahr al-Saghir. Count Robert of Artois, the brother of King Louis, guided a surprise assault on the Ayyubid camp. The enemies fled, and Count Robert and his crusaders, ignoring orders to wait, followed the fleeing Ayyubids into Damietta. The commanding officer Rukn al-Zahir Baybars, rallied the Egyptians, and they turned on the small group of crusaders who were disoriented, unable to escape in the narrow streets, and were mercilessly slaughtered.

The main force of the crusaders were still on the march when the Egyptians, lead by Baybars, left Damietta and engaged into a fierce battle. The crusaders managed to hold their position, and the Egyptians retreated into their fortress al-Mansourah. The king decided to stay for a siege but the Egyptians time and again ventured out and destroyed the barges bringing supplies for the crusaders. In spring 1250, King Louis retreated to Damietta. During their march, the army faced repeated attacks from the Egyptians, and the king fell seriously ill. The surrender determined that Damietta was returned to the Sultan Turan Shah. The shah decided that there were too many prisoners to be fed, and every day for a week 300 Christian soldiers were executed. King Louis was captured, chained, and marched into prison. A high ransom was demanded for his release.

The capture of the saintly King Louis IX of France, loved for his kindness, and the failure of the seventh Crusade provoked an outpour of sorrow and unhappiness. In 1251, a vast ransom was paid and King Louis was released. He remained for another three years ruling the Kingdom of Jerusalem and held court in Acre. In 1254, he returned to France because his mother Blanche of Castile (daughter of King Henry II of England and Eleanor of Aquitaine) who had been his regent during his absence had died.

During King Louis' absence from the Holy Land, the Mongols under their leader Hulagu, who was the grandson of Genghis Khan, invaded Persia and Armenia and in 1260, captured Damascus. Baybars, Turan Shah's general. rose up against him and founded a sultanate of Mamluks. Hulagu tried to conquer Egypt but Baybars defeated him in the battle of Ain Jalut in Galilee.

In 1265, Baybars launched an invasion on Caesarea and Outremer, and seized the garrison of the Knights Hospitaller who surrendered when given the promise that their lived would be spared. The promise was not honoured, and the Knights Hospitaller slaughtered. In 1268, Baybars utterly destroyed Jaffa and Antioch. The population was sold into slavery, or murdered.

Baybar's destruction of Outremer motivated King Louis IX in 1267 to take the cross again and declared the Eight Crusade, to free Tunis, and from there to Baybars headquarters in Egypt.

According to the suggestion of Louis' brother, Charles of Anjou, the crusaders landed in northern Africa and beleaguered Tunis but a large part of the army became sick from drinking muddy water, King Louis fell very ill with dysentery and died August 25, 1270, and his 25-year-old son Philip, Count of Orleans, was proclaimed

King Philip III of France. Charles of Anjou accepted the responsibility of leadership. The crusaders, unable to conquer Tunis, lifted the siege and negotiated a settlement which granted the Christian merchants free trade, including residence to monks and priests.

Prince Edward of England, later King Edward I, and his English army arrived in 1271 at the Holy Land to sustain the beleaguered surviving parts of Outremer, especially Tripoli and Acre. His aim to support the Eighth Crusade came too late. Sultan Baybars had recaptured the formidable fortress of Krak des Chevaliers and was besieging Tripoli but when he learned about the arrival of Prince Edward and his army he lifted the siege. He and King Hugh of Jerusalem accepted a ten-year truce with Tripoli.

Prince Edward's arrival and his actions can be considered as the Ninth Crusade.

In June, 1271, Sultan Baybars captured Monfort Castle near Acre held by the Teutonic Knights. Prince Edward tried to seek an alliance with the Mongol ruler of Iran, Iraq and parts of Anatolia, Il Khan Abagha against Sultan Baybars. Outremer's position strengthened when the Moguls attacked Mamluk Syria. In autumn, Prince Edmund of England arrived with reinforcements, and Edward led another mission to conquer the castle of Qaqun which was under Muslim control. Edward established a new order, the Order of St. Edward of Acre.

In May 1272, King Hugh III of Jerusalem and Cyprus accepted a truce with Sultan Baybars. It was agreed that the Kingdom of Jerusalem's borders would be maintained for ten years. A month later, the sultan's hired assassin tried to stab Prince Edward with a poisoned dagger while he slept. Edward woke up and drew the man out. He planned to attack Jerusalem but when he received the news that his father, King Henry III had died, he was forced to abandon his plan. Edward and Eleanor of Castile his wife, embarked for England, and in 1274, he was crowned as King Edward I of England in Westminster Abbey.

Sultan Baybars died in 1277. The ten-year truces were not honoured by the sultans Qalawun and Khalil and Tripoly was conquered in 1289 and Acre in 1291.

Pope Gregory X preached another crusade in 1274, and tried to enter into negotiations with the Mongols but died in 1276. Charles I of Anjou, King of Sicily (brother of King Louis IX) planned a campaign to retake Constantinople. Charles was faced with the uprising Sicilian Vespers, the revolt of the 1282 eponymous war of the Sicilian population against French officials. It happened on Easter Monday, March 30, 1282, when a Frenchman harassed a married Sicilian woman at the time the bells at the Church of the Holy Spirit in Palermo tolled for the Vespers. The enraged husband killed the offending French official and some of his French comrades. King Charles was forced to abandon his intended campaign. The occasion stirred up a massacre because the French officials were mistreating the Sicilian population who hated them.

In 1266, King Charles I of Anjou, with papal complicity had taken control of the entire Kingdom of Sicily, which included the suburbs of Rome and the entire land of Italy. The Sicilians hated the cruel rule of Charles and his associates and fought for their freedom. He was driven out in 1282 and the Sicilians allied themselves with King Peter III of Aragon. The ensuing war which lasted almost twenty years between the houses of Anjou and Aragon, are called the Wars of the Sicilian Vespers (1283-1302). In 1302, the Treaty of Caltabellotta determined the mainland of the kingdom to be ruled by Anjou as the Kingdom of Naples, and the island of Sicily to be ruled by the House of Aragon.

Charles of Anjou died in 1285 to be succeeded by King Henry III of Cyprus who was crowned King of Jerusalem at Acre in 1286. Sultan Qalawun besieged Tripolis in 1289 and moved on to Acre which fell in 1291 after a long siege and heavy fighting. The crusader towns of Beirut, Haifa, Tyre and Tortosa were abandoned and the refugees left for Cyprus. Many were captured and sold into slavery and Outremer was no more.

The fall of Acre was the end of the crusades but in the thirteenth century, plans were drawn up for re-establishing the Kingdom of Jerusalem.

The Late Middle Age (1300-1500)

The Knight Hospitallers traders from Cyprus and Venice attempted to form a maritime league to fight the authority of the Turkish emirates who had settled along the coast of Anatolia. The League was established in 1334 and overpowered a Turkish fleet at Adramyttium.

The second League, established in 1344, captured the port of Smyrna. Humbert II of Vienne attempted to gather an army in northern Italy to regain more territory but he failed due to rivalry between the cities of Genoa and Venice.

A third League formed in 1359, supported by Peter I of Cyprus in his efforts to repel the Turkish Emirates which were attacking his coastal territories. Peter captured the port of Adalia in today's south-western Turkey and other ports located along the coast. He set off in 1362 to Europe in the attempt of papal and European knight's support. His visit of the European countries resulted in 1365 in the embarkation of a fleet at Venice, called the 'King Peter's Crusade'. The fleet sailed to Rhodes to be united with the Knights Hospitaller. Peter's plan was to attack Mamluck Egypt and seizing Alexandria and to negotiate a change possession of Alexandria for the Holy City of Jerusalem.

In 1366, Amadeus of Savoy, an Italian nobleman, sailed with a small fleet to restore Byzantium. Amadeus allied with Francesco I of the Aegaen Islands and recaptured Gallipoli. They discovered that John V Paleologus had been taken prisoner by the

Bulgarians and brought to Sozopolis on the Black Sea. Amadeus, who was a cousin of John, demanded his release and John was finally liberated.

King Peter and the army attacked Alexandria, and after heavy fighting, conquered the city. Violence and looting broke out and during the rampage the famous library went ablaze. Afterwards, the army abandoned Alexandria and the exasperate King Peter headed homeward, but returned to Cypress, and continued to raid Turkish settlements like Tripoli. In 1367, he undertook another trip to Europe to raise one more crusade army but failed in his attempt. On 1369, he was assassinated by one of his knights.

During the Great Schism (1378-1417) the time of two popes (Clemet VII in Avignon and UrbanVI in Rome) one or the other pope was supported by either Scotland and France (the Avignon pope) or England and Italy (the pope in Rome). The crusaders finally came to the decision to wage another crusade against Tunisia in 1390. The Genoese merchants, whose ships were raided by Tunesian pirates, were supported by Pope Boniface IX and backed by King Charles VI of France. The chosen leader of the crusade was Count Louis of Bourbon. They sailed from Marseilles to the North African coast and began the siege of Mahdia. After nine weeks of fighting, the Genoas negotiated with Ahmad, emir of Tunis, and achieved the desired peace contract including the generous taxes they had hoped for.

The European Christian monarchs became increasingly alarmed at the threat posed by the expanding Ottoman Empire. The Ottoman Sultan Bayezid I, who conquered Saloniki, blockaded Constantinople and invaded Hungary. The Christian reaction was a Venetian-Hungarian crusade and supported by the two popes but it ended in defeat at Nicopolis but was a victory for Bayezit. The Ottoman Empire under the leadership of Osman I managed through political influence and marriage of his son Orhan into the Byzantine empirical family of John V Paleologus to gain lands in Thrace and Macedonia. Orhan's son, Murad I, expanded the conquests into Serbia and Bulgaria.

Murad's son, Bayezid I, ascended power following the death of his father who died in battle against Bosnian, Serbian and Bulgarian princes in 1389. Two years later he began a siege of Constantinople as well as extending his power into Europe and capturing large areas of the Balkans.

Both popes Boniface IX in Rome, and the Avignon Pope Clement VII proclaimed a crusade. It was supported by the Royal houses of Europe, King Richard II of England, King Charles VI of France and the Hungarian King Sigismund. They planned to free the Balkans of the Turks, lessen the siege of Constantinople and retake Jerusalem. A sizeable army gathered from supporters of Wallachia, Transylvania, Venice, Genoa, and the Hospitaller Knights from Rhodes.

In September, 1396, the army moved south and besieged Nicopolis. Bayezid I, whose nickname was 'Thunderbolt' abandoned the siege of Constantinople and approached the crusaders at Nicopolis. The Wallacian prince Mircea was familiar with the Ottoman strategy and proposed to engage an assault previous to the main attack of the army, but the crusade leaders disapproved of and preferred a complete assault. It proved to be a total disaster and the crusaders were overwhelmed by Bayezid's army. He built the Ula Mosque in Bursa in honour of his victory at the crusade of Nicopolis.

Bayezit met his match when he confronted Tamerlane (or Timur) the Turkish-Mongolian warlord who overpowered Bayezid in 1402 at the Battle of Ankara. Tamerlane captured Bayezid who died a year later in captivity.

Constantinople was repeatedly threatened by the Ottomans and the Western kingdoms sent assistance to the city. In 1430, Murad II, grandson of Bayezid, had recaptured Salonika and Serbia, and in 1444, the crusade at Varna ended in defeat.

In 1443, Pope Eugenius IV rallied the Christians to fight against the Ottomans. The smaller crusade army, led by King Ladislas of Poland and Janos Hunyadi (the White Knight who was regent of Hungary in 1446-53) were outnumbered and hoped for reinforcement from Constantinople. The army was trapped between the Black Sea, Lake Varna and the surrounding hills. King Ladislas chased Murad on the battlefield but was captured and beheaded by the Janissaries, the elite corps of the sultan. King Janos raised another Christian army consisting manly of Hungarians, and fought Murad II at Kosovo. Once again, Janos was greatly outnumbered though his soldiers fought bravely, but the sultan's Janissary unit won over the Hungarian knights and forced them to flee. Five years later, in spring of 1453, Murat II's son Sultan Mehmet II captured Constantinople and ended the Byzantine Empire.

After the conquest of Constantinople, Sultan Mehmet II sought new conquests and began the siege of Belgrad in July 1456. King Hunyadi had the foresight to strengthen the fortress of Belgrad, and raised a fleet of warships and relief force. He found help and assistance from the Italian-born Franciscan brother Giovanni de Capistrano, who preached against heretics and supported the crusade against the Ottoman Empire

The Hungarian army managed to break through the Ottoman naval blockade and held Belgrad. Mehmet launched an artillery bombardment that lasted a week, and after that ordered the attack. There was heavy fighting on both sides but the Christian army succeeded and drove the Turks back. Sultan Mehmed was wounded and carried away. He recovered and fell into deep despair when he learned of the humiliating defeat.

Giovanni de Capistrano and King Janos Hunyadi believed that they may be able to retake Constantinople, and Jerusalem, but both of them became victims of the bubonic plague and died shortly afterwards.

In 1459, when the Turks advanced into the Balkan, Pope Pius II called for a crusade and insisted that the Turks must be stopped.

Prince Vlad III the 'Impaler' encountered Mehmet in 1462 when he invaded Wallachia. The sultan's army occupied the capital but Vlad kept up a fierce guerrilla war against the invading Turks. Prince Vlad entered the enemy camp one night and almost killed the sleeping Sultan Mehmet who invested Vlad's brother Radu with the authority of rule. (Prince Vlad III has been used as the historical Dracula by Bram Stoker)

In 1464, Pope Pius II, inspired by the victory of Belgrade, called again for a crusade but the European rulers showed little eagerness to continue the crusades. Pope Pius died in 1164, and the crusades were finally abandoned.

The Knights Templar

After the First Crusade, the military brotherhood of the Knights Templar was established. In 1119, Hugues de Payens, a knight from the Champagne and Geoffroy de Saint-Omer were the first to establish the Order of the Templar Knights, called the Poor Knights of Christ, later assumed the name of the Temple of Solomon. King Baldwin I of Jerusalem granted part of his palace, known as the 'Temple of Solomon', to them. The order received its blessings of the Church at the Council of Troyes in 1129.

The knights took the monastic vows of chastity, poverty and obedience besides of strictest military discipline in the presence of Garimond, the Patriarch of Jerusalem to secure the Christian Realm.. The brilliant monk Bernard of Clairvaux defined the Knights Templar Rules.

The Knight had to be of noble birth, and at the age of fourteen, enter the service of a court as page. The next advance was that of Squire, and at twenty-one, dubbed as knight.

The Templar hierarchy divided into different groups. The Grand Master's authority was supreme, and his superior was no other but the pope. He served as such until to the end of his life. The Seneschal, next in rank to the Grand Master, participated in the administrative duties. The Marshall of the Order was the true soldier and responsible of the details of war. He served as Commander-in Chief, and reported directly to the Grand Master. The Marshall was served by two squires and allowed to own four horses. The knights were separated by rank and distinguished by clothing. In 1149, Pope Eugenius III granted the Knights to wear a red cross, sewn above the heart, on their white surplice. The forth rank were the common soldiers.

After approximately fifty years, the Order was established in most of the European countries. The Seneschal and the Grand Master governed over the provinces of Portugal, Scotland, England, Aragon, Hungary, France, Poitiers and Apulia.

At the beginnings of the crusades, the Knights Templar duty was to aid and protect travellers against marauding thieves and invading armies but the Knights Templar also engaged in battles. Their fearlessness and valour was highly praised.

The Templar fought to their death and no retreat or from the battlefield or being captured, was allowed.

The Knights Templar gained financial contributions from the aristocracy. Manors, lands and castles were donated by nobilities to support the cause and were obliged to donate their property and assets to the Order. The Order, who started from humble beginnings, became very wealthy and prominent. There were rumours that the Knights Templar found buried treasures in the ruins of Solomon's Temple, perhaps even the 'Holy Grail', the chalice from which Jesus drank during the 'Last Supper' with the disciples.

Over the next centuries, the Knights Templar developed techniques to protect the money of pilgrims and travellers from being seized by robbers. They were the first international bankers of their time, and laid the foundation of modern banking. The traveller received a letter of credit similar to today's banking practice. The affluence and leadership of the Knights Templar became their demise because it aroused the envy of the Church and the French king.

The first Knights Templar lived in poverty, and lived on alms. They were wholly committed to the duties they had accepted for themselves including combat if necessary. That the Knights Templar faced a shortage of horses is indicated by the oldest seal of the Order who depicts two knights sharing a horse and galloping towards their enemies.

Jacques de Molay, the last Knights Templar Grand Master

Jacques de Molay, a Burgundian nobleman, was born in Vitrey sur Mance (Haute Saone) in 1244. He joined the Order at the age of twenty-one, and rose quickly through the different ranks in which he distinguished himself. He lived for many years in Great Britain where he assumed the position of Visitor General and years later accepted the position as Grand Preceptor of England.

After the death of the Grand Master, Theobald Gaudin in 1292, Jacques de Moley was inaugurated as the 23rd Grand Master of the Order of the Knights Templar. He left Great Britain shortly afterwards to take up residence at the island of Cyprus, which, after the fall of Acre in 1291, had become the base of the Knights Templar. From there, he planned another attempt to recapture the lost regions of the Holy Land. In 1299, Jacques de Moley fought the Mamluks in Armenia.

In 1306, Pope Clement V summoned Jacques de Moley to France, apparently to discuss another crusade. The French King Philip IV envied the wealth of the Knights Templar, and was worried of their power and influence. He arrested the Jews, seized their assets and expelled them from France Philip also was hugely indebted to the Knight Templar who had been acting as bankers. He planned to break up the organization as to free himself of his crushing debts. On Friday, October 13, 1307, hundreds of Knights Templar in France, including the Grand Master Jacques de Moley were simultaneously arrested at the order of the king and charged of heresy, sodomy and blasphemy, and the veneration of a mysterious scull. The Knights Templar were allegedly answerable only to the Pope but Clement V was the king's pawn. The Templar property was confiscated and transferred to the Knights Hospitallers in Rhodes, and the Order of the Knights Templar was dissolved by the pope.

The Holy Grail, the chalice from which Jesus drank during his last supper with his disciples, was the priceless item long searched for. Chretian de Troyes wrote the story 'Perseval' (le Conte de Graal) for his patron, Count Philip of Flanders, around 1180-1191. The early Grail Legends centred about Perseval, and are interwoven with the Arthurian legends. The German poet Wolfram von Eschenbach (ca. 1280) wrote of the legendary Parzifal and the keepers of the Holy Grail 'san greal' (the old French translation of 'Holy Grail') at his castle of Montsalvath.

There was speculation that the Grail had been discovered by the Knights Templar and be in their possession as well as other fabulous treasures, buried under the Temple Mount and kept in their ownership. It was guessed that some of the Knights managed to slip away and hide the fortune. Another assumption held by the church was that the Cathars, in secret communication with the Knights Templar,hid the riches in a safe place.

Chretian de Troyes wrote the story 'Perseval, le Conte de Graal' for his patron Count Philip of Flanders around 1180-1191.The early Grail Legends centre on Percival and are interwoven with the Arthurian legends. The German poet Wolfram von Eschenback (ca. 1280) wrote of the legendary Parzifal and the keepers of the Holy Grail 'san greal' (the old French translation of 'Holy Grail') at his castle of Montsalvath.

The Templar fleet, anchored at their port in La Rochelle in western France, vanished during the night. Rumours had it that the fleet sailed to Scotland to aid Robert de Bruce in his struggle against King Edward I of England, and harbouring the Templar treasures.

The Grand Master and his knights were questioned by the Dominican Inquisitor, and submitted to the most agonizing and unbearable torture. The torturers used every means such as the rack, lies and trickery, to obtain confessions. One of the constantly repeated questions centred about the secret ritual of the initiation into the Order. It was rumoured that the initiate was required of trampling and spitting on the cross and denying Jesus to demonstrate obedience to the Order. Other committing atrocities during the ritual were worshipping a pagan god or mysterious skull, and accusations of fraternizing with the 'heretical' Cathars. One of the Templar Grand Masters, Bertrand de Blanchefort (1156-1169) came from a Cathar family, and since then the Knights Templar accepted Cathars into their Order.

Jacques de Moley and one hundred thirty-seven of his knights spent seven years in the dungeon, to be questioned and tortured at regular intervals. The confessions extracted under agonizing pain lead to their confessions of guilt, and the Templar were to be reconciled with the church. The solemn pronouncement of Pope Clement V was to be read to the repenting Templar in the attendance of the dignitaries of the church in front of Notre Dame. The Grand Master Jacques de Moley and Geoffrey de Charney shocked the attendant clergy and the assembled crowd by proclaiming their and the Knights Templar innocence, and revoked the inaccuracy of the assumed, under agonizing torture made confessions. The accused knights were men of courage and noblesse that had fought a good fight for the church and for what they believed to be true. They knew the outcome of the declaration but it was against their conscience to buy their life through admittance of atrocities they had not committed.

Grand Master Jacques de Moley, and Geoffrey de Charney, the Preceptor of Normandy, were arrested as relapsed heretics and on March 18, of 1314, at the Ile la Cite, close to Notre-Dame Cathedral, slowly burned to death at the stake. The dying Grand Master raised his hands in prayer and cried that he would meet the pope and king before the throne of God. Both Philip IV and Pope Clement died about a year later.

The heroic confession, resulting in the malicious death of the courageous and noble Knights Templar, bewildered the people, and the fearless victims aroused their sympathy. Countries like Germany, England, Scotland, Spain, and Portugal accepted the innocence of the Knights Templar and there were no persecutions of the Knights Templar.

Many of them, especially the Knights Templar of lower ranks, were never tried. They slipped away and re-established themselves by merging with the Knights of Christ in Portugal, or in Spain as Knights of the Order of Montesa. Others went to Switzerland or joined the Knights Hospitallers

Unconfirmed speculations suggested that a small number of Knights Templar managed to escape and sailed in 1398 to Nova Scotia and from there to New England, a journey undertaken by the Vikings 300 years earlier. Some discovered gravestones from Nova Scotia show Crusader crosses and runes. A hand-carved gravestone found in West-Massachusetts displays Templar imagery.

The Hospitallers

The Knights Hospitaller of St. John of Jerusalem was a monastic Order, and established after the First Crusade and the capture of Jerusalem.

The origin of the Order stemmed from the establishing of a hospital in Jerusalem to provide care for Christian pilgrims. The hospital was established as early as AD 600 by Abbot Probus and authorized by Pope Gregory the Great to house and care for Christian pilgrims who were visiting the Holy Land. Emperor Charlemagne, who promoted education, enlarged the hospital and included a library. In 1010, the hospital as well as the Church of the Holy Sepulchre, was destroyed by order of the Fatimid caliph of Egypt, Al-Hakim bi-Amr Allah. Italian merchants from Salerno and Amalfi rebuilt the hospital in 1023 with the permission of Caliph Ali az-Zahir of Egypt, ruler of Jerusalem.

Pope Paschal II, who ruled from 1099-1118, formally recognized the foundation and named it the 'Hospitallers of St. John of Jerusalem'. The name changed over time as of 'Knights of St. John', 'Knights of Rhodes', and 'Knights of Malta' according to the residence of the knights on the various islands.

In 1099, Gerard Thom, a Christian knight, became the Superior of the hospital and founder of the religious Order of St. John under Benedictine degree. "Blessed Gerard" as Gerard Thom was called, travelled to Europe to raise money, and Pope Paschal II decreed that the Order was- obedient to the pope only.

Gerard established hostels for pilgrims in Provence, southern France, and Italy located on the route to the Holy Land. Once there, the warrior monks escorted the pilgrims to protect them from attacks of bandits and enemy soldiers. He established and organized the Order into different sections such as military, clerical and medical sections, and established the first infirmities in Jerusalem. The Hospitallers took residence there after 1530, and the Order's symbol was the eight-pointed cross, known as the Maltese cross.

The loss of Jerusalem in 1187 made the Knights of St. John return to Acre, and after the fall of Acre in 1291, they resided on the island of Cyprus. The Hospitallers gradually transferred to the island of Rhodes and from there defeating seaborne enemies. The presence of the Hospitallers became an important part of controlling and protecting Christian ships sailing east. Fulkes of Villaret was the admiral of the Hospitaller fleet, and in 1307, the knights captured Rhodes and prevented Muslims from raiding Christian ships sailing eastward.

The Hospitallers, under their leadership of Grand Master Fulkes of Villaret, moved permanently to Rhodes and included several other small islands to their territory. From their bases they were able to control the western Mediterranean and engage in successful sea war against the Muslim raiders. The Hospitallers participated in various minor crusades like in 1345 the capture of Smyrna, and King Peter I Crusade of 1365. They witnessed the conquest and sacking of Alexandria, and in 1396, joined in the Nicopolis Crusade.

After the Knights Templar downfall, their property was assigned to the Hospitallers by Pope Clement V as had been suggested by King Philip IV of France who was heavily indebted to the Knights Templar.

Rhodes was isolated and vulnerable, and in 1426 the Muslims of Egypt conquered

Cyprus. In 1435, Sultan Baybar prepared for an invasion. The knights received reinforcement from Europe but this time the Egyptians withdrew. In 1444, the Egyptians besieged Rhodes for a month without succeeding.

In 1480, Ottoman Sultan Mehmet II launched an attack and a vast Ottoman fleet approached Rhodes. Grand Master Pierre d'Aubusson and his reinforced foot soldiers and knights from France prepared for a possible attack. The Ottoman began to besiege the citadel and partially succeeded but failed. The second attempt proved to be more successful and they raised the sultan's standard on the wall of the citadel. The Knights raised their banners representing Lord Jesus, Mary and St. John the Baptist on the walls of the citadel, and during the fiercest attack a golden cross appeared in the sky above the banners and the astonished warriors beheld the image of the Virgin Mary, and next to her a man in plain clothing, and a host of heavenly warriors behind him. The Ottoman's were paralyzed with fright and enabled the Hospitallers to drive them back. The siege was lifted and the fleet sailed away. The Hospitallers and the inhabitants of the island rejoiced at the miracle and their delivery but the Ottoman took a terrible revenge on the citizens of Otranto in Italy. They overran the port and killed Archbishop Stefano Agricoli in the cathedral. Any citizen, who refused to convert to Islam, was also slaughtered.

Grand Master Philippe of L'Isle-Adam prepared for the defence of Rhodes. His appeal throughout Europe to sent reinforcement to defend the last station of Christendom found no response except from a small party from Crete and Venice. The Grand Master tried to prepare for a siege by organizing provisions and prearranged the defence of the bastions and walls. The Ottoman fleet led by Sultan Suleyman arrived in June 1521, and a month later launched an assault. The walls were defended by knights of England and Aragon (Spain) using artillery and digging of mines. The Ottoman's efforts lead to no results, but on September 4, they managed to break into the bastion and gained control of the area. A heroic Hospitaller assault, led by the English knight Nicholas Hussey, drove the Turks back. The Ottomans mounted an assault on the town and concentrated the fire against the bastions of Spain, Provence, Italy and England. After fierce fighting, the attack was abandoned. Suleyman was so enraged at his commander Mustafa Pasha for not conquering the city that he ordered his execution but was persuaded to spare him.

The Ottomans launched another attack in November but were driven back again. The Knights and the citizens of the town were worn out and a truce was called. The citizens were requesting assurances and Sultan Suleyman ordered the artillery to attack again and his army took the bastion of Spain in December.

In 1522, Ottoman Sultan Suleyman besieged Rhodes and the Hospitallers left, first to take up residence in Sicily but in 1530 moved on to Malta. The Hospitallers launched their attacks on Muslim ships and the corsairs from North Africa. In 1551, the Ottoman admiral Sinan, in addition with the corsair Turgut Reis attacked Malta without success. They captured the nearby island of Gozo and the garrison of Tripoli. The Hospitallers expanded and strengthened the Maltese fortifications. In 1559, Philip II of Spain organized an expedition with the participation of the Knights to drive out Turgut Reis from Tripoli but the enterprise ended in defeat. Sultan Suleyman grew weary of having his ships attacked by the Hospitallers, and in 1565 he determined to stop it. A large Ottoman fleet carrying around 40 000-50 000 men landed on Malta. Grand Master Jean Parisot of Valette strengthened the fortifications of St.Elmo, Fort Angelo and Fort Michael. His summoned for manpower sent to members of the Order. His garrison numbered no more than 6 000 men.

The Ottomans launched their attack and pointed their guns at the fortress of St Elmo but were driven back by the defenders. The Ottomans suffered heavy loses but during another major attack the entire defending garrison was killed. The wounded Hospitallers fought until death. The fort was taken by the enemy. The Turks continued their attacks south of Fort St. Angelo, and heavy fighting lasted over several days. Attacks on Fort St. Michael failed and the Ottomans abandoned further attacks. A relief force from Sicily arrived and Malta had been able to hold out against impossible chances.

The Knights Hospitaller continued to fight for Christendom in Eastern Europe and on the Island of Crete. They were based on Malta until 1798 when General Napoleon en route to Egypt drove them out.

The Teutonic Knights

The Teutonic Order was founded as a hospital in Acre in 1190, and militarized. The Order was known as the Order of the Knights of the Hospital of St. Mary. The surplice of the Order was a white robe affixed with a black cross. The Order consisted of nobles, and the knights took the monastic vow of poverty, chastity and obedience. Their Grand Master was Hermann von Salza. The Order received land and donations of land in the Holy Roman Empire included Germany, Greece, Italy and Palestine. During Hermann von Salza's rule, the order changed from being a hospice brotherhood for pilgrims to a military order.

In 1211, King Andrew II of Hungary acknowledged their forces and the order defended Hungary against their neighbouring Cumans. In 1226, the Golden Bull of Rimini granted Prussia to the Teutonic Order, and the order subjugated Prussia and Livonia. After the fall of Acre in 1291, and the loss of the Holy Land the order moved its headquarters to Venice, and later in 1309, to the Marienburg (East Prussia, Germany).

Alexander Nevsky, Grand Duke of Vladimir-Suzdal, Prince of Novgorod (1220-1263) was the defender and protector of Russia. He defeated the Livonian Brothers of the Sword, and also the Lithuanians in 1242. Alexander accepted the rule of the invaded Tatars and was appointed as Grand Duke by the power of the ruling Khan. His acceptance and submission to the Khan saved the country from ruin, but caused much resentment among the local princes and the common people. On April 5, 1242, Alexander lured the Teutonic Knights on the partly frozen Lake Chudskoye on the Neva River, and many of the knights drowned in the icy waters. The defeat was disastrous, and the Teutonic Knights retreated from the Russian soil. Alexander Nevsky became a national hero and was canonized by the Russian Orthodox Church. (The battle is commemorated by the Cantata op. 78 by Sergey Prokoviev, and the movie "Alexander Nevsky" made by Sergej Eisenstein. Stalin used the movie as propaganda 'to fight for Mother Russia').

When Emperor Frederic II, was crowned as King of Jerusalem in 1225, the Teutonic Knights escorted him into the Church of the Holy Sepulchre in Jerusalem. The emperor elevated Hermann von Salza to the title of "Reichsfurst "(Prince Empire).The Teutonic Knights did not achieve the influence and distinction like the Knights Templar.

In 1290, wars of conquest subjugated Prussia, Poland and Livonia. The Teutonic Knights were deeply involved in the disputes between the nobles of Poland and Pomerania and purchased the castles of Danzig on the Baltic Sea. It increased their power because Poland's access to the Baltic Sea was blocked. The Treaty of Kalisz ended the war between Poland and the Teutonic Knights who lost some territory but retained Pomerania. The conflict between Poland and the Teutonic Knights culminated in 1410, when the Order suffered a decisive defeat at the Battle of Tannenberg in East Prussia. The disagreements and discord continued and culminated until the treaty of Torun in 1466 ruled that areas of both sides of the Vistula had to be returned to Poland. The headquarters of the Teutonic Knights became Konigsberg but the Grand Masters were obliged to swear an oath of allegiance to the kings of Poland.

In 1525, the Grand Master Albert of Brandenburg carried out Luther's recommendation of dissolving the order, and suggested the knights to renounce their vows. One of the groups regrouped in Mergentheim, the province of Frankonia, under a new Grand Master. The Order suffered further losses during the French Revolution in Alsace and Lorraine. In 1834, Austria revived its charitable calling to provide for hospitals and convalescent homes for soldiers. Austria recognized it as a charitable and spiritual Order and it is maintained as such.

The Church of the Holy Sepulchre

The Roman Emperor Hadrian (76-138) after the devastating revolt of the Jews in 135, erected a Temple of Venus over the ruins of Solomon's Temple, and, according to Eusebius, a statue of Jupiter was erected also. Emperor Constantine, who converted the Empire to Christianity, ordered the pagan temples to be destroyed, and a church was built over the area. It was erected in the Byzantine style and destroyed by the Persians in 614 to be rebuilt shortly afterwards. The Egyptian caliph Al-Hakim shattered the church in 1009, and ordered the tomb to be destroyed down to bedrock.

One of the most revered and visited sites of the Holy Land is the Church of the Sepulchre, originally built at the request of Helena, the mother of Emperor Constantine, who went in 326 to visit Bethlehem and Jerusalem. The Church of the Sepulchre commemorates the hillside of the crucifixion of Jesus, and the tomb of his burial. The excavation resulted in finding of several crosses of which one, Helena insisted, was the cross Jesus died on. Within the church is the rocky outcropping which was the place of the cross. The other tombs are, according to most updated archaeology, well-preserved tombs of the first century. One of them is most likely the tomb in which Jesus was placed.

The Knights Templar, responsible for building the great cathedrals throughout Europe, rebuilt the Church of the Holy Sepulchre as we know it today. The chapel within the church (the assumed place of crucifixion) is in the care of the Greek-Orthodox Church.

The Albigensian Crusade

The Cathars, a Christian sect, lived around the eleventh until the thirteenth century in southern France near and around Toulouse, a district referred to as Languedoc. Other Cathars were found in Spain, Cologne (Germany) Flanders, Lombardy and Tuscany. They lived simple and sober lives dedicated to the teachings of Jesus but not according to the doctrines of the Roman Catholic Church. Their teaching attacked the corruption and wealth of the Catholic Church and denied the pope's authority.

Cathars believed in dualism stating that there were two principle powers ruling the Universe, God, which was filled with the spirit of utter goodness and resided in pure light and spirit. The other God was Lucifer/Satan, also known as 'Prince of the World' who was absolutely evil and ruled the world of Matter (see: Gnosticism).

Cathars divided their congregation into two groups, the 'perfect' and the 'believers'. The believers were the common people who lived a pure, simple and devoted life. Both sexes were equal and telling lies, swearing or killing was prohibited. The Cathars wandered in pairs from place to place to visit the sick and poor and encourage and strengthen them in their beliefs. They were always of the same sex as not to be tempted, and this caused misinterpretations and false accusations by the church.

The title 'Perfect' (parfait) was affixed to a monk of the 'Cathars'. The Perfect were expected to embrace a life of renunciation and austerity, abstain from eating meat and sexual contact. The 'Perfect' men and women had to pass through three years of rigorous training before they were admitted as members into the spiritual-religious movement. They also believed in incarnation. According to them, Paul was the only one who identified Jesus as the only true son of God.

According to the church the Cathars were 'heretics' because they practiced the teachings of the early Christian writers like Maricon and Arius who lived in the second and third century. Maricon postulated that Christ was a teaching of love, and God could not be the Jewish God of Law and punishment. Marcion believed in salvation by faith and established his church based on this doctrine. His church became popular and widespread. Both of those early writers were not included into the canon but regarded as 'Gnostics'. Much of southern France of the twelfth century had converted to Catharism which centred about the city of Albi. The teaching had a large following among the peasants and the more educated classes, including the French nobility.

In 1198, St. Bernard of Clairvaux undertook the arduous and lengthy journey to the Languedoc Cathars to converse with them. Pope Innocent III tried a peaceful change of their supposedly wrong beliefs by sending his preachers but with little success. The nobles of southern France as well as the bishops protected the Cathars.

In 1204, Pope Innocent suspended the authority of the southern bishops by appointing papal legates to represent him. Any noble, who supported the Cathars, was excommunicated as it happened to the powerful Count Raymond VI of Toulouse who refused assistance. The pope called on King Philip II to take action against the nobles but the king refused. Count Raymond, who got involved into a fierce dispute with the papal legate Pierre de Castelau, was murdered.

The pope called for a Crusade against Languedoc, and offered the land of the Cathars to anyone willing to fight. With this proclamation, the southern and northern French nobility were drawn into the conflict. The clash, in which Christians opposed and killed Christians, was for the Crusaders successful at first but later they lost conquered land.

In 1229, the nobles made peace, and the Languedoc was in the hands of France. Toulouse became the centre of the Inquisition, and a systematic search of ridding the area of remaining Cathars took place. In 1233, the Inquisition under the leadership of Pope Gregory IX crushed the remnants of the Cathars. The town of Beziers was captured, and the soldiers called the Catholic population to leave the town. Afterwards, the entire Cathar populace were brutally massacred. The army systematically captured town after town. The church offered remaining Cathars to return to Catholicism, and some of them accepted it but the unrepentant Cathars were burned at the stake. The Knights Templar secretly helped by hiding fleeing Cathars, and burying their death.

Many of the Cathars escaped and took refuge at their fortress of Montsegur. It was their last stronghold and fell after a nine-month siege in March 1244.

On May 16, 1244, 200-224 Cathar 'perfect' were the subjects of a huge massacre, and burned in a gigantic fire at the 'prat cramats' near the fortress of Montsegur.

The small fortress of Queribus fell in August 1255. Some Cathars managed to escape to northern Italy and Spain. The last Cathar perfectus, Guillaume Belibaste, was burned at the stake in 1321.

In later years, descendants of the Cathars were required to live outside of towns.

Waldensians and Brethren of the Free Spirit living in the same area were also persecuted.

The Hundred Year War (1337-1453) fought between England and France began in 1357 with disputes to the French Throne.

Aquataine in southern France was King Henry II of England continental realm and in 1340 King Edward III of England announced his claim to the French Throne. In 1360, he failed to secure the French throne but approved large French territories. The English power and influence gradually slipped away and by 1374, most of the land was returned to France.

In 1420, King Henry V of England laid claim to the French throne. He invaded northern France during the summer of 1415, and fought and defeated the French army at Agincourt.

The French Royal family, Count Bernard VII, Duke of Orleans, and the Burgundian Duke John 'the Fearless' were divided concerning the legal heir to the throne of France. The French diplomats failed to extend the existing truce with England. While the French Royal family quarrelled, the English army conquered large areas of northern France and gained the support of the Burgundian Duke Philip III. He agreed to recognize King Henry V of England as the legal heir to the French throne because he rejected Charles of Ponthviev of the Valois dynasty as potential heir.

A high-spirited girl, Joan of Arc, born at Domrey-la-Pucelle, declared that, selected by Divine Guidance, she was chosen to lead the French army to victory and establish the rightful heir to the French throne.

Joan guided the French army and besides other victories, lifted the blockade of Orleans in nine days. Through her influence, she was indirectly responsible for the coronation of King Charles VII of France in the Cathedral of Reims on July 17, 1429.

Duke John's son Philip captured Joan and handed her over to the English. On January 9, 1471, Rouen witnessed the horrible death of Joan who was accused of witchcraft and burned at the stake. King Charles did not attempt to intervene to save the innocent girl's life. The French army continued the war and finally drove the English army out of France.

Joan of Arc inspired poets and common people alike because she demonstrated remarkable courage, sincerity, and devotion. She was beatified in 1909 and canonized in 1920, and is the patron saint of France.

Between 1378 and 1417, conflict within the Roman Catholic Church resulted in the election of two popes, one residing in Rome. Clement V moved the papacy to Avignon, France. In1377, Gregory XI moved the papacy to Rome but when he died a year later, the conclave cardinals chose the Italian cardinal Bartolomea Prignano as Pope Urban VI (1378-89) because the Roman crowd threatened to kill any non-Italian pope. The French cardinals in Avignon planned revolt, and in August 1378, declared in a manifesto Urban's election void. In September 1378, Rome declared Robert of Geneva to be the true pope. Robert, now Clement VII (1378-94 the 'Anti-Pope') resided at Avignon while Urban VI ruled in Rome. King Philip VI of France took Pope Clement prisoner. Clement was despotic and soon resented by his inner circle. The French cardinals in Avignon planned revolt and in 1378 declared in a manifesto Urban's election void and excommunicated him. The secular powers were undecided and supported one or the other of the popes. The church suffered unrest, instability and internal strife.

Pope Urban died in 1389 and was superseded by three more popes following each other in short succession: Boniface VIII was arrested by the French King Philip IV. Innocent VII, and Gregory XII. When Clement II died in 1394, the Avignon cardinals voted for a Spanish prelate to succeed as Benedict XIII. The election caused trouble with the French king Charles VI and the cardinal's family and a meeting at Pisa was scheduled. The Council of Pisa met in 1409. Benedict and Gregory were summoned but did not appear. Both were declared as deposed and a new pope, Alexander V, was elected. There were now three popes! Alexander died in 1410, and the cardinals at the Council of Pisa chose as his successor John XXII.

In 1417, the electoral committee of the Council in Rome chose Cardinal Oddone Colonna as Pope Martin V. The 'Great Schism'(referred to as the Babylonian Captivity) the time of chaos within the church, ended. The Roman Catholic Church never regained its former power (see also: Great Schism, 1378-1417).

Part 4

Chapter 20

The Renaissance

The Black Death, or called the 'bubonic plaque, a terrible epidemic, invaded China in 1300. It entered Europe during 1347-1352 and killed approximately 20 to 30 million people. Rats with infected flies made their way by ship from the Middle East and into Sicily. By 1349, the plaque reached England and Ireland. It affected the lymph nodes and the skin turned black. There were further outbreaks around 1500 and 1665. Some villages were totally wiped out

While during the 'Dark Ages' in Europe (300-650) man thought God, and his longing found expression in the architecture of the Gothic Cathedrals who were compared to 'hands in prayer'. The 'High Middle Ages' dating approximately from 1000-1300, changed Europe into ground-breaking urban and dynamic societies.

The Renaissance, (Late Middle Ages, 1300-1500) beginning in Italy and slowly spreading to northern Europe, lasted until 1600. It witnessed the rebirth (renaissance) of ancient Greek's and Roman civilizations, and expressed the Greek ideals expressed in sculpture and paintings. Scenes of Greek and Roman mythology were discovered and revitalized. The great writers Boccaccio and Petraccio articulated thoughts of life and love, and added to the search of man's self-discovery. For hundreds of years, the church had been the source of inspiration, and its influence in the arts had been supreme. The return to the classical epoch Greece and Rome changed man's outlook on life, art, and himself. The Renaissance created an incredible outburst of activities in areas of art, literature, architecture, painting and science. Florence was one of the great centres of art and produced men of genius such as Leonardo da Vinci, Michelangelo and Rafael. The manuscripts of classical Latin and Greek literature and drama were translated and performed, and. offered at the universities in their curriculum. The ideals of humanism was born but at times, clashed with the doctrines of the church.

Dante Alighieri (1265-1321) the towering genius of the Renaissance was born in Florence. As the first of the triangle of brilliant writers, he is best known for his masterpiece of World Literature, the 'Divine Comedy'. It is written in three sections: Inferno, Purgatory and Paradise.

Each of them divided into 33 cantos describing his journey with Virgil his guide (the writer of the Aeneid) through the Inferno and Purgatory. Beatrice Portinari, the lady of his love, guided him through Paradise.

During his journey, Dante realizes his errors made, and encounters many fascinating sinners. He realizes the consequences one has to face, and learns a great lesson. The final guide, who leads him to God, is St. Bernard.

In 1341, Giovanni Boccaccio (1313-1375) met the great poet Francisco Petrarch in Florence, and the two became lifelong friends. Boccaccio studied Latin and Greek, and tried to introduce Greek literature. Around 1348, during the bubonic plaque, Boccaccio wrote his 'Decameron'. 'Decameron', his most famous writing is a collection of 100 tales which are amusing, and sometimes impious. Decameron is set against the raging of the Black Death. The tales reveal a variety of different characters brought together, some of them self-seeking, ludicrous, cruel or loving. In contrast to the pious Dante, Boccaccio made fun of the clergy. Exposed to suffering and death, Boccaccio was open to goodness of man, and to the beauties and joys of life. He is regarded as one of the great writers of literature.

Francesco Petraccio (1304-1374), a lifelong friend of Giovanni Boccaccio, was born in Arezzo in 1304. His family moved in 1307 to Avignon to the court of Pope John XXII. His studies of law brought him first to Montpelier and later to Bologna. The dishonesty of the vocation disgusted him, and when his father died, he abandoned the studies. He and his brother Gherardo entered the church to serve within its ranks.

In 1327, he saw Laura de Noves first time and fell deeply in love. She was married, and a relationship was unthinkable but Francesco wrote hundreds of poems to her. His poems were widely read and translated into every language, and exercised a great influence on the literary geniuses of his time. Others, like Shakespeare, would study his works.

Lorenzo the 'Magnificent' (1449-1492) sponsored the arts in Florence. The spirit of the Renaissance celebrated the individual who was free to follow the inclinations of his choice.

Niccolo Machiavelli (1469-1527) born in Florence, became famous through his book "The Prince" He emphasized that a ruler should be strong and went so far as to advocate deceit, two-faced dealings and force. He was the son of a lawyer, and worked as secretary to a council, and later as diplomat. In 1512, the Republic of Florence was overthrown, and Machiavelli's courier ended. While in exile, he continued to write on other works, including a play. His book has been condemned though it circulated widely and is still studied today.

Galileo Galilei (1564-1642) and Johannes Kepler (1571-1630) changed the way of how we perceive the Universe. Johannes Kepler (1571-1630) confirmed the findings of Nicolaus Copernicus (1473-1543) that the solar system was heliocentric (sun-centred) and Earth was just another planet. It was contradictory to the beliefs of the church. Though the church authorities were not trained astronomers, the Catholic Church had adopted the teaching of Ptolemy, the Egyptian astronomer of the second century A.D. who postulated that the Earth was the centre, and Sun and the other planets circled around it. His geocentric theory agreed with the creation story of the Bible.

In 1610, Galileo observed with his self-made telescope the planet Jupiter and four its four largest moons (Io, Europe, Ganymede, and Callisto) and was the first who discovered and observed sun spots. In 1632, he supported in a book the theory of Copernicus. The church authorities put Galileo under house arrest for the remaining eight years of his life. The church felt challenged and failed to understand the new theories of the astronomers which overturned the old theory of Ptolemy, and this was regarded as heresy.

At the same time, St. Peter's Cathedral in Rome was built, and Michelangelo painted the ceiling of the Sistine Chapel. The paintings depict scenes from classical myth and the Old and New Testament. The vitality of the Renaissance permeated every aspect of life and its citizens.

In England, Geoffrey Chaucer (1340-1400) wrote the 'Canterbury Tales 'He served in the household of the Duke of Clarence, and was sent to fight in the wars of France. In 1367, he was granted the title of 'yeoman of the King's chamber' and at times travelled with King Edward III. 'The Canterbury Tales' tells the story of pilgrims on their way to Canterbury to pray at the shrine of St. Thomas Becket. The pilgrims are from different backgrounds: a knight and his squire, a miller and his wife, a prioress and a friar. For entertaining themselves on their pilgrimage, they agree that each of them tell a tale. It is a colourful and rich description of medieval life that describes the nobles, workers, priests and the low classes. The Canterbury Tales is the first book of poetry written in the English language. Before Chaucer's time, literature in England was written in Latin or Italian and available only to the educated few. He paved the path for the great poets to follow like Shakespeare, Dryden, Keats and Eliot to render their expressions in English in a beautiful and noble style.

Chapter 21

Foreshadows of the Reformation

The Inquisition and the Plight of the Jews

The Italian cities of the eleventh century were the first ones to establish Jewish ghettos. Other large cities with Jewish communities like Venice, Frankfurt and Prague followed the example.

The design of the inquisition was developed by Pope Alexander III in 1163 and more outlined by Pope Innocent III in 1199. He stated that heresy was 'treachery against God' and to be punishable by death. In 1231, Pope Gregory IX gave his blessings in the bull Excommunicanus. Anti-Semitism committed innocent people to panic and fear. The pope declared that a dutiful Christian must persecute heretics and this attitude was further confirmed and encouraged in 1252 by Pope Innocent IV.

The Inquisition and the ensuing heinous cruelties towards guiltless but accused individuals were incredibly malicious and hideous. It took no more but a jealous neighbour to condemn an innocent individual to the most excruciating tortures and abhorrent death: to die in the flames.

England granted in1290 the Jewish population three month to leave the country while France barred them in 1394. The Jewish communities throughout Europe faced persecutions and restrictions. One of the most cruel and heartless acts against Jews was the demand of distinct attire to smudge them as despicable and abhorrent, and to exclude them from most occupations accept finance and commerce. It was the resilience and spirit of the Jewish people to survive, and to be strong. Many members of the Jewish population, as well as Muslims (Moors) in Spain intermarried into high society or converted to Christianity, and became influential and wealthy. It aroused bad feelings and jealousy. King Ferdinand and Queen Isabella introduced the inquisition in 1478. It started in Seville in 1480, and was granted by Pope Sixtus IV. The Grand nquisitor, the Dominican priest Tomas de Torquemada used torture to obtain confessions. The sentence announced the punishment of flogging or burning at the stake, which was carried out in public. Since it was not possible to try Jews and

Muslims, therefore, Ferdinand and Isabella agreed to expel about 160.000 Jews in 1493 that had to leave their assets and possessions behind. Venice had a large population of Jews who were important members of commerce and finance but in 1516, the Senate ordained that Jews had to live in a section referred to as the Ghetto. Besides, the Senate ordered that all Marranos or converted Jews, to leave the city.

Some of the popes like Alexander VI, Julius II, Leo X, Clement VII and Paul III, received the Jews and allowed them to practice their religion. A bishop complained to Pope Paul that the Marranos had returned to the Jewish practice of circumcising their baptized children, and the pope, under pressure, established the Inquisition in Rome.

In 1555, Giovanni Pietro Caraffa became Pope Paul IV. He did not show tolerance towards the Jewish population. The Jews were confined to the ghetto that was periodically flooded by the Tiber River, and a hotbed for disease. Other ghettos were established in Siena and Florence, Ancona and Bologna. Paul IV ordered a secret decree that the Marranos in Ancona to be submitted to the Inquisition and their possessions confiscated. Some of the prisoners were burned at the stake as heretics, and others being sent to the galleys.

Some of the Jews were welcomed in Poland and prospered, and Germany had its Jewish communities. The fate of the Jewish population was never secure. They were frequently victims of periodic persecutions. In 1540, Charles V issued an order to expel the Jews from Naples.

Sultan Bajazet II (1556) welcomed Jewish exiles to make their home in Turkey. He knew that they were skilled in trade, handicrafts and medicine which were little developed among the Turks. Since they were non-Muslims, the Jews were subject to the usual tax but exempt from military service. The Jewish physicians were highly favoured and esteemed for their skills and knowledge of medicine. The Holy Land was under Turkish rule and only a limited number of Jews were allowed to live there.

The Inquisition continued in Spain and in the Spanish colonies at irregular intervals. In other countries like Italy, France, and Germany millions of innocent people were fated to die the dreadful death of burning at the stake. The Inquisition finally ended in 1834.

Chapter 22

The Mystics

The fourteenth and fifteenth centuries saw a rise of great mystics. Mysticism expresses the idea that each person may have a personal and direct relationship and unity with God. St. Bernard of Clairvaux (1091-1153) leader of the Cistercian Order (a branch of the Benedictines) believed that the world was illusive and wicked, and man unable to resist temptation and should withdraw from the world. Only through contemplation and surrender to God and indisputable accept His will was man able to communicate directly with Him.

The Kabbalah (Jewish Mysticism) declares that the ideal human condition is intimacy with the Divine, and development of mystical awareness. The union with God leads to a transformation of the person but God, the Infinite, can never directly be known.

Later mystics stated that man did not require the help and guidance of the church to attain the lofty goal of union with God. The most prominent sect in Germany called itself 'Brethren of the Free Spirit'. The sect believed that the world was God in outward appearance (referred to as 'pantheism') and that every living being returned to God at their death, therefore purgatory or hell did not exist.

The Brethren wandered from town to town begging for their food, and converting people. Many mystics were therefore looked upon as heretics.

Some women becoming nuns were seeking more than serving God within the framework of the Church. Mystical union with God was their aspiration and the descriptions of their experiences are inspiring.

The Beguines were religious women who were not taking vows like nuns but lead a life devoted to spiritual development and to ministering to the need of others. They supported themselves through working and were members of the lower classes. The first Beguines were two sisters, living about 1223 in Cologne, and Strassbourg, and their membership gradually increased. The Beguines established a home in Cologne that became a shelter for destitute persons or such who needed shelter while relocating. Pope Gregory IX officially recognized the Beguines in 1233, and granted them protection. In time, the hospitality of the Beguines was abused by Flagellants and others.

Hildegard of Bingen

Hildegard of Bingen was born in 1098 in Bermersheim, near Mainz (south-western Germany). Her parents were of noble decent. At eight, Hildegard entered the convent near Bingen. She was still very young when she experienced a great light that made her shiver. The light returned later in life and made her decide to write down her visions. Hildegard described it as 'a reflection of the living light'. At forty-three, Hildegard became abbess. She was highly intelligent, a composer, poet, healer and advisor to emperors and popes. Her writings and described visions found the attention of Bernard of Clairvaux and Pope Eugenius III. Both of them affirmed Hildegard's as mystic and prophetess. In 1165, she founded a new convent across the Rhine.

She wrote a visionary work titled 'Scivias' and two books, of herbal medicine and of compound medicine. She was highly reputed for her knowledge as healer and herbalist. Her 'Symphony of the Harmony of Celestial Revelation' described her devotions and spiritual life. It is accompanied by monophonic music to be performed during specific feasts.

Hildegard had not received a scholarly education but she had a brilliant mind and based her knowledge on the Bible, and her style is distinctly individual.

Albertus Magnus

Albertus Magnus (1193-1280) was born in Germany and taught in Cologne and Paris. He read Greek and Roman authors and was strongly influenced by Aristotle who had vigilantly observed the world around him and carefully wrote down his observations and attempted to organize them. Albertus Magnus emphasized on the Greek philosopher by praising his innate wisdom of reason

Thomas Aquinas

Dominican Thomas Aquinas (1225-1274) was a student of Albertus Magnus who attempted to unite St. Bernard's dependence on faith and Peter Abelard's and Albertus's stress on reason, combining it into a single philosophy. Peter Abelard (1079-1142) a contemporary of St. Bernard, and wandering scholar, questioned faith and reason, and quoted apparently conflicting quotes from the Bible although he never denied the importance of faith. He believed that reason instead of faith must be man's guidance.

Thomas Aquinas tried to reconcile Bernard and Abelard by explaining the difference between the active and passive intellects. The 'passive' intellect, he postulated, recorded the impressions of the world while the 'active' intellect analysed them, and applying reason and faith, examines to seek to find universal truth. In his book 'Summa Theologica' described God's vision of the perfect man, called 'essence', and described as the personal virtues as man's 'being'. Aquinas emphasized that each Christian should strife to attain his essence and to come as close as possible to the ideal of the perfect man. He combined St. Bernard and Abelard by stating that faith was the first requirement, and reason served as the tool to accomplish the task God gave man to carry out.

Julian of Norwich

The anchoress Julian of Norwich wrote in 1373 of her visions of Christ whom she described as love. The anchorites withdrew from the outside world and lived in enclosed cells. They aspired through meditation and prayer to reach intimate contact with God which was more difficult to obtain in a busy nunnery. The anchoress was able to watch through a window the church service, and give spiritual council.

Julian perceived how closely interconnected Creator and his creatures are: being drawn together through suffering and divine love. She perceived God as our hope and comfort. Julian was the first woman to express her thoughts and devotions in the English language.

Francis of Assissi

Francesco Bernardone was born in Assissi in 1181 to a wealthy merchant. He was a careless youth until he became a soldier and experienced the horrors of war. Francesco was wounded and returned home a very ill man. While he recuperated, he felt a call to add a deeper dimension of religion into the present world. His feelings were confirmed when one day while praying at the church of San Damiano, the statue of Christ said to him, "Francesco, restore my Church."

Francesco assumed that Christ meant the church of San Damiano who was in the state of decay. He went and sold a large quantity of his father's merchandise to pay for the repair of the church. His father became very angry and disinherited Francesco. He left the father's house to establish his life devoted to God, and to be wedded to "Lady Poverty." Some of his former friends joined him and their lives were lead by poverty, chastity and faith. In 1210, Pope Innocent III approved Francesco and his eleven companions to be travelling preachers. The brothers wandered throughout

Italy encouraging people to live in repentance and simplicity. In 1212, Francesco and Claire founded the community of the 'Poor Ladies'.

Around 1217, the many supporters of Francesco slowly became a monastic order. There were so many followers that communities were established in other parts of Italy and Europe. In 1221, Cardinal Ugolino revised and reiterated the vows of humility and poverty.

One day, Francesco was in deep prayer (1224) when stigmata like the bleeding five wounds inflicted on Jesus on the cross, appeared on his hands, feet and body. The stigmata never left him and he suffered greatly until "Sister Death" embraced him in 1226.

Francesco is one of the most beloved saints because of his purity and simplicity. Some great minds declared him to come closest to representing Christ on earth.

He left for us his wonderful writings like the "Canticles of the Creatures", "The Praise of the Virtues", "Dear Brother Fire"

Francesco was a soul totally immersed in his love of God and the universe, and saw nature and him as an expression of it.

Meister Eckhart

One of the distinguished mystics was (and is) the Dominican Meister (Master) Johannes Eckhart (1260-1328) born in Hochheim in Thuringia (Germany) and his disciples Johannes Tauler (1300-1361) and Henry Suso. Meister Eckhart received his theosophical training in Cologne and Paris. He studied briefly under Albert the Great who had been the teacher of Thomas Aquinas. In 1302 he accepted the position as professor of theology at the University of Paris. In 1413, Meister Eckhart was made prior, preacher and professor at Strassbourg. The book 'Breakthrough' written by Matthew Fox summarized Meister Eckhart's 'Sermons' into four parts: One: The experience of God in creation. Two: The experience of God by letting go and letting be. Three: The experience of God in breakthrough and giving birth to Self and God. Four: The experience of God by way of compassion and social justice.

Meister Eckhart's way of thinking was dialectical and poetic, and tried to imagine beyond the common expressions and away from the teachings of the university. He stated that creation was a celestial blessing, and Heaven was within us but we do not realize is because we are trapped in our dualism. Eckhart emphasized on the awareness of the intrinsic unity of all creature. The eternal life, he declared, was here and now. His emphasis of detachment was to give birth to oneself and God. The person who becomes unattached to belongings or to the outcome of actions develops a state of 'emptiness' what is necessary to become 'filled' with God's love and being lead by Him

Meister Eckhart confessed that he was deeply indebted to the Scriptures he loved so dearly. Eckhart had a creative and independent mind and tried to see God beyond the unity of all being as the miracle of creation. His teaching of non-attachment and God-realization stood in stark contrast to the teachings of the church and the flamboyant life style of the clergy in office.

He preached to the Beguines and was their spiritual adviser. At that time he became renounced as preacher for his spiritual perception. After the canonization of his spiritual brother, Dominican Thomas Aquinas (1225-1274), the Franciscan Archbishop of Cologne succumbed to rumours of heresy. Pope Paul XXII condemned the Beguines as heretical. Eckhart was summoned and appealed in 1326 to his right of trial by a papal court. He went to Avignon to defend his case, and died shortly afterwards.

Eckhart's writings remain the reader of Eastern philosophy. Meister Eckhart of course, never knew or studied Buddhism but readers may find a startling resemblance between his writings and the great literature of India when pondering thoughts like his writings on detachment and God-realization. He was an enlightened and misunderstood individual, and far ahead of his time.

His emphasis of detachment is also emphasized in the Bhagavad Gita, the Holy Book of the Hindus. Prince Arjuna, of the royal house of Bharata, had to enter into battle with his relatives, the Kurus. He was extremely unhappy about the situation but as a member of the Warrior-Caste (Kshatria) he was obliged to fight. Lord Krishna, the incarnation of Lord Vishnu, appeared and functioned as his charioteer. He explained to the desperate Arjuna that he must carry out his royal obligation as warrior without craving for honour and false pride of victory. Lord Krishna instructed Arjuna on whatever the outcome of the battle if it is victory or defeat, to detach him from the result of it.

Detachment is a valuable guide to develop rational and clear-headed thinking and acting. It is not to be associated with aloofness and emotional coldness.

Other mystics like Thomas Aquinas, St. John of the Cross, Thomas a Kempis, and Teresa of Avila etc. are worthwhile to be studied and grant hours of inspiring reading.

Part 5

Chapter 23

Disillusions

William of Ockham

The first signs of disillusionment with the church came from England. William of Ockham, of the Franciscan Order, a famous, though controversial, philosopher (1300-49) taught for six years at Oxford (and perhaps at Paris). He wrote commentaries on Aristotle and Peter Lombard, and in his copious writings he expounded that nothing could be known except through direct perception which he applied to the knowledge of the existence of God and to the Trinity. In his writings he declared that Christ was the One and only head of the Church, and the pope had no lawful civil power. Ockham also insisted that the Church should be without worldly possessions.

This highly critical commentaries regarding the Catholic Church resulted in a summons to appear at the papal court at Avignon (referred to as the 'Babylonian Captivity). Pope John XXII ordered inquiries into Ockham's 'abominable heretical writings' and was shortly afterwards imprisoned there. He and two other imprisoned Franciscans managed to escape and flee to Aiguesmortes where they embarked in a boat. A galley picked them up and brought the fugitives to King Louis IV of Bavaria (Holy Roman Emperor) at Pisa. They were excommunicated by the pope and protected by the Emperor.

William accompanied the Emperor to Munich, and continued to apply his 'razor' to rites and dogmas of the Church. William of Ockham died of the Black Death in 1349. Long before his death, William found recognition as the most dynamic thinker of his age.

A discontented voice came from John Wyclif (1320-84) of North Yorkshire. He studied at Oxford and received his Master's Degree. For a year, Wyclif was Master of Balliol College. He was brilliant and wrote a large amount of Scholastic treaties on theology, logic and metaphysics, all of them in Latin. Wyclif condemned the ecclesiastical wealth and taught that the word of God to be the only authority binding all Christians, and denied the authority of the pope. He believed in 'predestination', that is, God had determined the course of one's life. To learn about God one must study the Bible. He denied transubstantiation and believed that Christ was mysteriously and spiritually present along with the bread and wine.

In 1408, Archbishop Arundel disapproved of the circulation of Wyclif's translations of the Scriptures and forbade further distribution.

Wyclif emphasized the time of the early beginnings before the Christian church had established rituals and wealth. In a pamphlet, he called for the separation of the English Church from Rome. He translate the Bible (New Testament) from the Latin Vulgate into English and declared that anyone able to read and write in English would befit firsthand without the need of interpretation. Most of Wyclif's writings appeared in English. He favoured the 'Lord's Prayer' spoken in English instead of in Latin which was not understood by the uneducated parishioners. Wyclif insisted that the Host and Wine did not transubstantiate (Christ was spiritually present) and his denial affected Catholic teaching. Luther and his contemporaries hotly disputed the same subject of transubstantiation

The Catholic Church's emphasis was on worship and in relation to the Holy Eucharist. The church exercised power within including the lives of the parishioners. Wyclif's canon diminished the power of the church because he stressed knowledge of the Bible and to a lesser degree on the worship.

Wycliff wrote some 300 sermons in English for the Lollards, the lay priests of limited learning. They were barefoot and clad in black wool robes preaching to the country folks. The common people flocked to listening to their preaching and their importance of simplicity and piety. The Lollards were thought of being a threat of the established social and religious order and it resulted in prosecution of the 'heretics'. In 1410, the Lollard tailor John Badby, was condemned by the Church, and burned at the stake.

Wyclif's ideas appeared radical to the church authorities and made many enemies within the church. Any of his writings found were destroyed.

In 1384, Pope Urban VI summoned Wyclif to Rome but in December Wyclif suffered from a stroke and died. He was buried but according to an order of the Council of Constance (1415) his bones were exhumed and thrown into a nearby stream.

Chapter 24

Jan Hus

Wyclif's ideas influenced the Bohemian reformer Jan Hus (1369-1415). He was a brilliant scholar, and in 1401, became ordained as priest. At the same year, he was chosen as dean of the Faculty of Arts at Prag and earned a reputation as inspiring and gifted speaker. Hus was familiar with William of Ockhams' and Wyclif's writings, and adopted many of their ideas. He condemned the sales of the indulgences sold by the Dominican friar Johann Tetzel by which a person was able to buy himself free of committed sins. Hus stated that no power except God could forgive sins. He also criticized the Church for being rich and worldly. The Church at that time faced severe internal problems, and two popes, Gregory XII (the Roman pope) and Benedict XIII (the Avignon pope) who both claimed the papacy, were disposed of by the third Pope John XXIII (the anti-pope) at a council at Pisa in 1409. The pope excommunicated Hus who preached against the sale of the indulgencies.

Pope John summoned a Council in 1414 at the lakeside city of Constance near the Swiss border. Hus received command to attend the council to attempt a resolution. The German Emperor Sigismund secured him safe conduct for attending the Council and for his safe return. At the Council, Hus defended his preaching and writings as based on the gospels. He refused to accept the pope as infallible and declared transubstantiation as wrong teaching and the doctrine of it without foundation. Hus was condemned as heretic and Antichrist, and burned at the stake at Constance.

The news of Hus' death caused a great uproar in Bohemia. An assembly sent to Constance declared Hus as a devout Catholic. Furthermore, the document stated that papal commands to be obeyed only if they agreed with the Scripture.

Chapter 25

Johannes Gutenberg

Johannes Gutenberg, living around 1400-1468, changed history by inventing the printing press. He lived in Strasbourg for forty years but became in 1448 a citizen of Mainz. Gutenberg experimented with cutting metal types, and enrolled into a contract with the wealthy goldsmith Johann Fust. Gutenberg mortgaged his press and when Fust sued him for money, he was unable to repay and left Fust. With borrowed money, he established himself with another press. In 1456-57, he produced the first type-printed book made with movable types, the beautiful 'Gutenberg-Bible' consisting of 1282 double-columned pages and leaf-illuminated pages. His printing press was praised throughout Europe although the professional copiers feared for losing their subsistence. The Bible, as well as classical literature and pamphlets became available to anyone able to read, and were no longer the realm of the elected and the privileged classes of the aristocracy, the clergy and scholars. Printing presses were established in Venice, Paris (Sorbonne) Utrecht and Cologne.

The letters of the indulgence were printed by Johannes Gutenberg at Mainz in 1445. A printer in Paris printed Erasmus' 'Praise of Folly' and 'Colloquies'. The printing press changed society by informing them of the ideas and ills of their rulers and their social order.

The printed books opened the path to the common people, and made the possession of a Bible possible. It also encouraged vernacular literature for large audiences to be printed and distributed.

The 1385 'Wycliffe Manuscript New Testament' was hand-written in 'Middle-English'. Wycliff's follower William Tyndale created the first English language 'New Testament' to be printed. The 1539 'Great Bible' published in 1539 was authorized by King Henry VIII and Parliament.

In 1539, the Matthew-Tyndale Bible, translated from the original Greek and Hebrew, was printed by John Rogers who operated under the assumed name of 'Thomas Matthew'.

The 'Bible of the Protestant Reformation' was the 1560 Geneva Bible (first edition). The Geneva Bible, edited and approved of by John Knox, John Calvin, and others, was the 'Study Bible' and the Bible of the Pilgrims and Puritans.

Chapter 26

John Colet

The humanistic movement centred in England with John Colet (1467-1519), the son of Sir Henry Colet, as the leader. John Colet studied at Oxford and was intrigued by the humanist ideals. Colet travelled to France and Italy, and met Erasmus in Paris. Savonarola's struggle moved him deeply, and the conduct of Pope Alexander VI (Rodrigo Borgia) and his cardinals shocked him. On his return to England, he decided to teach in Oxford. He lectured directly from the Bible. Later he founded a school to teach boys humanistic learning. He lived humbly and used the inherited wealth to charity.

Germany was lead by the Hebrew scholar Johannes Reuchlin (1455-1522).He was fluent in Latin, Greek and Hebrew, and was at the age of thirty-eight appointed professor of Hebrew at the University of Heidelberg. Reuchlin was criticised for teaching from the Bible like the d'Estables in Paris. The humanists of northern Europe were members of the priesthood who wished to reform the Catholic Church and modernize it according to their humanistic principles. Their pamphlet and books were widely distributed, and they unintentionally added fuel to the brewing discontent.

Chapter 27

Girolamo Savonarola

Girolamo Savonarola was a Dominican priest of Florence (1494) and contemporary of Pope Alexander VI. Savonarola protested against the corruption of Alexander and his family, the infamous Cecare Borgia, and Alexander's daughter Lucrezia. Like Wyclif, Savonarola stressed the studies Of the Bible. At the Carnival of Florence, he ordered a great 'Bonfire of Vanities' in which items such as wigs, perfumes, lewd books and immodest dresses were cast. Savonarola attacked the Church by accusing her of being proud and lascivious. His doctrine was orthodox, and he was fearlessly criticising the Vatican and the flamboyant lifestyle of its court.

Florence was a Republic and ruled by Lorenzo de Medici, the "Magnificent". After his death, his weak son Pietro the "Unfortunate", followed him. Savonarola managed to override Pietro by influencing the population of Florence with dire prophesies. He proclaimed Florence to be the "City of God" and a theocratic republic lead by him, Savonarola.

Pope Alexander was reluctant to excommunicate Savonarola as a heretic but he kept writing letters to the princes with the suggestion of overthrowing the non-Christian Pope. Savonarola had gone too far! He was arrested and tortured because he refused to recant. On May, 23, 1493 Savonarola was burned at the stake.

Chapter 28

King Henry VIII of England

The English Church was tossed into the confusion of the European chaos between reformers and the struggle of the Catholic Church who tried to keep the upper hand in matters. The parish priests heavily taxed the parishioners, corruption of the clergy and heresy were widespread.

William Tyndale (1492-1536) educated at Cambridge, was fluent in eight languages, and around 1520 accepted the position of tutor in the family of Sir Walsh in Gloucestershire. He devoted himself to the study of the Scriptures and the doctrines of the Reformation. With encouragement from his employer and the financial aid of Sir Humphrey Monmouth and others, Tyndale decided to undertake a Bible translation from the original Hebrew and Greek to translate the texts into English as spoken of the day. Since translations were forbidden in England, he went in 1524 to Wittenberg to continue with the translations under Luther's guidance. At Cologne, he began to print his New Testament translated from the Greek text as edited by Erasmus, and Hebrew. The translation of the New Testament appeared in 1525-26, Pentateuch in 1530, Jonah in 1531.

English agents learned about and instigated the authorities against him. Tyndale left Catholic Cologne and found refuge in Protestant Worms where he printed 6000 copies. King Henry's Court Chancellor Cardinal Wolsey ordered his arrest but Philip, Landgrave of Hesse, granted Tyndale his protection. The copies were smuggled into England where they added to the fuel of the developing Protestant movement. Tyndale was finally captured and for torturous sixteen months imprisoned in the castle at Vilvorde near Brussels, and his Bible was banned. Although Thomas Cromwell, Henry's minister tried to intercede for Tyndale, on October 6, 1536, he was burned at the stake. His last words expressed the hope that 'God may open the King's eyes'.

King Henry Tudor (1509-1547) grew up a devout Catholic who attended Mass regularly. He was very intelligent, and a gifted musician and composer. Catharine of Aragon, daughter of King Ferdinand II and Isabella of Spain and Leon, was married to Henry's older brother Arthur. After his death, Henry married the young widow, an act to be frowned at by the church authorities. She was a number of years his senior and had the misfortune of suffering numerous miscarriages, and finally gave birth to a healthy baby girl named Mary. Henry desired a son to carry on the Tudor dynasty. He pointed out the Cardinal Wolsey that his conscience tortured him because of his illegal marriage to Catherine which, according to the Old Testament, Leviticus 20:21, 'forbade marrying the wife of your brother.' He too had grown tired of Catherine, and demanded from Pope Clement VII an annulment of his marriage because he was in love with Anne Boleyn, a young lady in the Queens entourage. Henry desired to marry Anne and hoped that she would give birth to the desired heir. The Pope denied the request to dissolve the marriage.

Holy Roman Emperor Charles V (1519-56) the nephew of Catharine of Aragon, made war with France and in 1525, Francis I, and King of France (1515-47) was taken prisoner at Pavia. In 1527, Imperial catholic and protestant troops captured Rome. Pope Clement VII (the Avignon Pope) became for a short time the Emperor's prisoner, unable and unwilling to resolve Henry's marriage problems.

Cardinal Wolsey who had failed to procure Henry's annulment of marriage, was charged with high treason on ground of his subservience to the authority of the pope. The Cardinal was removed from the court and sent to serve as archbishop in rural communities. His possessions were confiscated and he died of natural causes a few years later.

Thomas Cranmer, a Cambridge theologian, suggested that the universities to exam the validity of the marriage. Henry married Anne Boleyn in January 1533. Cranmer, the new Archbishop of Canterbury, declared the marriage with Catherine annulled, and pronounced Anne Boleyn to be Henry's legal wife but Pope Clement declared the marriage as void and excommunicated the king. The outraged Henry broke up his connection with Rome and declared himself as Protector and Head of the Church of England. The clergy were obliged to acknowledge and sign the recognition forwarded in a statement. Henry closed down the convents and monasteries in 1535 because of the 'abominable living of the canons, monks and nuns'. He did not oppose the Catholic Church but scorned the authority of the pope. The Act of Supremacy issues in November 1534 declared the king and his successors to be the supreme head of the Church of England (Anglicana Ecclesia). Henry was conservative concerning doctrine and reluctant to permission to a new doctrine about his new church, and only slight alterations in worship were made.

The dethroned Queen Catherine did not accept the divorce. She was sent to a convent and died a few years later. Catherine's and Henry's daughter Mary stayed a devout Catholic but Anne Boleyn's daughter Elizabeth, later Queen Elizabeth I of England, was Protestant. Henry and Anne's married life was not a happy one. He grew tired of her hot temper and demands, and in 1536, Henry trumped up charges of incest between Anne and her brother, and Anne was beheaded. Soon afterwards, Henry married Jane Seymour, a lady of the court who died in childbirth. Their son Edward was brought up in the Protestant faith and was strongly influenced by his relative, the Duke of Somerset.

The Matthew Bible of 1537, a conversion of the banned Tyndale Bible, the New Testament and Miles Coverdale's Old Testament were revised in 1539 as the 'Great Bible'. In May 1541, a Royal Proclamation ordered every parish to have a copy of the 'Great Bible'.

Henry married three more times and after his death, his only son was crowned as Edward VI. He was of poor health and died in 1553, and his half-sister Mary Tudor succeeded him. She married King Philip II of Spain, and tried to fulfil her royal obligations well. Queen Mary was a devout Catholic and allowed no compromises. Mary feared a conspiracy, and for a short time sent her Protestant half-sister Elizabeth to the tower. Queen Mary jailed Henry's Archbishop Cranmer who declared that he had wronged, and recanted by repudiating the reformers Zwingli and Luther. Afterwards his conscience tortured him, and overcome by remorse and weeping, he withdrew his recantation. When he was burned at Oxford in 1556, he held his hand into the flames because 'this hand had signed the recantations.' More bishops and distinguished Protestants, including the Queen's godmother Margaret of Salisbury, perished on the stage. Queen Mary, daughter of Catherine of Aragon and Henry VIII, was to be branded as the 'bloody' Mary. She died in 1558, succeeded by her brilliant half-sister Elizabeth who became Queen Elizabeth I of England.

The Church of England's reform was introduced by various leaders. The 'Anglican' (Church of England and Episcopal Church in the United States) finally adopted a halfway between Calvin and Catholic established traditions though changed little concerning the liturgy or the vestments of the officiating priest.

Luther's influence in England was noticeable, and Queen Elizabeth I of England did not lay emphasis on strict interpretations of religious doctrines. Some of the English Calvinists sought to purify the Church of England of customs not directly based on the Bible. They wished the bishops to be replaced by assemblies of the ministers or elders according to the Presbyterian Church of Scotland. The 'Seperatists' who later became the Congregationalists, were even stricter and refused altogether to compromise with the Anglican Church.

The Puritans who did not believe in church authority headed by a pope, left the country and immigrated to the New World. Here they felt free to worship according to their conscience and spiritual needs based on the 'Geneva Bible'. They were later joined by various other European groups of people including the Quakers who wished to live simple, pious and peaceful and in religious freedom in the British colonies of the New World.

Chapter 29

Thomas More

Sir Thomas More (1478-1535) a lawyer, educated at Oxford and London, was the privy councillor of Henry VIII of England. Thomas was befriended with, and follower of John Colet, dean of St. Paul in London. Colet preached in 1512 against the worldliness of the priesthood and stated that they were the servants of men instead of God.

More was a man of many interests such as wildlife, geometry and astronomy. Erasmus introduced him to his humanism and became a lifelong friend. He observed Sir Thomas' fondness of his children and the tenderness toward his wife. Thomas was the author of the book 'Utopia' which described a society not governed by a king but by reason. He described the ideal life exercising freedom of religion and equality. Prosperity should be equally distributed and the population prosperous and free. His gentle criticism focused on the evils of inequalities. He promoted clean towns and restricted manual labour, and education for everyone. King Henry and Sir Thomas were in disagreement concerning the planned annulment of Henry's marriage to Catherine. Cardinal Wolsey had been unable to obtain an annulment of King Henry's marriage to his wife Catherine of Aragon from Pope Clement VII, who was at the present a prisoner of Emperor Charles, and resulted in his dismissal as privy councillor. Sir Thomas was appointed to that post, also opposed the annulment. He also disagreed of the anticlerical legislation of 1529 and supposed that this threatened the foundation of social order.

King Henry declared through an Act of Parliament to be the head of the Church of England, and his servants had to vow allegiance to him. Sir Thomas refused to sign the document because he supported the pope's authority. He retired to his estate and occupied himself by writing against the Protestant movement.

Thomas Cromwell became the appointed court secretary of King Henry. He was instrumental in perusing the king to dissolve the convents and to include the estates to the crown.

The king charged Thomas More with connections of conspiracy. He was accused of denying the royal superiority, and imprisoned in the Tower of London. For fifteen months he suffered but refused to acknowledge Henry as the head of the Church. More' wife and daughter Margaret pleaded with him and begged him to recant but Sir Thomas refused. During the months of interrogation, he wrote on Christ's Passion including "Dialogue of Comfort against Tribulation'. He was tried and convicted and on July 7, 1534, Sir Thomas More, after asking the spectators to pray for him and for the king, was beheaded.

England and Europe were terrified realizing the heartlessness of King Henry, and Erasmus deeply mourned the death of his friend.

Chapter 30

Erasmus of Rotterdam

Desiderius Erasmus of Rotterdam (1469-1517) was born in the Netherlands. He was a prominent Catholic scholar of great knowledge of classical literature and internationally known. Erasmus lost his parents at a young age, and his guardian persuaded him to accept a monastic career. Erasmus wished to attend a university but finally took vows as an Augustinian canon and in 1492 became an ordained priest.

Erasmus studied at the University of Paris where he noticed that the professors emphasized on the lesser aspects of the Christian faith at the expense of the important ones. He agreed with others in the request of reform within the church.

He loved books, and to obtain the money to indulge in his passion, he gave private instructions to students. Erasmus taught himself Greek in which he became very efficient. One of his rich students invited him to a visit to England where he met the young Thomas More who became a cherished friend. He also made the acquaintance of John Colet who professed true Christianity and teaching of the Bible. After his return in 1500, he decided to study and revise the Greek text of the New Testament and a new Latin translation with a commentary as to the true spirit of Christianity that had been concealed by dogma. He presented the revised Greek text parallel to the Latin translation.

Erasmus received some good offers concerning high ranking offices within the church but he turned it down and preferred to by a free lance writer (with limited income). He published some noteworthy writings based on the classical authors that were translated into English, German, French and Italian but the proceedings were meagre. In 1502, Adrian of Utrecht offered him a professorship but Erasmus declined.

In his book 'In Praise of Folly' (1509) he gently attacked the ecclesiastical corruption and luxury which was widespread. He was also critical of the common beliefs that prayers to the saints would be a remedy for toothache and labour pains.

He agreed with Wyclif to translate the scriptures into every language to make it available to the populace. Erasmus also observed the tendency of the common people to plead for help to the Mother of Jesus which, according to him, resulted in distancing and alienation of Jesus and his teachings. In 1517, Luther stepped forward criticizing the church which lead to bitterly opposing religious parties. Erasmus refused to accept the belief that the church must be overthrown. He promoted compromise and reason but the extremist groups attacked his humanist views.

Erasmus advised Luther to be cautious in his attacks on the pope's authority. He declared himself to be Luther's friend which alienated his own friends in high positions. Luther shocked Erasmus by burning Pope Leo X Bull of excommunication. A German prince asked Erasmus to be present at the Diet of Worms where Luther justified his beliefs but Erasmus refused. He was of the opinion that it was too late to intervene. Erasmus regretted Luther's refusal to submit because he believed that it would have helped and strengthened the progress for reform, and he feared civil confrontations and conflict. Erasmus continued to influence the political arena by advising humanly treatment and courtesy in treating others. Always encouraging moderation, he condemned monastic depravity and dogmatism as the most challenging reasons of the Reformation.

In the last years of his life, Erasmus was severely ill. He was still visited by many of his friends who loved and cherished him. He passed away on June 6, 1536 and received a significant funeral at Basel, Switzerland.

Part 6

Part 6

Chapter 31

The Reformers

Huldrych Zwingli

Huldrych Zwingli, the Swiss reformer (1484-1531) was born in the small village of Wildhaus in Switzerland. His father was a magistrate and his mother's brother a priest. He attended a Latin school at Basel and the college at Bern. Later he transferred to the University of Vienna. Huldrych received his master's degree at the age of twenty-two, and became an ordained priest.

Zwingli continued his studies and taught himself Greek to read the New Testament in its original language. He read classical literature like Homer, Plutarch, Cicero and Seneca, with great interest. Zwingli adored Erasmus with whom he kept a lively correspondence, and whom he visited at Basel.

After changing to Einsiedeln and accepting the offered position as his preaching gradually changed to emphasize a religion that was based on the teachings of the Bible. Formerly, the sermon had been short and the Mass and communion dominated the ritual but Zwingli based the service on the sermon and emphasised simplicity of worship. He spoke strongly against the sale of the indulgencies promoted by Pope Leo X, son of Lorenzo the Magnificent, who was the instigator of the Indulgencies, and endorsed the sale in 1517. Anyone who obtained a letter of Indulgence was forgiven of sins committed. The money for obtaining them was used to build St. Peter's Cathedral in Rome.

Luther's writings and Huss's treatise 'On the Church' stirred Zwingli. He publicly attacked the invocation of saints, purgatory and monasticism. No reference in the New Testament mention the avoidance of consuming meat during Lent, and Zwingli told his parishioners to ignore the rule. The Bishop of Constance objected, and Zwingli replied in a book 'Beginning and End' in which he predicted uprising against the Catholic Church. Zwingli summarized his system of belief by stating them in two Latin treatises. He believed in the triune God (Father, Son and Holy Ghost) and the Virgin Birth. Zwingli stated like Luther, that good works alone could not bring salvation but the belief in the redeeming death of Jesus. Grace was a gift of God bestowed on us although we did not deserve it. Luther and Calvin accepted predestination of every event foreseen by Gods will and plan, and to occur as such to which Zwingli agreed. He also affirmed their beliefs that no priest but only God can forgive man's sins. Zwingli insisted that the Lord's Supper was symbolic of the spiritual union between Jesus and the communicant but the bread and wine could not actually become flesh and blood of Jesus.

Zwingli's Reformed Church maintained that the sermon during the remaining year replaced the Lord's Supper. He agreed with Calvin and Luther on the doctrine of predestination, and that no priest but only God can forgive sins.

Not all Swiss Cantons followed Zwingli's teachings, and some of them remained Catholic. By 1524, the Reformation in Switzerland caused a split in the Confederation of Cantons, and five of them, Lucerne, Uri, Schwyz, Unterwalden and Zug, created a Catholic League. The reason was the suppression of Lutheran, Zwinglian and Hussite activities. It came to blows and to destroying a monastery and images in a number of churches. Erasmus, who resided at that time in Basel, was very distressed to see worshippers carried away by rage and anger.

The Swiss Confederation was split up and threatened. Archduke Ferdinand of Austria encouraged the Catholic cantons to unite against Zwingli. The reformed town of Zurich and Zwingli acted in response and sent a dispatch of missionaries to announce the Reformation. In 1529, a Protestant missionary from Zurich tried to preach in the town of Catholic Schwyz, but was seized and burned. The event gave Zwingli the opportunity to declare war. At Kappel, he met with a representative of the League, and they engaged in negotiations. Zwingli finally agreed to the terms and the peace treaty lasted for twenty-eight months. On May 15, 1531, the assembly of Zurich and her allies, voted to compel the Catholic cantons to grant freedom of preaching in their region. The cantons refused, and Zwingli planned war. The cantons declared war as well, and again the armies met at Kappel. The Protestants, outnumbered with only 1500 men fought the 8000 Catholics. Zwingli fought the Catholics with his men and met his death.

Zwingli' successor in Zurich was Heinrich Bullinger, who with Calvin, brought the Genevan and Zurich Protestants together and established the "Reformed Church". The Catholic Church regained its hold in the Catholic cantons while some areas stayed undecided.

Chapter 32

John Knox

Around 1523, the writings of Luther reached Scotland and a translation of Wyclif's New Testament into Scot's dialect circled among the population and enflamed the readers for the Christian values based on the Bible. Patrick Hamilton (1505-1528), a student of Greek philosophy and the writings of Erasmus, travelled to Witttenberg to meet Luther. He returned to Scotland and preached with enthusiasm the new doctrine of the Reformation.

The Archbishop of St. Andrews, Cardinal David Beaton, requested explanations. Patrick Hamilton did not recant his beliefs and was burned in 1534. Several of Hamilton's followers found their death through burning or hanging.

John Knox, born around 1505 near Haddington, went to Glasgow to study for the priesthood and was ordained in 1532. He was brilliant and made a name for himself for his knowledge in canon and civil law. Knox knew and valued George Wishart who had visited Luther in Wittenberg and enthusiastically preached justification by faith. He was instrumental in introducing a more Calvinist teaching into Scotland.

Wishart was invited by James, the uncle of Cardinal David Beaton, to give account of his philosophy, and he stood firm in his belief. The Cardinal had him arrested and charged for heresy. At his order Wishart was strangled and burned in 1546. On Easter, 1547, Knox and a band of men avenged Wishart and killed Cardinal Beaton in the Castle of St.Andrew.

A French fleet sailed up and bombarded the castle and after four weeks, conquered it. Knox and his comrades were seized, and for nineteen months Knox laboured in chains in a French galley.

In February 1549, the captives became free and Knox took the position of a Protestant clergy in England. He served as chaplain to young Edward VI of England but fled to Geneva when Queen Mary Tudor ascended the throne As Queen of England.

John Knox visited Calvin in Geneva. He praised Calvin's influence and teaching and declared that Geneva was truly the place were Christ was present.

Knox was horrified at the rule of the Catholic Mary Stuart in Scotland. After Queen Mary's Tudor's death and the ascension of Elizabeth I as Queen of England, many exiled Scottish Protestants returned home. Knox too, returned and preached at St. Andrews and Perth. He was a fiery puritan of stern disposition and in his blasting writings he equalled Luther.

In 1557, a meeting at Edinburgh signed the "First Scottish Covenant" and called for reformation in government and religion. The meeting passed the decision to establish reformed churches throughout Scotland and to adopt a Book of Common Prayer for the Scot congregation.

In 1560, a Protestant Confession of Faith, written by Knox and his aides, was delivered to the Scottish Parliament which described complains of the Scots against the Catholic Church. The Confession was accepted and the Papal jurisdiction in Scotland banned and outlawed. The Scottish Reformation was the least violent and the most enduring.

Chapter 33

John Calvin

Jean Chauvin, born 1509 in Noyon, France, attended college in Paris. He Latinized his name as Johannes Calvinus. John studied and excelled in Latin, and at the request of his father, took up the study of law. Calvin was a very diligent student, pious and shy, and well liked by his friends. He loved classical literature, and after receiving his Bachelor of Laws in 1531, Calvin published an essay on Seneca's De Clementia. He sent a copy of the essay sent to Erasmus who pleaded for purified Christianity.

Calvin met like-minded men who desired Church reform, and were familiar with Lutheran theology "Salvation through faith and grace". His friend, the chosen rector of the university, Nicholas Cop, escaped arrest for his inaugural address in which he cited Erasmus, Luther, and a plea for tolerance of religious thoughts. His speech created an angry outburst, and Cop fled to Protestant Basel. Calvin and his friends heeded the warnings and left for Basel to meet Cop there as well as other Protestant leaders.

While living in Basel (1536) Calvin published his book in Latin titled "The Institutes of the Christian Religion". The book found an eager audience and became the most significant writing of the Reformation.

Calvin's love for God was deep and sincere, and he felt small in the presence of God. He pondered how man in his insignificance tried to understand God's Majesty, and declared the Bible to be the absolute last word. Calvin believed that man must devote himself to doing good deeds but still it would not earn him deliverance. The sacrificial death of Christ was the only means of salvation for man. He concluded that everything, including the fall of Adam and Eve, was preordained, and predestination was the plan of God for man. God knew the destiny of man because He created it. Like Augustine, Calvin spoke of the 'elect', the chosen ones from the beginning of time to be the faithful children of God. In Matt. 24:24, the disciple speaks of 'the very elect' Luke 18:7 speaks of 'the elect' also, and so does Paul in his various letters.

Predestination assumes that some people be elected to eternal salvation. Calvin declared that such individuals do not love the world though they are here to live their lives. Divine grace chose and saved them. The doctrine opens up many worrisome questions like 'did Jesus die for the 'elect' only? Did he not state that anyone who believed in him and followed his teaching has eternal life?

Luther opposed Calvin's ideas as too extreme. Calvin desired the religious service to be humble and plain. Christ is in the Holy Communion present but only in spirit, and the wafer and wine are symbols. He considered the veneration of idols as infringement of the second commandment: "Thou shalt not have other Gods before me". Calvin accepted only two of the sacraments, the baptism and the Lord's Supper, and church attendance was compulsory.

The Protestant movement grew members in France, and on October 18, 1534, ardent Lutheran admirers decorated the walls in Paris and Orleans with anti-Catholic slogans The enraged King Francis I led a procession to the cathedral to pray for redemption of the 'Lutheran poison'. Calvin, who had returned to France, left, and fled to Switzerland. After a short stay in Strasbourg, Calvin settled down in Geneva in 1536.

Geneva was in the state of change caused by the fierce preacher and reformer Gulliaume Farel. After meeting the sombre and stern Calvin, Farel decided that he was the right man to go forward with the reform. Calvin was unwilling to accept the challenge because his planes were those of writing and study but he finally accepted. He gave at the church of St. Peter several addresses on the Letters of Paul.

The Genevese were merry people, and the senior and junior ministers of St. Peter (Farel and Calvin) discovered to their dismay that the people loved a good time. They cherished dancing, singing, and worse, gambling, and intoxication. The two pastors decided to rededicate Geneva to God.

Farel released the 'Constitution of Faith and Discipline', and Calvin a Catechism. The writings found approval by the Great Council in November 1536. Anyone who continuously ignored the code faced excommunication, and expatriation.

The Genevese opposed Calvin's new orders and tried to rid themselves of their two overzealous pastors who did not appreciate their light-hearted lifestyle. Calvin recommended a way of life based on the Bible, shared by husband and wife who lived a mutual and orderly life He encouraged pastors to marry and raise a family in the biblical tradition, and compared his ideal with some Catholic priests who had concubines and children. Calvin married, and when his wife died several years later, he praised her for her fine qualities.

Calvin's restrictions were too severe because it uncompromisingly affected the population in every aspect of their lives. They protested against the joylessness of life his strict discipline created by denying the most harmless pleasures. Calvin's standard of establishing a theocratic regime lead to dictatorship. His ideas of discipline created intrusion into the private lives of the parishioners who did not tolerate such. Farel and Calvin, who faced banishment from Geneva, left for Strasbourg.

The population of Geneva returned to their old way of life: gambling and intoxication. The four syndics that had been instrumental of expelling Farel and Calvin were men who had created trouble and were blamed for disorderly conduct. In due time, they were arrested and sentenced for various crimes. On May 1, 1541, the Council reinstated the two reformers with honours. Calvin was reluctant to return to Geneva because he had made many friends in Strasbourg. He finally agreed to pay a visit, and arrived in September 1541 in Geneva. Calvin received a splendid reception, and many of the former enemies apologized and promised cooperation, and he finally agreed to stay.

Calvin reorganized the Reformed Church by establishing the Small Council to develop a new ecclesialistic code. The Great Council approved on January 2, 1542, the Ordinances ecclesiastiques. The basic characteristics are still acknowledged by the Presbyterian and Reformed Churches of Europe and America. Calvin agreed with Luther's doctrine of election by faith. Calvin supported Zwingli's belief that the bread and wine served during the Eucharist was spiritually changed into the Body and Blood of Christ. He insisted that the laws of a Christian state must be based on the Bible. Calvin tried to regulate the lives of the Genevese into hard-working and sober citizens, but he also seemed to realize that he imposed a joyless life on them, and encouraged them to enjoy harmless pleasures and games. One critique praised the life of the city of Geneva for the morality of the inhabitants, their helpfulness and charity.

The differences between Catholics and Protestants were unbridgeable. Calvin insisted that the Catholic Church possessed very few Christian traces while Catholics believed that salvation outside of the Catholic Church was impossible.

Calvin and the brilliant physician Michael Servetus corresponded with each other. Servetus was a disillusioned Catholic and studied the scriptures in Greek and Hebrew. He did not accept the concept of the Trinity. In a mistaken belief of seeing in Calvin a kindred spirit he sent his manuscript 'Christianismi Restitutio' to him. Calvin thanked him for the transcript. Servetus expressed the wish to met Calvin.

Servetus "Christianism restitution" a very controversial manuscript rejecting predestination concepts, was printed in Vienna. Calvin in turn sent him a copy of his "Institutes". Servetus returned the copy with insulting comments and disdainful letters. The matter came to the attention of the inquisitor Matthieu Ory at Lyons who checked out the case. Calvin supplied him with Servetus' handwriting and letters as evidence. Servetus was arrested and Ory interrogated him at Lyons. Servetus managed to escape from prison and received in his absence the death sentence issued on August 6, 1553. He walked to Geneva and tried to cross the lake to reach Zurich where he felt safer among the Zwinglians. Since there was no boat available until Monday, he attended the church service in Geneva which was compulsory. Servetus was recognized and arrested.

The trial lasted from August 14 to October 26. There was little hope for continued existence, and Calvin described him as 'monster' His greatest crime consisted in his denial of the Trinity. Servetus insisted in his writings that the application of force was erroneous even in protecting and defending Christianity. The final sentence condemned him to be burned alive. The sentence was carried out on October 27, 1553. As Servetus walked to his death, he prayed that God would forgive his judges. Calvin preferred beheading but did not show too much compassion for his victim. He complained rather that such unfortunate and miserable beings caused him much pain and agony. He would have preferred that they lived prosperous and contended lives Calvin delivered his last sermon on February 6, 1564. He was a dying man and thanked God for having been able to preach the doctrine of salvation. He died on May 27, 1564.

Chapter 34

The Huguenots

French Calvinist Protestants were known as Huguenots, and made gains in the south and west of France. Lutheran teaching reached France and found fertile soil.

Jacques Lefevre, who taught at the University of Paris, published in 1512 a translation of Paul's Epistles. He added a commentary that emphasized that not through good works but only through the grace of God and the supreme sacrifice of Jesus one could find redemption. He added that through Christ's presence during the Eucharist the transubstantiation of bread and wine took place. Lefevre agreed with Luther to return to the Gospel. He and Erasmus shared the same wish to reinstate and elucidate the New Testament from the myths and other additions. In 1523, he issued a French translation of the Psalms and the New Testament. In one of his comments he criticized the clergy for their worldly habits of drinking, hunting and gambling.

The Sorbonne declared him a heretic, and Lefevre fled in 1525 to Strasbourg. The high-spirited Queen Marguerite of Navarre, sister of King Francis I and protector of the Protestants, interceded, and Francis appointed him as his royal librarian at Bois. Lefevre became tutor of the king's children. He stayed at Marguerite's court until his death in 1537.

King Francis I tolerated the Lutheran teachings as long as it did not interfere with his regime or caused disturbances. He did not wish to have the Peasant's War in his own country as it had happened in Germany.

The Calvinist teaching spread across the border from Geneva into France. Some people went in 1559 to Geneva to obtain Bibles and Calvin's writings. At the same time, they inquired about a pastor, and decided on a man named Geoffrey Brun who was brought under the cover of night to Castres (Languedoc) and to stay with a family. The congregation grew fast and nightly meetings were held in barns and private homes protected by men bearing arms. In 1562, approximately seven thousand Huguenots met in the market square at Rouen to sing and listening to a preacher.

The duke of Guise and his revenue stopped at a monastery to attend Mass. During the ensuing scuffle, forty eight Huguenots were killed. The news of it sparked violence in Toulouse and resulted in the slaughter of three thousand Huguenots who revenged themselves by attacking and destroying statues and glass windows of various Catholic churches. In 1556, Pope Paul IV (1555-1559) persecuted Jews and Protestants and decreed that Jews must wear yellow patches to mark them as of the Jewish faith. On both sides were religious fanatics, and the mob was uncontrollable. A Huguenot murdered the Duke of Guise, and Queen Catherine de Medici plotted a massacre against the Huguenots. On the eve of St. Bartholomew Day, August 23, 1572, two days after the attempted assassination of the political leader of the Huguenots, Admiral Gaspard de Coligny, about ten thousand Protestants murdered. The slaughter spread through Paris and expanded to other urban areas and the country side.

The French throne was weakened. The crown was passed on to the boy King Charles IX in 1560 who was the ten-year old son of Catherine de Medici. Under the pretend of religion, two powerful parties, Francis, Duke of Guise and his brother, Cardinal Charles of Guise, opposed the Calvinist Huguenots led by the king of Navarre, Antoine de Bourbon. The conflict created severe political tensions. Catherine's third son took the throne in 1574 as Henry III. He allied himself with Guise but turned on him by having him assassinated in 1588. Henry was murdered by a Catholic monk who was incensed by Henry's deceit.

In 1593, Henry of Navarre, who was heir to the throne and a Protestant, renounced his belief and became Catholic. The Catholic priesthood refused to anoint him as king until Henry pledged to forsake heresy and live as a devout Catholic. He was crowned at Chartres as King Henry IV of France. The Catholic Church was recognized as the established Church of France but the Protestant faith survived. In the Edict of Nantes in 1598, Henry, not forgetting his Protestant roots, granted the Protestants liberty. They were allowed to establish their own schools, and all offices were open to them.

The Princess Renee d'Este of Ferrara, daughter of Louis XII, was a fervent Protestant. She had been strongly influenced by Queen Marguerite of Navarre and by her governess Mme. Soubise. Calvin visited the princess in 1536. She and her husband Ercole d'Este, received Protestant guests at their home. Calvin visited Renee and her husband in their home. King Henry IV of France died in 1610 of being fatally stabbed by a Catholic fanatic, Francois Ravaillac. The Edict was honoured until 1685, when Louis XIV revoked it, and thousands of Protestants were persecuted and some Protestants converted to Catholicism. Many refused conversion and fled to England, Geneva, Prussia (Germany) and the Netherlands, or sought a new home in America and South Africa.

Chapter 35

The Anabaptists

A new sect calling themselves Anabaptist (baptized again) developed in Switzerland around 1534. The members insisted that infant baptism should be repeated as the mature individual was able to make the choice. The sect split because some of them denied Christ's divinity and declared that Jesus redeemed not through his sacrificial death but through his exemplary life.

The Anabaptists emphasized on orderly conduct and simplicity in attire. Forceful government service like joining the military, and killing a human life was considered as sinful, and rejected. They disagreed with reformers like Zwingli, Know, Calvin and Luther by preaching religious tolerance. Anabaptists waited for Jesus to return while they were living.

The movement made headway in southern Germany. The city of Augsburg, lead by Hubmaier and Denck found listeners among the lower classes. Holy Roman Emperor Charles V learned about and decreed that re-baptism was to be punished as capital crime. At the Diet of Speyer (south-western Germany) the Emperor's proclamation ordered the Anabaptists to be killed without trial. By 1530, two thousand Anabaptists had found their death. In spite of the killings, the sect enlarged and gained new members in northern and western Germany.

Under the leadership of Hans Hut, the Anabaptists established a communal centre at Austerlitz (where Napoleon fought the famous battle in 1805). They occupied themselves with farming and small industries. The landed aristocracy supported them because they rendered cheap labour. The Anabaptists lived as a commune with one kitchen, a school, common laundry and a brewery besides a hospital. The children were brought up within the commune but monogamy was upheld.

Melchior Hofman, a German, preached the Anabaptist Gospel in the Netherlands with great success. One of his pupils was Jan Beuckelszoon or more commonly referred to as Jan van Leyden (immortalized in Meyerbeer's opera 'The Prophet'). He was familiar with the writings of the German reformer Thomas Munzer, a former priest and admirer of Luther, and propagator of the theory of 'the elect'. Munzer was not too well received and frequently expelled from the various towns were he preached. He was beheaded on May 27, 1525 after recanting his preaching's and writings.

The Peasants War started in 1525 after some demonstrations in various parts of Germany (1432) and Scandinavia (1434). The peasants revolted against being forced into serfdom. In 1517, peasants banded together to attack castles, kill the lords and destroy their manors.

Jan van Leyden received an invitation from the Anabaptist Jan Matthys to preach in the rich city of Munster in Westphalia. He entered the city on January 13, 1534. The city was subject to the Bishop Franz von Waldeck but had gained prosperity through commerce and industry. Its citizens were represented through the various guilds which were chosen by the city council. Jan van Leyden and the cloth merchant Knipperdollinck roamed the streets of Munster and called on its inhabitants to repent their sins. The city was in an uproar because of the proclamation that the sinful world would be destroyed very soon. The Lutherans and Catholics, frightened as they were, submitted themselves to re-baptism. The bishop of Munster responded to the upheaval with arms and fortified the city with hired mercenaries. The Anabaptists, men and women, who lived in the district, were burned, beheaded or drowned.

Matthys found a violent death when he ventured out one morning. Jan van Leyden entered into an ecstasy that lasted three days. After recovering, he told that God had made known to him that the city must be modelled after ancient Israel. He was to serve as absolute prophet and appoint twelve elders beneath him. The population was known as of Israel. Meals were consumed communally, and Knipperdollinck was chosen as sword bearer. Leyden approved of polygamy, and was married to three women. He continued to marry until he had fifteen wives and encouraged his flock to follow his example.

One man named Dusentschur declared that God had granted him the revelation that Leyden was chosen to become king and inherit the throne of his father David. Leyden was in due course anointed King of New Jerusalem with all the necessary pageantry.

The spreading heresy deeply disturbed the rulers of the Rhineland. At a meeting in Koblenz, they agreed to support and supply the bishop of Munster with money and manpower. When Easter of 1535 arrived, the beleaguered city of Munster was hopelessly surrounded. Hunger raged and people died. Some of them fled the city but did not find a friendly welcome from the bishop's men. During the night of June 24, 1535, the bishop's men stormed the city, and the defenders were beaten. Many of the Anabaptists tried to flee but were killed during the following days. Three of the captured men were kept alive: the king, his friend Knipperdollinck and another man. Both of them refused to see a priest and were executed. Leyden agreed to confess his sins and he stated that he deserved execution. He refused to accept errors concerning the teachings of baptism and the nature of Jesus. The prisoner commended his spirit into God's hands and kept silent as he was tortured to death.

Anabaptists divided into two groups, the Baptists and the Mennonites. Both groups immigrated later to the United States and Canada.

One group, whose leader was Menno Simons (1496-1561) founded a sect what was similar to the ideals of the Anabaptists. The followers called themselves 'Mennonites' and settled in Poland, Hungary, Russia and North America. In England, members founded the Baptist Church.

Chapter 36

Martin Luther - A Mighty Fortress Is Our God

The Augustinian monk Martin Luther (1483-1517) ignited the Protestant Reformation that was long stirring and brewing.

Martin Luther was born on November 10, 1483, at Eisleben in Saxony, to Hans and Margarete Luther. His stern father believed in severe physical punishment, and his timid mother followed the example of her husband in harshly punishing the boy for small misdemeanours. They believed in superstition and demons of many kinds. The joyless childhood and severe discipline at home shaped his character. When Martin grew older, the father realized that his son was of exceptional intelligence, and sent him to the Latin school at Mansfeld. After changing school twice, Luther entered in 1501 the University of Erfurt who was at that time one of the best universities in Germany. In 1505 he received his master of arts. His father wanted him to pursue the study of law but to his dismay, Martin decided to become a monk One day while returning from Erfurt to Mansfeld, Luther was knocked down to the ground by a lightning bolt. The shocked young man, always fearful of God's judgement, vowed to become a monk.

The young Luther perceived God as angry and punishing mankind according to the teachings of the Old Testament and Jesus as the figure of the Last Judgement. Luther saw himself as a sinner condemned to hell and punishment. He suffered from depression and anxieties regarding his salvation, and felt that his refuge lay in the quietness and safety of a monastery where he would live a life of discipline and devotion. In 1505, Luther entered the monastery of the Augustinian Eremites in Erfurt. He was a devoted and ascetic monk performing the lowest duties with humility, praying and fasting, and closely observed the monastery rules. His mentor, Johann von Staubitz, noticed that the novice was troubled and advised him to read the Bible and the writings of St. Augustine. The writings of the German mystic Johannes Tauler (1290-1361) assured him of overcoming the gulf of man's sinful nature and

God's supremacy. Luther admired Tauler and Meister Eckhart. He came across a treatise of Jan Hus and wondered why such a Christian man had been condemned and burned.

Luther received his ordination as priest in September 1507 and continued to study advanced theological literature. He received his doctorate in theology from the University of Wittenberg in 1512, where he taught biblical theology. One day, while studying the Bible, he came across a line in Paul's Epistle to the Romans (1:17) "The just shall live by faith." Luther pondered the words and it guided him to the doctrine that man can become just and be saved from hell. He believed that good works (and sacraments) alone not suffice to atone for sins but only by reading the Scriptures, live a humble life devoted to the loving surrender to Christ and his supreme sacrifice for mankind.

Luther underwent a slow change in outlook. The morality of the clergy in high offices as well as among monks declined to shameful lows. The common people developed contempt and hatred for the corrupted and gambling monks and their equally degraded high church authorities. Humanists like Erasmus, More and Colet feared a break within the church which remind them of the split between the Roman Catholic and Greek Orthodox Church. Some popes and members of the clergy were distraught about the decay within the church and attempted to bring a change about but were defeated by the cardinals. Rome exercised a relentless power.

Luther complained that the clergy diverted from the Bible by telling the populace too many fables. He discovered an old manuscript that supported his ideas of total dependence of the soul on divine grace and published the edited version as Theologica Germanica (German Theology). A few months later he challenged the world with his ninety-five theses that he had nailed on October 31, 1517 on the Wittenberg Church door. The theses circulated and were widely read and applaud.

Luther's conflict with the church was ignited by the sale of the Indulgencies by the Dominican friar Johann Tetzel. To obtain one paid for the remission of sins of the past and future, and was granted by the Pope Leo X son of Lorenzo the Magnificent, the instigator of the Indulgencies. He promoted their sale in 1517 to rebuild the Cathedral of St Peter with the obtained collections. Luther was deeply troubled by such false claims that affected ordinary people's salvation, and he vigorously attacked the sale of it. Half of the earnings went to Albert, the Archbishop of Mainz who was deeply in debts. Money was sent to Italy and those dealings unsettled the German population. Pope Leo X was unruffled. He regarded the disputes as arguments between the Dominicans and Augustinians, and referred to the disgruntled people as to deal with Luther. The pope did not foresee the grave consequences that followed Luther's protest nor did Luther attempt to break with the church. He voiced his disapproval with events that took place within the church. In 1520, Pope Leo X condemned in a bull forty –one of the statements made by Luther. He ordered the public burnings of the books in which the statements had appeared, and urged Luther to renounce his errors. Luther refused to appear before the pope and make a public recantation. Frederick the Wise, the Elector of Saxony, and Emperor Charles V discussed with Erasmus the ensuing conflict and encouraged the authorities to give Luther a chance of defending his writings.

In June 1520, Pope LeoX issued a writing which condemned forty-one statements of Luther's writings and ordered them to be publicly burned. He was encouraged to abjure his mistakes or to be cut off from Christendom. Luther responded with more writings, and in September, Dr Johann Eck of Ingolstadt and Jerome Alexander promulgated the bull of excommunication in Germany. Luther responded with a manifesto titled 'The Babylonian Captivity of the Church emphasising the one thousand year captivity under the papacy of Rome.

At the Diet (legislative assembly) at Worms in Spring 1521, presided by Emperor Charles V and Girolamo Alesandro as the representative of Pope Leo X, Luther refused to recant his writings and assault on the pope.

Luther, still wearing his Augustinian monastic garb, arrived on April 17, 1521, at Worms. The Emperor Charles V, archbishops, bishops and the nobility gathered in the palace when Luther entered the hall. The pope's envoy, Girolamo Alesandro, opened the examination.. Johann Eck, an official of the archbishop pf Trier pointed at the books before him and asked Luther if he had written them. After reading the titles, Luther confirmed them as his writings.

The examination continued on the following day. Luther pointed out that he had attacked only those who had harmed Christendom, body and soul. "I dispute not for my life but for the doctrine of Christ. My conscience is submissive to God's word. Therefore, I cannot and will not recant. To act against my conscience is unholy. Here I stand. God help me. Amen".

As outcome, the church excommunicated him. His friend, the Elector Frederick, staged a kidnapping and concealed Luther at his Wartburg castle near Eisenach in Thuringia as 'Junker Jorg', where Luther translated the New Testament from the Greek into the German language The first printings were done with movable type were the Indulgences printed in 1445 by Johannes Gutenberg in Mainz. The invention helped to spread the writings of Luther, and permitted the translation of Luther's New Testament into German in 1521 (the Greek text edited by Erasmus with a Latin account in 1516) and published in 1522 to become available. Luther translated the Old Testament twelve years later with the assistance of Philip Melanchthon (1497-1560) who used the Greek translation of his German name, and some Jewish scholars.

Philip (Schwarzert) Melanchthon was a brilliant theologian and humanist who had been appointed in 1518 by the Elector of Saxony to teach Greek at the University of Wittenberg. He was a distant relative of Johann Reuchlin. Philip Melanchthon was soft-spoken and loved by the students who crowded his lecture room. He was broad-spirited and inclined to science due to his studies in astronomy, physics, mathematics and medicine. Erasmus praised him for his gentle nature. Melanchthon who loved peace was overwhelmed by the dynamic character of Luther who was a fighter. Nevertheless, the two became friends though Melanchthon tried in vain to soften Luther's sharp and harsh pen. .

The Emperor Charles V and Luther's opponents saw in Luther's teachings a threat to the empirical control of his German lands. The Emperors possessions stretched from Hungary to Spain, and he allied with the Catholic prelates, the pope and loyal German princes.

One of the hotly disputed topics was the transubstantiation (the physical body of Jesus being offered as bread and wine during the Holy Eucharist and consubstantiation (Jesus spiritually present in the offered bread and wine) during the Holy Eucharist (or Last Supper). According to Wyclif, Zwingly and Calvin, Christ appeared spiritually and substantially during the Holy Eucharist by consubstantiation and not by transubstantiation. Luther and the theologians were of different opinions. Zwingli and Calvin insisted that the bread and wine had a spiritual significance.

Luther's conception of God was based on the Old Testament seeing God as the punisher and Christ as the final adjudicator. He believed in the existence of hell and heaven and its angels. Luther was very superstitious and firmly believed in evil spirits living in the woods and in the wilderness. Man himself was wicked by nature and prone to the temptations of the ever present devil.

His doctrine of 'Salvation through faith' became the cornerstone of the Lutheran Church. Other leaders of the Protestant faith followed and established their distinctive worships but similar doctrines. At the Catholic Church as well as the Episcopal Church, the Mass is the centre of worship. In comparison, the service at a Protestant Church is more austere. It emphasizes on the teachings of the scriptures chosen from the Bible, and on the observation of the Last Supper commemorated at specific Sundays. The architecture and interior of the churches are less decorative and nearly without pictures.

Luther married Katharine von Boa, a former nun of minor aristocracy. He loved his 'Kathie' and they raised five children. Luther encouraged marriage because it was the natural impulse of a man to have a wife and family.

The Peasant rebellion against their masters, the aristocratic landowners, dragged on for many years. It started in 1359 in the city of Bruges, spread to Florence in 1378 and the starving peasants in southern France engaged in warfare against nobles and clergy. They revolted in England in 1450 bringing their grievances to Henry VI and

169

his court. The Archbishop of Canterbury and the Bishop of Worchester listened and granted some of the demands.

During the years of 1520 most of the princes in northern Germany adopted Lutheranism. The peasants in Germany stated their just grievances in various pamphlets and encouraged their fellow men to rise against their superiors, princes and priests. They hoped that the new belief would help to solve their problems and grievances. In 1525, they revolted and there was widespread plundering and burning of castles and monasteries in the hope to end the feudal system. The most noted rebels leading the peasants were Florian Geyer, Munzer, and Gotz von Berlichingen (J.W. von Goethe immortalized him in his play 'Gotz von Berlichingen). Luther issued a pamphlet in May 1525 in which he turned sharply against the plundering and killing peasants, and startled with his writing the aristocracy as well as the pillaging peasants. He feared that through the excessive violence government and law may be overturned.

The uprisings in the various German provinces were crushed, the rebels tortured and executed. The revolt in Austria continued a year longer and in 1526 was brought to an end. The losses of property and lives in Germany were high, and were exceeded only by the Thirty Years War. The peasant's uprising had hurt the Reformation and its cause, and Luther himself became unpopular.

Melanchthon and Luther had hoped that the revenues of church properties would be devoted to establishing new schools to replace the closed monasteries. The enrolment into the universities had reached the lowest level possible. Luther issued an Epistle to the Burgomasters (mayors of towns) in which he appealed to the authorities to establish schools He proposed that the elementary education should be made compulsory and at community expense. Melanchthon devoted himself to the task of revitalize education, and under his guidance many schools were opened. He advised a plan for organizing universities and schools and devoted himself to write textbooks of Greek and Latin grammar.

At the Diet (legislative assembly) at Augsburg on June 20, 1530, under the presidency of Emperor Charles V, and the assembly, Christian Bayer read Melanchthon's "Augsburg Confession" which with some changes was to become the creed of the Lutheran churches. It stated Luther's doctrines on salvation by faith, the priesthood of the believers, and the authority of the Bible. Melanchthon had prepared the statement and tactfully tried to soften the differences between the Catholic and Lutheran views and pointed out the various differences between the two concepts, especially the disputed differences of transubstantiation and consubstantiation. He separated Lutheran from the Zwinglian reform, and alleviated the doctrines of consubstantiation, predestination and justification by faith. The reply of the Catholics was uncompromising and inflexible, and the assembly refused to accept it until it had been revised. The new Catholic report insisted on transubstantiation, the prayer to saints, the seven sacraments, and celibacy of the clerics, the Latin Mass and communion in bread only (wine to be omitted for parishioners).

Emperor Charles accepted the new Refutation and stated that the Protestants must accept it as such. A party of Catholics entered into discussions with Melanchthon and he made other concessions like fasts, and confessions It caused more disagreements among the Protestants, and the Emperor gave them six months time (until April 15, 1531) to regulate themselves to the will of the Diet. Emperor Charles had imminent worries to address namely the involvement with Suleiman and his advancing Turks. In 1531, Charles suspended the Augsburg decree and asked for Protestant aid against the Turks. The princes and Luther responded, and in July 1532 the Catholics and Protestants signed the Peace of Nuremberg. When Suleiman faced a large army of Catholic and Protestant Germans, Italians and Spaniards, he returned back to Constantinople.

The Protestant cause gained strength and acceptance and in 1540 Pope Paul III encouraged Charles to invite the Catholics and Protestant leaders to get together. The meeting was held in Worms and the debate between Dr. Johann Eck and Melanchthon cautiously accepting the position recognized at the Augsburg confession. Emperor Charles was encouraged and summoned the two groups to further discussions at Regensburg. Between April 5, and May 22, 1541, Melanchthon, Charles and the delegate of the pope, Gasparo Contarini, finally worked out the issues of permitting marriage of the Protestant clergy, and communion of wine and bread. The parties were unable to agree on the issues of transubstantiation and the dominance of the popes.

The new church grew, and Luther suggested to call the movement' Evangelical'. The service as constituted by Melanchthon was approved by Luther who wrote the "Kleine Kathechismus" which incorporated the Ten Commandments and the Apostles Creed. The Divine Service included candles and vestments, and Mass was partly in German. The prayers to saints or the Virgin were dismissed, and the main service was dedicated to the sermon. Paintings and statues were omitted. Music and song became one of the pleasant additions to the church service. Luther, who loved music, wrote various songs and composed the music.

Luther's intolerance was reflected in his pamphlet "Concerning the Jews and their Lies" written in 1542. In his writing, he raged against them for not accepting Jesus and declared that God hated them. He accused the Jews of poisoning wells and murdering Christian children, and went so far as to incite violence against Jews, their lives and property. The anti-Semitism uttered by Luther influenced the Electors of Brandenburg and Saxony to expel the Jews living in their territory.

Luther had not directly participated in the conferences. He was affected with various health problems and his sufferings made him even more intolerant. He emphasized on the state and its power to rule. The later years of life did not soften his outlook on the pope, and his furious writing 'Against the Papacy' (1545) shocked even his most devoted friends.

In January 1545, during wintry and cold weather, Luther went to Eisleben where he was born, to settle an argument. During February, he fell ill and weakened fast. His friends realized that he was dying and after declaring his faith in Christ, he died on February 18, 1546.

Luther's aim had not been a rebellion against the church but against its corruption, its worldliness and the abuse of the uneducated and poor adherents as it was demonstrated by the sale of the Indulgencies. In his outlook were church and state one unit, and therefore he opposed the Peasant's war by pointing out that the people owed loyalty to their ruling princes.

Between February 5 and September 25, 1555, negotiations ended the religious war in Germany. The Peace at Augsburg recognized the Lutheran states. The Protestants gained the freedom to practice their faith in all of Germany. Catholic worship was banned in Lutheran areas. The aristocratic landowners chose between Catholicism or Lutheranism and their subjects were to accept the religion of their rulers as their own. Toleration for each other had been lost The Peace of Augsburg broke all facade of religious unity in Germany. The princes were now the absolute heads of their church in their region and possessed the right to appoint the clergy. The state ruled the Church.

Philip Melanchthon died in 1560, five years after the Peace of Augsburg. He had tried very much to soften the hard blows dealt by the rough fist of Luther but the cause, the Reformation, needed a forceful man like Luther. Melanchthon stood for moderation, and although supporting Luther's doctrine, tried to deliver his ideas in a more acceptable and moderate language. Martin Luther had been the driving force, the spirit of the Reformation while his faithful and gentle friend blessed it with his benevolent strength.

Chapter 37

The Jesuits

Don Inigo de Onez y Loyola (1491-1556) had been born at the castle of Loyola (Basque) and of noble decent. The family belonged to the upper Spanish nobility, and destined him to become a soldier. Loyola received only a rudimentary education.

He was knighted and engaged in war between the French and the Spaniards, and injured in 1521. During his painful and slow convalescence he read 'Life of Christ' by Ludolfu, and the lives of the saints. Both books touched him deeply, and he resolved to become a soldier of Christ and Mary.

Loyola practiced ascetic exercises almost to the point of death. He gained spiritual strength through visions and premeditated his Spiritual Exercises of contemplation, prayer and penance by which the body could be restrained to gain self-control. He finally decided that he was purged and ready to visit the sacred shrines at the Holy Land.

He sailed from Barcelona in 1523. Jerusalem was in the hands of the Turks who allowed the Christians to visit the holy shrines but not to convert Turks to Christianity. Loyola could not resist the temptation, and the Franciscan local, who was placed by the pope for peace's sake, bade him to leave.

After returning to Barcelona in 1524, Loyola began to study Latin, philosophy and theology, and tried to teach. His teaching got him in trouble with the Inquisition that jailed him but released him after he convinced them of his beliefs.

Loyola went to Paris where he begged in the streets for tuition and food. He entered the College de Montaigue, and his concentrated and absorbed study earned him the respect of the students whom he introduced in his spiritual exercises

Loyola found nine students to accept the call to livelong devotion to Christ. They took the vows of chastity and poverty and later included the vow of obedience. Loyola expected them to accept military discipline, and he called his little band the "Soldiers of Jesus." He planned to go with his students to the Holy Land, and to live as much as possible the life of Christ It was difficult to materialize the plan because Venice was in war with Turkey and passage was impossible.

Loyola and his 'Soldiers of Jesus' arrived at Rome and worked at the Spanish hospital tending the sick. In 1538, Pope Paul III received Loyola and his disciples, and was impressed by their wish to go to Palestine. He encouraged Loyola in his aspirations who felt that he was led to serve God. A forth vow was taken to serve the Pope as God's representative on Earth, and accept any command the Pope ask to do. On September 27, 1540, the Pope established the Society of Jesus, and a year later, Loyola was nominated general. Though highest in rank, he did not reject to perform the most humble and menial duties He made Rome his home and permanently headquarters. New members were required to pass through two years as novitiates under strict discipline and submission. After completing the degree of novitiate, the member entered the 'second class' being lay brother. Some members who aspired the priesthood studied theology and philosophy to become school –and college teachers. After two more classes passing further tests, the aspirants would finally rise as 'professed priests' and accepts missions assigned by the Pope. All of them were requested to eat moderately and keep body and mind fit. Loyola himself gave a living example of his demands on others. Ignatius Loyola died in 1556 as one of the most influential and remarkable man of the century.

At Loyola's death, the society counted about a thousand members of whom thirty-five were 'professed.' The Jesuits went abroad to spread Christianity among the poor. In Europe, they established orphanages and educated without charge. Schools were opened and Jesuit colleges sprang up and scattered from Mexico and Brazil into Africa, Japan and India. The curriculum included philosophy, meditation, prayer and religious belief.

The Jesuits emphasis of education, diplomacy and discipline helped to re-establish the Catholic Church in Poland, Germany, Bohemia and Hungary. They were highly respected, influential, and recognized as the most brilliant creation of the Catholic Reform.

Part 7

Part 7

Chapter 38

The Counterreformation

Some of Luther's writings reached Milan in 1519. Cardinal Caraffa (later Pope Paul IV) informed Pope Clement VII that the Venetians did not observe the confessions or the fasts, and religion was not much practiced. The Lutheran doctrine was in fact widespread, and in 1535 around 30,000 adherents to Luther were reported.

Pope Clement VII (1523-1534) was among the most humane and generous popes. He was open-minded but not a good administrator. He defended the Jews and abstained from the greed that surrounded him. His successor, Pope Paul III, elected in 1534 was a true man of the Renaissance. He loved the time he was born into and promoted new buildings to beautify Rome. He supported and financed artists like Michelangelo and Titian. Paul participated in splendid receptions and received musicians, singers and dancers. He experienced difficulties understanding the Reformation, and after two unsuccessful attempts to reach a meeting with the Catholic and Protestant leaders, he sent Cardinal Gasparo Contarini to Ratisborn (Regensburg, southern Germany) to call for a conference.

The assembly admired the Cardinal Contarini's patience with which he directed the disputes between the Catholics Dr.Eck, Gropper and Pflug and the Protestant leaders Melanchthon, Pistorius and Bucer. The meeting reached agreements on free will, baptism, original sin, holy Orders and confirmation. The one concession could not be made namely that of the Eucharist. The Protestants insisted on transubstantiation (spiritual presence of Christ) while the Catholic viewed the transformation of bread and wine into the body and blood of Christ as the centre of the worship. The pope was displeased with the outcome but he was steeply involved with the political scene of Germany ruled by Charles V, Francis I, and the Papal States. He feared that a strengthened Germany under the rule of Emperor Charles V, being reconciled with the Lutherans and Protestants, may end the power of the papal Rome.

Chapter 39

The Council at Trent

Pope Paul III called the Council at Trent, a town south of the Brenner Pass in the Alps. It was held on December 13, 1545. Paul was nearly eighty years old and stayed in Rome but was represented by three of his cardinals. The traditional doctrine was examined and compared with Protestant criticism covering the major areas. The council scrutinized in the light of Protestant criticism all mayor areas of teachings like justification by faith, transubstantiation, the seven sacraments, existence of purgatory, celibacy, and the legality of the indulgencies. The Latin Vulgate was affirmed as to be sacred and canonical. The power of the pope was affirmed and his authority confirmed.

The Council was held under the guidance of various delegations of the popes, and lasted until 1563. Internal reforms within the Catholic Church continued.

Pope Paul IV (1555-1559) a man of strong will and high temper showed little tolerance for Ignatius Loyola's Jesuits and mistrusted them. He equally disliked that a Catholic monarch agreed with the Peace of Augsburg signed in 1555 and recognizing the Lutheran states. In 1556, he decreed that Jews living in Rome must wear yellow hats. They were confined to live in a crowded walled section of Rome which was often flooded by the river, and had only one single exit. The ghetto existed until 1870.

In 1559, the pope published the Index that condemned forty-eight editions of the Bible as 'heretic' and banned publishers and printers. Thousands of books were burned in the various cities, and caused the humanistic movement to disappear.

Hundred years later the Thirty-Year War (1618-1648) devastated large areas of Germany Catholics and Protestants and nearly all of Europe had been involved in the conflict that shattered the population, commerce and agriculture. Large areas were unpopulated and the land uncultivated because the inhabitants had fled or were killed.

The Peace of Westphalia brought recognition between Catholics and Protestants. The power of the Holy Roman Empire was diminished and hopes for unity destroyed. The result was the break-up and division of many princely states throughout Europe.

Chapter 40

Conclusion

Mankind has gone a long way since Moses took the children of Israel on the daring and strenuous journey to their Promised Land. Although instructed by Moses, the children of Israel had been wilful and disobedient to the will of God more than once, to the grief and desperation of their great leader.

Jesus tried desperately to deliver his message of God's unconditional love and of His Kingdom to his listeners, and even his devoted disciples did not always understand their master.

We have gone far away from the 'Ten Commandments' and the 'Sermon on the Mount'. To some individuals they seem to be written for special events and to be read on special days to commemorate an occasion. For the rest of the week and months, the lessons are forgotten. Somebody once stated that 'Christianity was impractical and out of time, and must be modernized.' It may be that many Christians feel the same way.

Moses' Ten Commandments' and the teaching of Jesus are eternal. They cannot be modified or 'modernized' but must be lived as thought. Many people feel very uncomfortable about that but one cannot obey seven of the 'Ten Commandments', and ignore three others. Sorry!

It would be wonderful if mankind would be able to learn lessons from the past! Why did Hitler not learn from Napoleons defeat by trying to conquer Moscow? Why did the popes not listen to the many voices within and outside of the Roman Catholic Church asking for reforms? The Church (Catholic and Protestant) created great men, popes, martyrs and saints who should have been the model for those in power. The wisdom of Pope Gregory the 'Great', the devotion and courage of men like Thomas Becket, Martin Luther and Thomas More, the humility and unconditional love of St. Francis, the gentleness and tact of Philip Melanchthon are the perfect examples for anyone to strife for and to imitate. The Reformation could have been avoided if the popes in power would have lived the humble lives they were supposed to live as spiritual leaders, and of great and exemplary sons of Man.

What horrible blood spill and terror destroying precious lives were worse: the Inquisition or the devastation of Europe of the Thirty Year War? The tragedies, the loss of innocent lives and destruction of cities and villages may have been avoided if power- hungry individuals would have curbed their lust for wealth and rule.

Christianity and Judaism are closely connected and deeply connected. Judaism is the foundation of Christianity because it was the heritage of Jesus. The destructive flames of anti-Semitism could be extinguished if both would have a more profound knowledge and mutual appreciation and respect for each other. Prejudice stems from ignorance and in its trails follow evil deeds and worst of all, hate. Without knowledge, kindness and love toward one another we are shallow and empty as Paul said in his letters to the Corinthians, (I, 13:1) Though I speak with the tongues of men and of angels, and have not charity (love) I am become a sounding brass or a tinkling cymbal".

As Christianity and Judaism should attempt to become closer in accepting each other so also must the various Christian Protestant branches to come closer to each other and the secret attitude 'I am better than others' or 'Catholics are non-Christians' is an offensive and disgusting viewpoint.

The path of Christianity is marked by suffering and hardship caused through intolerance, lack of love, greed and ungodliness but the same stony path had been tread and conquered by heroic souls through courage, love and forgiveness. If we cannot return to the teachings of Christ and overcome greed, violence, intolerance and abominable life styles, we doom ourselves to self-destruction and annihilation.

The Native Americans rightfully fought when strange people appeared and took the land which had been theirs for thousands of years. The Indians were brutally driven off their land and resettled in areas the white settlers did not want because the soil was unproductive. Starvation and illness reduced great numbers of the Indian population. They were lied to, promises broken – and all of it was committed by Christian leaders. The government tried to forbid them to practice their customs and strip them off their dignity. The Catholic Church took the American Indians in her fold, and tried to help and improve their lives. Although some of the beautiful casinos are run by Indians and are a lucrative enterprise, most of their brothers and sisters, the 'forgotten Americans" still living under abject poverty on reservations without good roads, sewage, water and electricity. They still suffer from discrimination, depravation and malnourishment.

The Indian Elders still teach the younger generation the virtues of life: respect, generosity, courage and wisdom. Should we not strife to reach the same wholesome aspirations and rectify the appalling evil deeds committed against them?

The Kingdom of Heaven – Jesus message to us – can be reached by accepting Him as our Saviour, and living according to His teachings. Jesus added a thought to be heeded: "Except ye be converted and become as little children (trusting and pure) ye shall not enter the Kingdom of Heaven" (Mt. 18:3).

Bibliography

Ariel, David, Kabbalah, Rowman & Littlefield Publ. 2006, Oxford, UK

Arnold, Eberhard, Salt and Light, The Plough Publishing House, 1967

Atlas of the Medieval World, Rosamond McKitterick, Oxford University Press, NY, 2004

Barlow, Frank, Thomas Becket, Univ. of California Press, Berkely, CA 1986

Bhagavad Gita, Transl. Swami Prabhavananda and Chr. Isherwood, Mentor Books, 1954

Borg, Marcus, Jesus and Buddha, The Parallel Sayings, Ulysses Press, Berkely, CA. 2004

Cathar Perfect, Wikipegia, The Free Library

Daniels & Stephen G. Islop, Almanac of World History, Nat. Geographic, Washington, DC., 2003

Durant, Will, The Story of Civilization: Ceasar and Christ, Simon & Schuster, NY 1944

Durant, Will, The Story of Civilization, The Reformation, Simon & Schuster, 1957

Ehrmann, Bart, Peter, Paul and Mary Magdalene, Oxford University Press, NY, 2006

Ehrmann, Bart, Lost Scriptures, Oxford University Press, NY 2003

Evans, Craig A., The Dead Sea Scrolls

Fadiman (editor) Essential Sufism, James & Frager, R. Harper, San Fransico, 1997

Fox, Emmet, The Sermon on the Mount, Harper & Collins, 1989

Fox, Matthew, Breakthrough (Meister Eckhart) Image Books, Doubleday, 1980

Girsone, Joseph F., Trinity, Doubleday, 2002

Grant, Michael, Jesus, Rigel Publications, 1977, London, UK

Hayes, Charlton, J. Frederick F. Clark, Medieval and Early Modern Times, Macmillan Publ.C., 1966

Hock, Ronald F. The Banned Book of Mary, Ulysses Press, Berkely, CA, 2004

Idel, Moshe, and McGinn, Mystical Union in Judaism, Christianity and Islam, Continuum Publ.ication, NY, 2009

Jeffery, Arthur, The Koran and Selected Sutras, Dover Publications Inc., Mineola, NY, 1958

Isbouts, Jean-Pierre, The Biblical World, Illustrated Atlas, National Georgraphic, Washington, DC 2004

Keller, Werner, The Bible as History, Hodder & Stoughton, UK, 1980

Kramer, Joel L. Maimonides, Doubleday, New York, 2008

Merovingian, Wikipegia, The Free Library

Meyer, Marvin W. The Secret Teachings of Jesus, Vintage Book, Div. of Random House, NY, 1984

Monyahan, Brian, The Faith, Doubleday, 2002

Philips, Charles, An Illustrated History of the Crusades, Lorenz Books, Annes Publishing Ltd, Hermes House, London, UK

Picknett, Lynn & Clyde, Prince, The Templar Revelation, Simon & Schuster, 1997

Rowland, Ingrid D., Giordano Bruno, Farrar, Straus & Giroux, New York, 2008

Shanks, Hershel & Witherington III, Ben, The Brother of Jesus, Harper, San Francisco, 2003

Simon, Bernard, The Essence of Gnostics, Chartwell Books, Edison, NJ, 2004

The Holy Bible, Old and New Testaments in the King James Version, World Aflame Press, Hazelton, MO,

Underwood, Evelyn, Mysticism, One World Publication, Oxford, UK, 1993.